MINERAL COLLECTOR'S HANDBOOK

Barry Krause

Sterling Publishing Co., Inc.
New York

Library of Congress Cataloging-in-Publication Data

Krause, Barry, 1947–
     Mineral collector's handbook / by Barry Krause.
          p.   cm.
     Includes index.
     ISBN 0-8069-0874-2
     1. Minerals—Collection and preservation.   2. Rocks—Collection
and preservation.   I. Title.
QE366.2.K73   1996
549'.075—dc20   95-26034
                                                                CIP

Designed by Judy Morgan

10   9   8   7   6   5   4   3   2   1

Published by Sterling Publishing Company, Inc.
387 Park Avenue South, New York, N.Y. 10016
© 1996 by Barry Krause
Distributed in Canada by Sterling Publishing
% Canadian Manda Group, One Atlantic Avenue, Suite 105
Toronto, Ontario, Canada M6K 3E7
Distributed in Great Britain and Europe by Cassell PLC
Wellington House, 125 Strand, London WC2R 0BB, England
Distributed in Australia by Capricorn Link (Australia) Pty Ltd.
P.O. Box 6651, Baulkham Hills, Business Centre, NSW 2153, Australia
Printed in China

Sterling ISBN 0-8069-0874-2

ACKNOWLEDGMENTS

Gemological Institute of America (GIA), Santa Monica, California—for permission to reproduce copyrighted photographs from its library files; special thanks to Dona Mary Dirlam, director of the Liddicoat Gemological Library and Information Center, and her staff, especially Judy Colbert, G.G., slide librarian.

Natural History Museum of Los Angeles County, Los Angeles, California—for permission to reproduce photographs of museum mineral specimens; special thanks to Dr. Anthony R. Kampf, curator of Minerals and Gems. The museum owns the mineral specimens depicted in, as well as the copyright to, all specimen photographs attributed to it in this book.

The photographers whose photo credits are cited in the book.

United States Geological Survey, U.S. Department of the Interior, Washington, D.C.—for providing information for use in this book; special thanks to Jane E. Jenness, geologist in the Minerals Information Office.

United States Bureau of Mines, U.S. Department of the Interior, Washington, D.C.—for providing information for use in this book; special thanks to Harold A. Taylor, Jr., physical scientist.

Nevada Department of Minerals, Carson City, Nevada—for permission to quote passages from one of its publications; special thanks to Doug Driesner, administrator of the Division of Abandoned Mine Lands.

The staff of Sterling Publishing Company, Inc., New York, New York—for guiding the author's manuscript for this book to successful publication; special thanks to editors Sheila Anne Barry and Hannah Steinmetz.

CONTENTS

INTRODUCTION

Pick up a rock. Feel its edges and texture. Look at its color and lustre. Is it heavy or lightweight? Scratch its surface with your fingernail. Is this rock hard or soft, brittle or cohesive, smooth or rough, flat or round, interesting or boring?

Is this rock made of minerals, whose tiny crystals sparkle in the morning sunlight? Will this rock melt in a candle flame, dissolve in water, or crumble under pressure? Could this rock be *basalt*—a cold lump of volcanic minerals, which once flowed restlessly as blistering molten lava before human beings existed on Earth? Or is this rock actually a pure mineral—perhaps a *gemstone*, a precious piece of *diamond* or *emerald* or sky-blue *sapphire*?

Swing a small magnet near this rock. Does the magnet move towards the rock's magnetic field? Is this rock a *nickel-iron meteorite* that hit the Earth from outer space when the dinosaurs roamed the planet?

Walk along the beach, and curl your toes around the pebbles in the sand. Is that glistening "sea glass" really a wave-tossed *quartz* crystal? Or could it be a piece of a *petrified* seashell, tumbled free from its rocky tomb of 60 million years, a stony time traveller whose once-living body crawled along these very shores?

Climb the *marble* steps of your library or courthouse. Spin road *gravel* with your car or bicycle tires. Lean a moment against that *limestone* bench in your shaded city park. Gasp in awe at the price tag on a *ruby* and *platinum* ring prominently displayed in a jewelry store window—and realize that everything for sale in that store was found somewhere in nature by mineral prospectors!

We live in a world of rocks and minerals. They surround us, protect us, support us, nourish us, teach us, amuse us, and enrich us. Human civilization has been built mainly from rocky raw materials. Our very bodies hold perfectly balanced, dynamically stable (always changing, but always the same) concentrations of life-sustaining minerals!

Why collect rocks and minerals? Because they're beautiful and fascinating and part of our past and future. Make time in your life for *amethyst* geodes and *tourmaline* clusters, for *gold* nuggets and *silver* ores, for Stone Age *flint* arrowheads and *opalized* rainbows.

Explore national parks and private quarries, mountain peaks and enchanted caverns, bubbling hot springs and sleeping volcanoes, glacier-cut valleys and mineral-rich deserts, eroding crystal cliffs and newly fallen rock slides. Look for rocks and minerals in their natural environments, at rock shops and mineral shows, or in nature museums and mineralogy books—and, as time goes on, enjoy the beauty of rocks and minerals in your own personal collection!

Watch fluorescent rocks glow with ghostly glory under the gentle coaxing of your portable mineral ultraviolet lamp. Pour some mine concentrate through a sifting screen, and pick out the *topaz* and *garnet* trapped in the metal mesh. Touch *halite* to your tongue, and taste this salty mineral from an evaporated prehistoric ocean!

* * *

The chapters in this book deal with the origins and classification of rocks and minerals, field collecting your own specimens, mineral properties and tests, and handling and housing a collection.

The color photos provide many museum-quality mineral examples, as well as the more routine specimens likely to be encountered by the beginning and intermediate collector. All mineral photos were selected for showing handsome specimens and/or normality of mineral type—important traits that are admired and sought by the dedicated mineral student and collector.

At the end of the book, the Appendices summarize the mathematics and chemistry that most rock and mineral collectors find helpful.

———————————— ◆ ————————————

A 30 × 22 millimetre, cut and polished, fossilized dinosaur bone agate cabochon, set in a sterling silver ring. Photo by Mike Havstad. © GIA.

Azurite mineral cluster, 10 × 7.6 centimetres, from one of the world's earliest-mined copper deposits near Lyon, Chessy, France. Azurite is a blue copper carbonate ore. © GIA.

THE ORIGINS OF ROCKS AND MINERALS

"In the beginning, God created the heaven and the earth."
Genesis 1:1, *Old Testament*

Our Earth is about 4.6 billion years old. The oldest rocks found on Earth—from Australia, Canada's Northwest Territories, and Greenland—have been radioactively dated to approximately 3.5 billion to 4 billion years old. Stony meteorites and certain rocks retrieved by our astronauts from the surface of the Moon have been radioactively dated at 4.6 billion years—which is thought to be when the Earth and the rest of our solar system formed.

Rough and faceted moldavite *"tektites" from Bohemia and Moravia. Tektites are objects of uncertain origin, but may be formed from Earth rocks during a meteoroid impact explosion on our planet's surface. Moldavites are typically dark, translucent olive-green in color, but often faceted into gemstones when highly transparent.* © *GIA.*

OUR EARTH'S HISTORY

We can view our Earth's history as 10 important "stages" in our planet's past, occurring in this order:

1. *Condensation of the Earth* from a solar nebula. This took place about 4.6 billion years ago, along with the formation of the rest of our solar system.

2. *Elemental separation* due to relative density. Molten *iron* and *nickel* sank towards the middle of the young Earth, while lighter elements "floated" towards its surface, eventually to become the silicate rocks of the Earth's crust. The lightest elements of all (such as hydrogen and helium) formed the first atmosphere of the Earth, and they gradually escaped into space to be replaced by other gases.

3. *Cooling of the Earth's surface*, especially the outermost few miles of molten material. It is believed that our Earth was originally much hotter, and has been cooling over the ages.

4. *Crustal solidification and continental congealing.* As the lightweight elements in the molten Earth rose to its surface, they cooled and solidified, but they were still too hot to support liquid surface water.

5. *Atmospheric evolution.* The Earth's first relatively stable atmosphere is thought to have been a mixture of hydrogen (H_2), methane (CH_4), ammonia (NH_3), and carbon dioxide (CO_2)—similar to Jupiter's atmosphere today (some planets still retain much of their original atmosphere of 4.6 billion years ago)—plus water vapor (H_2O).

6. *Volcanism* produced both new surface rocks and new gas molecules for the young Earth's atmosphere. On the primitive Earth, free oxygen (O_2) and methane combinations could have produced water and carbon dioxide (CO_2)—but much water, carbon dioxide, and free nitrogen (N_2) came from volcanism. The present high nitrogen content (78 percent) of our atmosphere may have come from escaping volcanic gases when the Earth was young.

7. *Ocean formation.* Escaping water vapor from ubiquitous volcanism on the primeval Earth occurred in large quantities as the Earth's surface was cooling. This water condensed in planetwide cloud covers and fell as warm rain back towards the hot crustal surface rocks, from which the water instantly evaporated again to form more clouds. This cycle

repeated itself over and over for thousands (or millions?) of years.

Finally, the Earth's surface rocks were cooled just below the boiling point of water (100° C). On that day, the falling rain stayed in a puddle. Later, it accumulated in a pond, then a lake, then (with time) small seas. And still it rained, for perhaps thousands of years, to create the Earth's first oceans. These oceans were acidic rather than salty, due to the increasing dissolved carbon dioxide and the lack of much mineral content yet.

The Earth formed at the right distance from the Sun for water to exist in a liquid state. The next planet in, Venus, is as hot as a pizza oven and, long ago, had its water boiled into permanent vapor—a runaway greenhouse effect. Mars, the next planet out from the Earth's orbit, has half the Earth's diameter, and it therefore was too small gravitationally to retain a surface ocean of water—which, in any case, would have frozen due to Mars's distance from the Sun.

8. *Rock cycles* began as soon as liquid water formed on our planet's rocky surface. They eroded the exposed rock into particles, which were carried away, some of them dissolving as salt in the newly formed seas and some piling up as sediments on the ocean floor, eventually forming the first sedimentary rocks. *Metamorphism* created new rock types, and continual mountain building (including volcanism) raised new rock outcrops to be eroded by water and wind. These rock cycles have never ceased.

When the sea water evaporated by absorbing the Sun's energy, the dissolved rocks (sea salt) stayed behind, making the

Grossular garnets, *rough in matrix and faceted. Grossular garnets are calcium, aluminum silicates. Photo by Mike Havstad.* © GIA.

Earth's seas saltier and saltier. Because our seas are not yet a saturated solution of salt in water, the oceans are becoming saltier still—although, within one brief human lifetime, no change is discernable.

By chance, our continents are mostly exposed above sea level at the present time. In other words, the Earth's oceans coincidentally fill the ocean basins at this time in geologic history.

Natural inclusions in amber, *fossilized tree resin, sometimes termed an "organic gemstone." Such inclusions are often faked in manufactured amber.* © GIA.

A 10-centimetre-long amethyst quartz *"scepter" crystal, from Inyo National Forest in California. Amethyst is the purple-color variety of crystalline quartz. Photo by Robert Weldon.* © GIA.

Fossil ammonite *on lucite display stand. Ammonites are an extinct order (Ammonoidea) of Mesozoic era cephalopod mollusks.* © GIA.

9. *Creation of life and its evolution*. Scientists believe that life originated in the sea from simple molecules there, increasing in complexity over a long span of time. The oldest-known *fossils* (rocky evidence of past life) are of so-called "blue-green algae" in rocks radioactively dated to about 3½ billion years old. Photosynthesizing plant life evolved from bacteria, and it produced a high-oxygen content in the Earth's atmosphere about 2 billion years ago, permitting the extensive support of animal life. The present oxygen content (21 percent) of our atmosphere is due to plants, many of them still in the oceans as descendants of the first plants eons ago. Animals and plants have changed and increased in bewildering variety and intricacy during the last 600 million years.

10. *Human development and civilization*. We appeared on Earth a few million years ago. Our civilization dates from the close of the last Ice Age, say, about 10,000 years ago. Human beings are the most intelligent creatures on Earth, and are among the most curious, whether or not they're rock collectors.

Green beryl crystal cluster in matrix. Deep green beryl is the gemstone emerald. Photo by Robert Weldon. © GIA.

Victorian brooch with carnelian cameo set in gold with half pearls. Courtesy of Elise Misiorowski. Photo by Robert Weldon. © GIA.

THE EARTH'S ATMOSPHERE

The Earth's *atmosphere* is the air that surrounds the *hydrosphere* (surface water) and *lithosphere* (rocky portion of the planet). Our present atmosphere weighs about 5.7 quadrillion tons—about one-millionth as much as the rest of the Earth. Over 99 percent of our atmosphere's weight is below 50 miles in height off the Earth's surface, but some air extends 1,000 miles off the ground, gradually dissipating into space. Atmospheric pressure at sea level is 14.7 pounds per square inch ("1 atmosphere"), and it decreases with increases in altitude. The atmosphere has the same composition up to about 60 miles in altitude: about 78 percent nitrogen (N_2), 21 percent oxygen (O_2), 0.9 percent argon (Ar), 0.03 percent carbon dioxide (CO_2), and traces of other gases, with variable water vapor (H_2O).

The *troposphere* is the lowest, densest part of the atmosphere, averaging 6 to 8 miles above sea level. It is the atmospheric zone where weather occurs, as well as weathering of rocks, surface volcanism, and all life on Earth. Because of the air's high oxygen content, rocks that are exposed on the Earth's surface are subject to strong oxidation, which tends to be accelerated in climates of high humidity.

There is a constant exchange of gases between the atmosphere, hydrosphere, and lithosphere. Volcanism is always adding carbon dioxide and water vapor to the air, and human activities produce localized and long-range effects in atmospheric composition, but they are subtle on a global scale.

THE EARTH'S HYDROSPHERE

All of the water on the Earth's surface weighs about 180 quintillion tons, about 0.03 percent of the Earth's total weight. The seas contain 98 percent of the water on Earth, with the remaining 2 percent in all the lakes, rivers, ice, groundwater, and atmospheric water combined (a relatively insignificant total amount of water exists in all the plants, animals, and hydrated minerals on Earth put together).

Water covers 71 percent of the Earth's surface area, and the average ocean depth is 2½ miles. The salt concentration of sea water varies slightly, but it averages about 3½ percent by weight. It is mostly sodium chloride, with appreciable amounts of magnesium chloride and sulfate. Virtually all metals are in the sea, albeit in trace amounts per unit volume; but it has been estimated that if all the gold in sea water could be extracted, gold's market value would be made essentially worthless.

Barite *cluster from Rumania. Composed of barium sulfate, barite is a common mineral that is soft and heavy, and known by miners of sulfide ores since earliest times. Courtesy of Natural History Museum of Los Angeles County.*

The four main ocean basins are the Arctic, Atlantic, Indian, and Pacific—with all the others being parts of these oceans.

The *hydrologic cycle* consists of the path that water takes from the sea to clouds to precipitation on land to surface water and/or groundwater . . . and back to the sea. This cycle has been occurring for 4 billion years, as essentially all water on Earth (including that in your blood right now) has been here since the creation of our planet.

When rocks are naturally exposed on the Earth's surface, they are assaulted by the combined weathering effects of water, air, and gravity.

THE EARTH'S LITHOSPHERE

The Earth's *lithosphere* is sometimes defined as the solid rocks of the Earth's crust and upper part of the mantle—say, about 60 to 100 miles deep. The "centrosphere" is the term that some people give to the Earth's interior below the lithosphere. Then there are those who prefer to use "lithosphere" to mean all of the Earth from the crustal surface to, and including, the central core. So, let's just discuss the four major zones of the Earth's interior:

Crust The outermost layer of the Earth's solid structure, averaging 20 miles thick, from 3 miles thick under the basaltic ocean floor to about 40 miles thick under the granitic continents. The oceanic crust is sometimes called "sima," because basalt is rich in silica and magnesia. The continental crust is termed "sial," because

granite is rich in silica and alumina. Of the 92 natural elements found in the Earths' crust, eight of them make up almost 99 percent of the crustal rocks by weight: *oxygen* (O), 47.2 percent; *silicon* (Si), 28.2 percent; *aluminum* (Al), 8.2 percent; *iron* (Fe), 5.1 percent; *calcium* (Ca), 3.7 percent; *sodium* (Na), 2.9 percent; *potassium* (K), 2.6 percent; and *magnesium* (Mg), 2.1 percent. Most minerals contain silicon and oxygen, and are called "silicates."

Epidote, *a basic calcium, aluminum, iron silicate mineral. This specimen is from Prince of Wales Island, Alaska. Courtesy of Natural History Museum of Los Angeles County.*

The granitic crust "floats" on the underlying basaltic crust, which, in turn, floats on the denser mantle (see below). The Earth's crust has not been completely drilled through to the mantle yet, although there are gold mines in Africa that are two miles deep and Texas oil wells five miles deep. The seven continents are Africa, Antarctica, Asia, Australia, Europe, North America, and South America (Greenland is actually part of the North American continent).

The highest point on the Earth's crust is Mount Everest (on the Nepalese-

Tibetan border): 29,028 feet *above* sea level. The lowest point on the Earth's crust is the Marianas Trench (off the Philippines): 36,198 feet *below* sea level. The average surface temperature on Earth is 57° F. Deep crustal temperatures may get up to 1,600° F—which can melt rocks. Crustal density varies from about 2.6 to 3 on the average—in other words, it's about three times as heavy as water.

A 29.99-carat cabochon fashioned from a pallasitic meteorite. Pallasites are stony-iron meteorites, the rarest meteorite group. They have a composition of olivine crystals in a nickel-iron matrix, believed to have formed when molten metallic core material intruded into the olivine-rich mantle of an asteroid, before it exploded by interasteroidal collision. Photo by Maha DeMaggio. © GIA.

Natural rough spinel *crystal, from the Pamir Mountains north of Afghanistan. Photo by Robert Weldon. © GIA.*

Mantle   The 1,800-mile-thick layer between the Earth's crust and outer core. We have never sampled the mantle's chemicals directly, but we believe them to be a mixture of iron and magnesium silicates, free iron, and iron sulfates—all in a hot "plastic" state—a chemical composition similar to stony meteorites. The mantle is probably olivine and pyroxene rocks. Since olivine is common in meteorites, we can theorize that such extraterrestrial rocky visitors would have ended up in the mantle of a terrestrial planet if they had been part of one.

The mantle is neither liquid nor rigidly solid. It is plastic, and it can bend or flow slowly over time. Either the mantle itself or crustal rocks heated from the mantle produce subterranean and surface igneous rock flows. *Magma* is molten rock beneath the Earth's surface. *Lava* is molten rock on the surface. Much of the mantle is heated by radioactive decay. The mantle's density varies from about 3 to 5.

Outer core   The 1,375-mile-thick layer between the Earth's mantle and inner core. We believe the outer core is a dense liquid (mostly molten iron) for two reasons: it is impervious to "S" seismic waves that don't go through liquids, and the Earth has a strong magnetic field, which can best be explained by a liquid interior. The outer core's density varies in perhaps the 8 to 15 range.

Inner core   The last 800 (or so) miles from the lower boundary of the outer core to the middle of the Earth. It is believed to be a solid mixture of about 90 percent free iron and 9 percent free nickel—similar to the chemical composition of nickel-iron meteorites (which are analogously equivalent to terrestrial planetary cores). The lighter elements, such as aluminum and oxygen, do not exist in the core, but they are richly concentrated in the crust.

The temperature in the middle of the Earth may be around 9,000° F, almost as hot as the "surface" (photosphere) of the Sun. At that temperature, all known substances would instantly vaporize on the Earth's surface, but the middle of the Earth is solid because it is under 3.7 million "atmospheres" of pressure, caused by 4,000 miles of planetary radius of rocky materials. Despite this tremendous pressure, the average density of the inner core is only about 16 to 20, six or seven times the density of typical rocks in your collection, which is proof that solids have their compressibility limits—in small planets, anyway.

ROCK AND MINERAL DEFINITIONS

GEOLOGY is from the Greek roots *geo* ("earth") and *logos* ("the study of"). Subbranches of geology are rock and mineral investigations, the subjects of the rest of this book.

MINERALOGY comes from the Medieval Latin root *mineralis* ("mineral"), from *minera* ("a mine" or "ore"), and it is the study of minerals, those naturally occurring substances (usually solid, sometimes liquid) having similar chemical compositions, internal structures, and physical properties. Minerals are generally considered as being crystalline in the solid state, although noncrystalline solids are often called minerals also. The most common minerals in the Earth's crust are the so-called "rock-forming minerals," including *amphiboles, calcite, feldspars, micas, olivine, pyroxenes,* and *quartz.*

Amazonite, *a bluish-green variety of* microcline feldspar. © *GIA.*

MINERAL SPECIES are minerals with the same chemical composition and structure. More than 3,000 mineral species have been identified by professional mineralogists. Most minerals are *compounds*—molecules made of two or more different elements chemically bonded with covalent and/or ionic bonds. *Quartz* is the most common mineral species in the Earth's crust.

MINERAL VARIETIES are minerals of the same species, but possessing impurities or structural variations. *Aquamarine* and *emerald* are respectively the blue- and green-color varieties of the mineral *beryl.*

Rough green beryl, 278.6 grams. Beryl is an aluminum silicate mineral that forms many gemstones, including emerald and aquamarine. © GIA & Tino Hammid.

Beryl, *variety* aquamarine, *crystal cluster, 6 centimetres wide, Pakistan. Typical of well-formed, but clouded, aquamarine crystals from this region. Courtesy Gene Meieran. Photo by Jeff Scovil.*

MINERALOIDS are amorphous (non-crystalline), pure, natural substances—such as *amber*, *coal*, *obsidian* (volcanic glass), and *petroleum*.

ROCK is a word derived from the Middle English *rokke*, from the Old French *roche*, from the Medieval Latin *rocca*. Rocks are natural formations made either from several minerals interlocked (for example, *basalt* and *granite*) or from single minerals forming bedrock (for example, *dolomite* and *limestone*).

*Rough "lapis lazuli" (*lazurite) *from Afghanistan. The opaque blue gemstone known as "lapis lazuli" is actually a rock composed mostly of the complex silicate mineral* lazurite, *often mixed with* calcite *and* pyrite. *Photo by Tino Hammid. © GIA & Tino Hammid.*

Petrography is the study of rocks. It is derived from the Greek word roots *petros* ("rock") and *graphein* ("to write"). *Petrology* is the study of rock origins and variations, and it is based on *mineralogy* (the study of mineral origins and variations), which, in turn, is based on the *chemistry* (study of matter) and *physics* (study of energy) of *crystallography* (see below), which is ultimately learned from atomic and molecular structure and interaction (the behavior of the electrical particles that compose matter).

CRYSTAL is a word derived from the Middle English and Old French *cristal*, from the Old English *cristalla*, from the Latin *crystallum* ("crystal" or "ice"), from the Greek *krystallos*, from *kryos* ("frost"). Indeed, the ancients believed that rock crystals were perhaps permanently frozen water, like the icicles they observed in cold mountain regions. A crystal is a natural, geometrically symmetrical solid. *Crystallography* is the study of crystals (see Chapter 6 for a summary of mineral crystallography).

Faceted Burmese ruby. © *GIA and Tino Hammid.*

Phosphophyllite *on matrix. A hydrous phosphate of zinc, with iron and manganese present. Photo by Mike Havstad.* © *GIA.*

STONE is linguistically derived from the Old English *stan*, which, in turn, comes from (or is of parallel origin with) the German word *stein*, from the Indo-European root *stai* "to compress," "to stiffen," or "to thicken"). "Stone" is a very general term that is not used much in scientific mineralogy, except where it customarily names a rock or mineral (for example, "sandstone" or "gemstone").

GEM is from the Latin *gemma* ("a swelling" or "precious stone"). A gem (or "gemstone") is a mineral that can be cut and/or polished for jewelry and lapidary purposes.

MINERAL AND ROCK FORMATION

Minerals form inside or on the surface of the Earth's crust, from (1) hot gases, (2) molten rock, and (3) hot or cold supersaturated solutions. Most minerals have an igneous origin, crystallizing out at a proper temperature and pressure for a given chemical. A mineral may crystallize alone out of a subterranean solution and form gorgeous *amethyst* crystals, for example, inside of a volcanic geode pocket, which was first formed by expanding igneous gases inside solidifying igneous rock. When minerals crystallize together in an interlocking pattern, they are called a rock (for example, *granite*, which is composed commonly of *quartz*, *mica*, and *feldspar* minerals).

HOW ROCKS ARE CHEMICALLY BUILT

SUBATOMIC PARTICLES   (such as protons, electrons, and neutrons)

(combine to make)

ATOMS   (the smallest part of an element that still retains the properties of that element)

(which comprise)

ELEMENTS   (substances made of one kind of atom; i.e., atoms with a constant number of protons in their atomic nuclei)

(which themselves form)   (or which combine to form)
Mono-elemental   Multi-elemental
MINERALS   MINERALS

(containing one element)   (compounds; i.e., with more than one element)

which combine individually or in group combinations to make

ROCKS

(hard natural substances, sometimes of one mineral, but usually of two or more minerals interlocked crystallographically)

Primary mineral deposits are formed at the same time as their surrounding rock matrix. Secondary mineral deposits are formed after their surrounding "country rock" has solidified.

The first minerals on Earth were crystallized as igneous rocks slowly cooled near, or on, the young Earth's crustal surface. When the crust cooled enough for liquid water to exist on it, the *sedimentary* *rock cycle* began with erosion of exposed bedrock; transport by water, wind, and gravity (and, later, ice); deposition; consolidation of deposited rock particles into sedimentary rock; uplift of the sedimentary rock beds; and re-erosion of the sedimentary rocks. This basic "rock cycle" has been going on ever since, predating life itself on Earth. Sometimes preexisting rocks are changed by heat and/or pressure into *metamorphic* rocks. New minerals are often formed along contact zones between hot igneous rocks and cool sedimentary rocks. The three basic rock types—*igneous*, *sedimentary*, and *metamorphic*—are discussed in detail in the next chapter, but here is some information specifically on the formation of the two most common rock types; igneous and sedimentary.

Faceted specimen of moss agate, *showing its diagnostic natural dendritic inclusions.* © *GIA.*

A 235-carat orthoclase feldspar *specimen from Madagascar. Feldspars are common rock-building minerals. Photo by Robert Weldon.* © *GIA.*

Close-up detail of the mosslike inclusions in the moss agate *specimen in the previous photo. These inclusions can be green, brown, or red in moss agate, and they consist of hornblende or of iron and manganese oxides, whereas the agate mineral itself is colorless to milky-white.* © *GIA.*

Natural rough and faceted rose quartz *specimens, showing typical cloudy translucency. Rose quartz is the pink to rose-red color variety of crystalline quartz, and scarce in large transparent crystals of deep color. Photo by Robert Weldon.* © *GIA.*

Igneous Rock Formation

Igneous rocks mostly form deep inside the Earth's crust, where temperatures and pressures are high due to the heavy weight of overlying rock beds. Rock about seven miles below the Earth's surface is about 1,500° F and under 50,000 pounds per square inch of pressure. Rock deep in the Earth is "semiplastic"—that is, not rigidly solid. It can be bent, squeezed, or stretched. Of course, conditions may be right for rock to liquify completely into a molten state called *magma*, which may work its way up towards the surface of the crust. Magma (molten rock) that solidifies below the Earth's surface is called *intrusive igneous rock*. Magma that hardens above the Earth's surface is *extrusive igneous rock*, lithifying from magma that is forced upwards by subterranean heat and pressure to escape through volcanic vents or crustal rifts and fissures.

Bicolored natural tourmaline *crystal, showing tourmaline's characteristic lengthwise external striations on crystals. Specimen from Afghanistan. Photo by Mike Havstad. © GIA.*

Intrusive Igneous Rock Masses

The four basic types of intrusive igneous rock masses are batholiths, dikes, laccoliths, and sills:

Batholiths Large masses of intrusive igneous bedrock that have no well-defined floor. Batholiths may be more than 1,000 miles long, and they typically occur as the core of folded mountains. The granitic Sierra Nevada Mountains of eastern California are an uplifted and exposed batholith.

Dikes Vertical masses of igneous rock that solidified in large, vertical, preexisting rock cracks. Dikes may be from a few inches to miles wide, and many miles long. The Great Dyke of Zimbabwe is 300 miles long and as much as 5 miles wide.

Laccoliths Intrusive, dome-shaped, igneous rock masses that push up overlying sedimentary rock layers. Unlike the huge, virtually bottomless batholiths (above), laccoliths have a "floor" that delineates the deepest part of their intrusion into overlying rock. Laccoliths are common in South Dakota near the Black Hills.

Sills Horizontal masses of intrusive igneous rock that forced its way between parallel rock layers and solidified. The most famous sill in the United States is the Hudson River Palisades, formed 190 million years ago, and now comprising a *basaltic* cliff from Jersey City into New York state. Sills and dikes (above) often occur together—and if a sill arches the overlying sedimentary bedrock, it is called a laccolith (above).

INTRUSIVE IGNEOUS ROCK MASSES

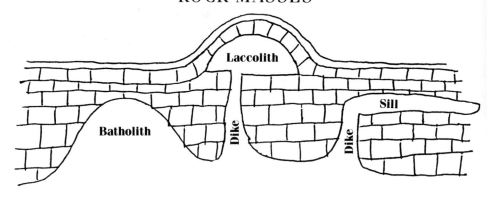

Extrusive (Volcanic) Igneous Rock Formation

The word *volcano* comes from the Latin *Volcanus*, which comes from *Vulcan*, the Roman god of fire and metalworking. A volcano is a vent (opening) in the Earth's crust through which igneous material escapes to the surface. Volcanoes are usually mountains built up of volcanic rocks. "Volcanic rocks" and "extrusive igneous rocks" are used synonymously and refer to rocks that cooled and hardened above the Earth's surface. When magma reaches the Earth's surface, it is called *lava*; another name for "volcanic rocks" is "lava rocks." The ocean floor is made of *basalt* from undersea lava flows.

The highest mountains on Earth, measured from the ocean floor, in this case, are volcanic: the Hawaiian Islands. Mauna Loa, the largest volcano on Earth, constitutes half of the island of Hawaii. It rises almost 6 miles from the ocean floor, is 70 miles wide at its sea-level base, and contains a volume of 10,000 cubic miles. Mauna Loa is not an explosive volcano, so it is safe to visit.

Most lava is ejected from the sides, not the *caldera* ("crater"), of a volcano. Volcanoes are classified by their activity as active (currently erupting or about to), dormant (not erupting, but may in the indefinite future), and extinct (unlikely to erupt again). Mount Saint Helens in Washington state suddenly turned from dormant to active in its spectacular explosion in 1980. Northern Oregon's Crater Lake rests in the caldera of the "extinct" volcano Mount Mazama.

Volcanism constantly creates new rocks and alters existing ones. All existing volcanic mountains are relatively young geologically, some created in this century.

Volcanoes can cause a lot of damage to humans and their property. Over a million people have died from the eruptions of Mount Etna on Sicily. The August 24, 79 A.D. eruption of Vesuvius buried the Roman towns of Pompeii and Herculaneum. One reason that people risk living near volcanoes is that the soil is often excellent for crops.

Volcanic rocks cool quickly as they lose their heat to the relatively cold atmosphere on the Earth's surface, so they don't have time to grow large mineral crystals. Two typical volcanic rocks, *obsidian* (volcanic glass) and *pumice* are not only "amorphous" (noncrystalline), but they are also chemically identical, having formed from lava that solidified without much gas content in obsidian, and with a "honeycomb" effect due to escaping volcanic gases in pumice.

Peridot crystal cluster from Pakistan, 49.68 cts. © GIA & Tino Hammid.

Types of Volcanoes

Volcanoes can be classified in three basic types, based on their external shapes and internal structures:

Shield volcanoes (also called "lava domes" or "dome volcanoes") Composed mostly of lava, with gentle slopes of about 2 geometric degrees near

the base to 10° near the summit. Mauna Loa and the other four peaks on the island of Hawaii are shield volcanoes.

Cinder cones (also called "pyroclastic volcanoes" or "debris cones") Volcanoes composed mostly of explosively ejected pulverized lava, blown out in the form of so-called "bombs" (large rocks), cinders, ashes, and so forth. The rock bentonite is made from compressed volcanic ash, and, as such, it can be classified as a hybrid, as it is half igneous and half sedimentary in origin. The angle of cinder cones is steeper than on shield volcanoes, often 30° to 40°. The Mexican volcano Parícutin is a pyroclastic cone that formed in a farmer's cornfield in the 1940s.

Composite cones (also called "strato-volcanoes") An alternating mixture of cinder debris and lava flows, in stratified layers. Slope angles tend to be intermediate between cinder and dome volcanoes, with about 5° near the base to 30° near the summit, and often alternating with steep and gentle grades, according to the respective types of volcanic eruptions.

Mount Fuji is an extinct composite volcano on the island of Honshu in Japan, and, at 12,388 feet, is the tallest Japanese mountain. The 8,000-foot Mayon is an active composite volcano on Luzon island in the Philippines. A volcano can change its classification: Mount Etna in Sicily is a 10,758-foot composite volcano that was long a shield volcano.

Fumaroles and Volcanic Gases

Fumaroles are volcanic vents that emit gases. Steam (water vapor) is the most common volcanic gas, often comprising

80 percent by volume of Hawaiian volcanic gases. Carbon often makes up 10 percent or more of volcanic gas composition. Volcanic gases are frequently released at temperatures of 500° C or higher. They are often extremely poisonous and invisible, so you need to be especially cautious when exploring near active fumaroles.

Here are some common volcanic gases, in alphabetical order: *carbon dioxide* (CO_2); *carbon monoxide* (CO); *chlorine* (Cl_2); *hydrogen* (H_2); *hydrogen chloride* (HCl)—i.e., hydrochloric acid; *hydrogen fluoride* (HF)—i.e., hydrofluoric acid; *hydrogen sulfide* (H_2S)—i.e., hydrosulfuric acid—which often oxidizes on contact with air to form sulfuric acid (H_2SO_4) or sulfur (S_2); sulfur (S_2); *sulfur dioxide* (SO_2); *sulfur trioxide* (SO_3); and *water vapor* (H_2O)—"steam."

Sedimentary Rock Formation

The formation of *sedimentary rock* begins with the *weathering* (breaking into small fragments) of preexisting bedrock outcrops on the Earth's surface. There are two kinds of rock weathering: mechanical and chemical.

Mechanical (also called "physical") *weathering* is of various types:

+ *Abrasion*—grinding away of exposed bedrock by water-carried gravel, glacier-carried gravel, and windblown sand.
+ *Cracking*—due to temperature changes causing alternating expansion and contraction of rock.
+ *Frost wedging*—rock splitting when water freezes to ice in rock cracks.

+ *Biological mechanical action*—for example, when tree roots grow into rock cracks and expand.

Chemical weathering is mostly done by acidic rain and groundwater chemically attacking bedrock. Atmospheric carbon dioxide gas (CO_2) mixes with rain water (H_2O) to form dilute carbonic acid (H_2CO_3), which dissolves calcium rocks such as *limestone* and *marble*. Organic acids from decaying plants in soil also dissolve rock by percolating down to underlying bedrock. Rain, streams, groundwater, and seawater dissolve soluble minerals from rock, causing the rock to break up into pieces. Wave action against shorelines is both mechanical and chemical in its rock weathering.

Magnesium calcite marble in dolomitic calcite marble. Note the spinel crystals and the graphite stains. This specimen is from Kootchinskoye in the Ural Mountains of Russia. © GIA & Tino Hammid.

Rough ametrine *specimens from Bolivia.*
Ametrine is the bicolored quartz *combination*
of purple amethyst *with yellow* citrine. *Photo*
by Robert Weldon. © GIA.

Transport of Weathered Rock Fragments

After weathering, rock particles can be transported by water, wind, gravity, or glaciers to sites of deposition. Most transport of weathered rock is done by moving water, which carries solid rock particles and dissolved-rock aqueous solutions away from the weathering site.

Mechanical weathering of desert rock outcrops occurs by abrasion. *Deflation* is the blowing away of such dust and sand by the wind. Underground streams will dissolve and erode *limestone* rock beds into caverns, shafts, and tunnels. Gravity will pull down weathered rock fragments to form rockfalls at the base of cliffs. A rockfall is fallen rock. An avalanche is fallen snow. A crevice is a rock crack. A crevasse is an ice crack (usually a large glacier crack).

Deposition of Transported Rock

Wind- and water-carried sediments are usually well sorted by particle size when they are deposited (reach their final resting place). *Moraine* deposits (glacial sedi-

ments) differ from water-deposited sediments, in that glacial deposits are generally not rounded fragments, sorted by size, and neatly layered. But streams from melting glaciers will often transport and physically transform glacial deposits into the more typically appearing water deposits, which may end up far from the glacier of origin. *Erratics* are glacial boulders that have been carried far and deposited by glaciers on different bedrock formations.

Sedimentary Rock Lithification

Sedimentary rocks form from deposited rock fragments if sufficient pressure develops from the cumulative weight of overlying sediments, according to the geologi-

Weathered sedimentary *rock strata in the Grand Canyon, Arizona. Photo by Paul McCallum.*

cal *law of superposition*, whereby, in normal sedimentary rock layers, the younger strata are on top of older strata. The deposited sediments may lose moisture, but they keep their particles visible in *clastic* sedimentary rocks. *Nonclastic* sedimentary rocks are of chemical or organic origin. *Tillite* is glacial erosion deposits that have been cemented together. *Travertine* and *tufa* are light-colored mineral deposits that chemically precipitate at mineralized hot springs. Silica cement can produce hard *sandstones* when sand deposits lithify. *Shale* is stone made from mud, and *conglomerate* is sedimentary rock composed of rounded pebbles cemented together. *Limestone* is either chemically precipitated from seawater or consists of cemented lime fragments. *Halite* and *gypsum* beds are sedimentary rocks from evaporated seas. About 75 percent of the land regions on Earth are covered with sedimentary rocks over igneous bedrock.

Halite *("rock salt") crystal cluster, with inclusion impurities. This mineral dissolves readily in water, and it must be stored in low humidity.* © *GIA.*

Metamorphic Rock Formation

Metamorphic rocks have been changed by heat, pressure, or fluid permeation acting on preexisting rocks. Igneous and sedimentary rocks are most commonly metamorphosed, but metamorphic rocks themselves can be further metamorphosed.

Pressure can be dynamic or static in metamorphism. Dynamic pressure results from compression due to faulting or folding of rock beds. Static pressure occurs from a bedrock overburden of 30,000 feet or more, creating a plastic flow in underlying rock formations.

Heat for metamorphism comes from *magmatic intrusions* into existing rock or from friction due to rock motion and deformation. Heat accelerates chemical processes that contribute to the formation of new minerals in rocks.

Igneous gases or fluids, as well as mineral-rich groundwater can also cause rocks to metamorphose. ·

Metamorphism typically results in mineral recrystallization, coarser rock texture, formation of new minerals, and/or rock stratification in mineralization. Metamorphism can be done by degrees, from simple to highly changed rock material, so that we often see intergrades of metamorphic rocks.

Unconformities

An unconformity is a bedrock gap in geologic sequence; that is, the bedrock formations are not continuously, chronologically superpositioned, due to erosion or nondeposition. Sometimes used inter-

Cuprite, *a copper ore, cut and rough.* © *GIA.*

Brownish-yellow stained, etch channel inclusions in an otherwise colorless topaz, *which has been cut and polished. Photo by W. Videto.* © *GIA.*

changeably, the basic types of unconformities are:

◆ *Angular unconformities*—successive rock layers aren't parallel to each other, indicating past faulting or folding of angular strata.

◆ *Disconformities*—relatively parallel successive layers of sedimentary bedrock, but with a geologic gap between them; not to be confused with "discontinuities," which are contacts between major zones in the Earth's interior (such as mantle/outer core).

◆ *Nonconformities*—sedimentary bedrock that rests on eroded igneous or metamorphic rock, the eroded material

being the geologic gap due to its absence.

Mountain Formation

Scientists used to believe that the Earth's interior was cooling and shrinking, causing the crust to buckle and form mountains. Now we believe that continental drift is responsible for major mountain ranges. Mountains may appear to be permanent, but they are constantly changing: uplifting, faulting, folding, and eroding. Large areas of Canada are still rising about ½ inch per year due to "crustal rebound," after being under the weight of the last Ice Age continental glacier, which melted 10,000 years ago.

Museum curator Peter Russell, of the Department of Earth Sciences at the University of Waterloo, Ontario, Canada, shows specimens in the university's Biology–Earth Sciences Museum's rock garden to graduate students. This particular rock is a piece of Lorrain jasper conglomerate, from the Canadian shield near Sault Sainte Marie. Photo courtesy of curator Russell, and originally published in Rocks & Minerals *magazine, Washington, D.C.*

Examples of folded mountains are the Alps, Andes, Himalayas, Rockies, and Urals. The classic faulted-block mountain range is the Sierra Nevadas in western North America. Existing volcanic mountains are geologically young, such as Etna, Fujiyama, Kilauea, and Vesuvius.

Continental bedrock tends to be the oldest in the middle of a continent and progressively younger towards the conti-

The Rock Cycle

Natural Causative Agents	Geological Events	Geological Results
Igneous pressure or faulting or folding, producing uplift of bedrock	Uplift and exposure of bedrock at the Earth's surface	Bedrock outcrops
Mechanical and chemical forces on the Earth's surface	Outcrop weathering	Weathered-rock fragments at outcrop site
Moving water, wind, glaciers, and gravity	Erosion of weathered-rock fragments	Transport of rock fragments from outcrop site to site of deposition
Natural physical obstacles and gravity prevent further transport of rock fragments	Deposition of rock fragments	Sedimentation: the layered accumulation of transported weathered-rock fragments

nent's edges. Currently forming mountains tend to be located along a continent's edges, whereas ancient, solidified lava flows (the continental shields) in the continent's geographical middle may have been long ago covered up with successive layers of superficial new rocks. Eroded hills from medium-aged mountains tend to exist between the ancient, continental central cores and the youngest mountains along the continental edges.

Pressure, compression, cementation, and/or dehydration	Lithification (solidification) of deposited sediments	Formation of new sedimentary bedrock
Weight of rock strata overburden that continually accumulates	Subsidence ("sinking") of previously formed bedrock, often sedimentary	Old bedrock gets pressed deeper towards the hot regions of the deep crust
Heat, pressure, or fluid permeation	Metamorphosis of existing bedrock (sedimentary or otherwise)	Changing of existing rocks into new metamorphic bedrock
Subterranean heat	Melting of subsided bedrock; also fresh magma intruding upward from deep crust	Magma formation underground
Cooling of magma underground—or in surface lava flows	Solidification of magma or lava	Formation of new igneous bedrock

ROCK CLASSIFICATION AND IDENTIFICATION

"When we examine into the structure of the earth's crust . . . we discover everywhere a series of mineral masses, which are not thrown together in a confused heap, but arranged with considerable order . . ."
Charles Lyell (1797–1875), *Principles of Geology*

There are more than 600 basic rock types, with perhaps several thousand subtypes and intergrades, depending on how we classify them: (1) chemically (such as acidic as against basic; types of elements or minerals included; simple or complex molecules), (2) structurally (for example, grain shapes, sizes, and relative arrangement; gross rock texture; appearance of rock formations), (3) optically (color and luster), (4) by method of formation (intrusive against extrusive igneous rocks; water-, wind-, or ice-transported sediments; contact versus regional metamorphism), and so forth.

Igneous, *sedimentary*, and *metamorphic* are the three major kinds of rocks in the Earth's crust, based on how they formed. These three massive divisions are logical separations in how most collectors organize their rock collections, and in how this chapter is divided. Igneous rocks come from magma (molten rock), sedimentary rocks consolidate from deposition and precipitation of transported rock particles, and metamorphic rocks are derived from preexisting rocks that have been changed by heat and/or pressure within the Earth's crust. All three major kinds of rocks can be eroded and turned into sedimentary rocks, and all three can be metamorphosed. All rocks were originally igneous, so all sedimentary and metamorphic rocks are, in a sense, secondary (rather than primary) rocks.

When you are rock collecting in the field, you are most interested in first identifying whether a rock outcrop or loose specimen is igneous, sedimentary, or metamorphic. Then you will try to make a preliminary identification of the rock's specific name, and you will follow up your suspicions with chemical or physical tests, if necessary, in the field or at home.

Mineralogy and gemstone books in the GIA Bookstore, Santa Monica, California. The serious rock and mineral student needs reference books from bookstores and libraries. © GIA.

Title pages of three early books on mineralogy and gemology: Robert Boyle's 1672 An Essay About the Origine and Virtues of Gems; a 1717 edition of Camillus Leonardus' Latin Speculum Lapidum ("Mirror of Stones"); and Thomas Nichols' 1652 Lapidary, or the History of Pretious Stones, which is the earliest-known English language work on gems. The Sinkankas book Collection, GIA Library, Santa Monica, California. Photo by Robert Weldon. © GIA.

Rare gemological books in the 14,000-volume Sinkankas Collection, which is now part of the GIA Library in Santa Monica, California. Books in this famous collection date from the early 16th century. Photo by Robert Weldon. © GIA.

Natural rough smithsonite from the Kelley mine in Socorro County, New Mexico. Smithsonite is a simple zinc carbonate mineral that forms from the weathering of zinc ores. Courtesy of Natural History Museum of Los Angeles County.

Blue crystal cluster of smithsonite, *a simple zinc carbonate mineral, whose hexagonal crystals are normally rounded and indistinct. Smithsonite's crystals are rarely well-formed; hence, this blue cluster is especially handsome, although this mineral is often pseudomorphic.* © GIA.

For example, igneous rocks have no layers or bands, and most igneous rocks have uniformly distributed interlocking mineral particles. Both sedimentary and metamorphic rocks are layered or banded in typical formations (there are exceptions), but sedimentary rocks have separated mineral particles and are usually dull in lustre, whereas metamorphic rocks have interlocking mineral particles and often sparkling lustres. Rocks have a strong tendency to integrate into other rock types, however, and even experienced field geologists sometimes have trouble making positive identifications for similar-appearing rock types in the field and need to perform analytical tests to verify or deny their opinions.

Unconformities are where different rock types meet in their natural bedrock formations. The typical unconformity is an igneous/sedimentary contact zone, indicating alternating processes of uplift, erosion, sedimentation, and subsidence over time. The mineral collector seeking rare specimens or large crystals will naturally be attracted to igneous/metamorphic/sedimentary unconformities, where hydrothermally deposited minerals, for example, will tend to be concentrated in the igneous/metamorphic zone of contact.

————————————— ◆ —————————————

Man-made hydrothermal sphalerite. *Photo by Kurt Nassau.* © *Kurt Nassau & GIA.*

This 896-carat lapidary "egg" has been fashioned from the rare arsenate mineral of mansfieldite. *Photo by Maha DeMaggio.* © GIA.

IGNEOUS ROCKS

The word *igneous* comes from the Latin *igneus*, from *ignis* ("a fire"), from the Indo-European root *egnis*. *Igneous rocks* have not been on fire, but they do form from magma—hot, molten rock beneath the Earth's surface. When magma reaches the Earth's surface, it is called lava.

Igneous rocks have no layers or bands. They have interlocking crystalline particles (when crystalline) and uniform texture no matter from which direction the rock is broken. Over 99 percent of the chemical composition of igneous rocks consists of nine elements: oxygen, silicon, aluminum, iron, calcium, sodium, potassium, magnesium, and titanium. Igneous rocks are usually hard (over 5½ on the Mohs' Scale). The noncrystalline igneous rocks are dense and glassy (for example, *obsidian*) or spongy with holes (for example, *pumice*).

Spessartite garnet *in matrix from Ramona, California. Photo by Mike Havstad.* © GIA.

Natural specimen of splintery fractured hematite, *a common iron ore with simple iron oxide composition.* © GIA.

A 5.72-carat "cat's-eye" apatite *cabochon from Madagascar. The word "apatite" is derived from the Greek term* apatao *("to deceive") because early mineralogists often confused apatite with other minerals.* © GIA.

Igneous rocks are made up mostly of eight minerals, although they may have accessory minerals (traces of other minerals), such as *allanite*, *apatite*, *garnet*, *hematite*, *ilmenite*, *sphene*, *spinel*, and *zircon*. The eight essential minerals of igneous rocks can be divided into two groups of four minerals each: the *felsic* and the *mafic* igneous rocks, discussed below.

Felsic Igneous Rocks

The *felsic* igneous rocks, also called *acidic* or "light-colored" igneous rocks, are rich in minerals that are both lighter in color and lighter in weight (lower in density or specific gravity) than the so-called "basic" igneous rocks (see below). Acidic rocks are rich in *silicates* (silicon and oxygen molecular groups). The rock *granite* is the most common felsic rock, being acidic, silica-rich, light-colored, and lighter weight (than basic rocks). Granite forms the core of most mountain ranges, as well as the continents themselves, which "float" on the underlying *basalt* of the Earth's crust.

The four essential minerals found in felsic igneous rocks are *quartz*, *feldspars*, *feldspathoids* (similar to feldspars but containing less silica; examples are leucite and nepheline), and *muscovite* mica. "Essential minerals" mean that, if a rock doesn't have any of them, it cannot be classified as a felsic igneous rock. Although, of course, it may be poor in one or more of these minerals, because they simply weren't richly present when the rock solidified.

Feldspar *"sunstone,"* also termed *"adventurine,"* an orange to reddish-brown variety of oligoclase. *The metallic sparkling lustre is due to intergrown* hematite or goethite *minerals. Photo by Robert Weldon.* © *GIA.*

A 4.6-centimetre-long cut slab of labradorite, *a* plagioclase feldspar *from Labrador, Canada. Courtesy of Fred Pough, photo by Jeff Scovil.*

Mafic Igneous Rocks

The *mafic* igneous rocks, also called *basic* or "dark-colored" igneous rocks, have *ferromagnesian* (iron and magnesium) minerals predominating, are low in silica, are usually dark-colored (compared with the felsic rocks described above), and are heavier in weight (higher density or specific gravity) than the "acidic" igneous rocks. The rock *basalt* is the most common mafic rock, being basic, ferromagnesian-rich, silica-poor, dark-colored, and heavier than *granite*. Basalt forms the ocean floor and the layer of the Earth's crust underneath the granitic continents.

The four essential minerals found in mafic igneous rocks are *olivines*, *pyroxenes*, *amphiboles*, and *biotite* mica.

Mesozoic mafic *volcanic rocks on Hayfork Creek, Trinity County, California, where* diamonds *have been found. Photo by R. W. Kopf.*

Olivine *nodule with* pyroxene, *two minerals often present in* mafic *igneous rocks, from Jackson County, North Carolina. Courtesy of Natural History Museum of Los Angeles County.*

Crystallinity of Igneous Rocks

Besides classifying igneous rocks as being either acidic or basic, we can also arrange them in four categories that describe their crystalline nature:

✦ *Crystalline* (also called *holocrystalline*)—rock composed 100 percent with well-defined crystals, such as *granite*.

✦ *Hemicrystalline* (also called *hypocrystalline*)—rock is mostly crystals, but it contains some glassy amorphous mass.

✦ *Hemihyaline* (also called *hypohyaline*)—rock is mostly igneous glass, but it has some crystal structure.

✦ *Hyaline* (also called *holohyaline*)—rock is completely glass.

Pectolite, *a hydrous, calcium, sodium silicate found in cavities in basic volcanic rocks. Specimen from California. Courtesy of Natural History Museum of Los Angeles County.*

Granularity of Igneous Rocks

Besides crystallinity (above), another important *textural* characteristic of igneous rocks is their granularity, which includes the relative sizes of the most common mineral crystals ("grains") in the rock. Some authorities classify the microcrystalline and cryptocrystalline grain sizes as subtypes of aphanitic grains, but here is the way I like to classify rock grain sizes:

+ *Phaneritic* (also called "coarse-grained")—individual mineral grains in the rock can be recognized without magnification; grains more than 0.2 inch (5 millimetres) in diameter.
+ *Aphanitic* (also called "medium-grained")—grains can only be recognized with a hand magnifier; grains between 0.04 and 0.2 inch (1–5 mm) in diameter.
+ *Microcrystalline* (also called "fine-grained")—grains can only be recog- nized with a microscope; grains between 0.0004 and 0.04 inch (0.01 and 1 mm) in diameter.
+ *Cryptocrystalline* (also called "very fine-grained")—grains cannot be resolved ("seen in focus") with a normal microscope; grains less than 0.0004 inch (0.01 mm) in diameter.
+ *Hyaline* (also called *subaphanitic*)— no grains at all; amorphous, glassy.

Color Classification of Igneous Rocks

We can classify igneous rocks into three categories based on their "color index," which is the percentage of mafic (basic, or dark-colored) minerals in an igneous rock:

+ *Leucocratic*—less than one-third mafic minerals (that is, a light-colored rock); examples are *granite*, *monzonite*, and *syenite*.
+ *Mesocratic*—roughly between one-third and two-thirds mafic minerals (a medium-colored rock); examples are *andesite* and *diorite*.
+ *Melanocratic*—over two-thirds mafic minerals (a mostly dark-colored rock); examples are *basalt*, *gabbro*, and *peridotite*.

Subterranean as Against Volcanic Lithification

We can also classify igneous rocks into two large groups based on where they solidified:

+ *Intrusive*—igneous rocks that solidified below the Earth's surface; examples are *gabbro*, *granite*, and *syenite*.
+ *Extrusive*—igneous rocks that solidi-

This miner is working a corundum mine in East Africa. © GIA.

fied above the Earth's surface; examples are *basalt*, *felsite*, and *obsidian*.

The "lithospheric site of consolidation" (precisely *where* the molten rock solidifies, above or below the Earth's surface) does not consistently correlate with a rock's chemical composition. It isn't possible to identify where a rock cooled by its chemical composition alone, because as soon as magma reaches the Earth's surface, it immediately becomes an extrusive rock. *Basalt* is the "volcanic equivalent" of *gabbro*: they both have similar chemical composition, but gabbro cooled *beneath* the Earth's surface, while basalt cooled *above*. But I have found that most beginning and intermediate collectors prefer to organize their igneous rock specimens into *intrusive* and *extrusive* subdivisions, and that is how I list them here.

Elementary school science teachers sometimes use the words "igneous" and "volcanic" synonymously, but this is not technically accurate. Volcanic rocks are a particular kind of igneous rock: extrusive igneous rock. Intrusive igneous rocks are not volcanic, because they never cooled on the Earth's surface.

Cabochons of jasper, *which can be considered an impure subtype of cryptocrystalline* chalcedony quartz. © *GIA.*

Intrusive Igneous Rocks

Intrusive igneous rocks (also called "plutonic rocks," as they were named for Pluto, the Roman god of the underworld) formed from magma that cooled and solidified *below* the Earth's surface. Intrusive igneous rocks have coarse- to medium-textured mineral grains, which can usually be seen without magnification. Rocks cool very slowly deep beneath the Earth's surface, so their crystals have time to grow to a large size. The greater the depth of cooling and the longer the time of cooling, the coarser the rock tex-

Chrysocolla, *a complex copper silicate mineral, from Arizona. Courtesy of Natural History Museum of Los Angeles County.*

ture. Some *granite* has taken millions of years to cool and harden underground.

DIORITE   A plutonic igneous rock, composed of a mixture of light and dark minerals—mostly amphiboles (like *hornblende*), *biotite mica*, *plagioclase feldspars*, and pyroxenes (especially *augite*). Grey to dark green in color, often darkly colored due to *hornblende*. Hardness: 5½–6. Texture similar to *granite*. Specific gravity: 2.8–3.0. Occurrence: nice specimens from Kern and Tuolumne counties in California, Dungannon County in Ontario. Diorite grades into *granite* as *granodiorite*.

GABBRO   A plutonic igneous rock, composed mostly of *plagioclase feldspars* and *pyroxenes*, with traces of *hornblende*, *ilmenite*, and *olivine*. Dark colored, dark grey to greenish-black. Granitic texture. Hardness above 5½. Specific gravity: 2.8–3.1. *Dolerite* (also called *diabase*) is a fine-grained gabbro, used as "trap-rock" crushed stone for roadbeds, concrete gravel, and so forth, because of its great strength. The lower Hudson River Palisades are diabase rock.

GRANITE   The most common and well-known plutonic rock, used extensively in buildings, monuments, and tombstones. Typically composed of about 30 percent *quartz* (white or clear, hard, and with glassy lustre), 60 percent *potash feldspars* (white, grey, pink, or red—giving the overall color to the granite), and 10 percent ferromagnesian mineral, such as *mica* or *hornblende* (dark colored). Often has a salt-and-pepper appearance, due to the *quartz* and *mica* mixture. Usually light-colored overall, but resulting color is based on the relative proportions of its constituent minerals. Hard (above 5½) and weather-resistant. Mineral grains can be identified with a hand lens. Specific gravity: 2.6–2.7. California's Sierra Nevada Mountains, which form the spectacular rock outcrops of Kings Canyon, Sequoia, and Yosemite National Parks, are mostly granite formed 65 million years ago. Placer *gold* deposits on the western slopes of the Sierras caused California's Gold Rush of 1848 and several years after. Of the common plutonic rocks—*diorite*, *gabbro*, *granite*, *peridotite*, and *syenite*—only granite has significant *quartz* content, making it hard, durable, and beautiful.

GRANODIORITE   A plutonic igneous rock, similar to *granite*, but its *feldspar* is mostly *plagioclase* (while *granitic feldspar* is mostly potash). Granite and granodiorite are often difficult to distinguish without a microscope, and they commonly grade into each other, which increases diagnostic confusion in. amateur collectors. Granodiorite color is similar to that of granite, but it is usually darker grey and less pink.

MONZONITE   A plutonic igneous rock, similar to *granite*, but with a *quartz* content of 10 percent or less, and similar to *syenite*, but with more *plagioclase* feldspar. *Potash feldspar* and *plagioclase feldspar* occur in roughly equal amounts in monzonite. Color: mostly light to medium grey. Hardness: 5½–6.

PEGMATITE   A plutonic igneous rock, often forming dikes or veins penetrating other intrusive igneous or metamorphic rockbeds. A coarse-grained rock, with crystals often growing to many feet in length. Many collector gemstones are found in pegmatitic cavities and pockets, where they crystallized out of igneous vapors and solutions. For example, in granitic pegmatites, of similar chemical composition to *granite* but more variable due to the small body of magma that formed the pegmatite, we sometimes discover the gem minerals *beryl, corundum, opal, spodumene, topaz, tourmaline,* and *zircon.* Pegmatites sometimes have *uranium* minerals. A pegmatite dike is characterized by its coarse grains compared to the bedrock that it invades, and it can be from a few inches to a couple of dozen feet thick—and over a mile long. The pegmatites of the Pala district of San Diego County, California, are famous for their rich concentrations of gemstones.

View of the Cruzeiro mine in the state of Minas Gerais in Brazil. This mine is considered to be one of the largest tourmaline mines in the world. © GIA.

A large pegmatite at Wolodarsk, Ukraine, produced this 314-gram yellow-green beryl *crystal. Photo © Sky Hall Photography.*

PERIDOTITE A dark colored plutonic rock, generally dark green to black, made mostly of ferromagnesian minerals—mainly *pyroxenes* and *olivine*, with possibly some *hornblende*. *Dunite* is a variety of peridotite that is yellowish-green, due to its almost total composition of olivine. Peridotite has a generally dull lustre, and it alters into *serpentine*. Peridotite sometimes bears the economically valuable ores of *chromium*, *nickel*, and *native platinum*. *Kimberlite*, a type of peridotite, is the famous diamondiferous ("diamond-bearing") rock of South Africa—where it appears yellowish on the Earth's surface, but bluish underground. Peridotite, with nice collectible minerals, is known from Arizona, Arkansas, Kentucky, New Mexico, North Carolina, and Washington state.

PORPHYRY Either an intrusive or extrusive igneous rock, and labelled according to its groundmass (for example, granitic porphyry or basaltic porphyry). Porphyry has *phenocrysts* (large crystals) mixed with a fine-grain *groundmass* (matrix), superficially resembling the sedimentary rock *conglomerate*, but thus having no uniform texture. So, porphyry itself is not a chemical rock type of standard composition.

SYENITE A plutonic rock, similar to *granite*, but with little or no *quartz*. Syenite is made mostly of *potash feldspars* with some *biotite mica* or *hornblende*. *Nepheline* (a feldspathoid mineral) may be present; nepheline looks similar to quartz, but it has a greasy (instead of glassy) lustre and is softer than *quartz*. Syenite is light-colored, usually a shade of grey, but it may have yellow or pink tints. Its lustre is less glassy than granite's. Its crystals are small, and the texture is relatively uniform. Hardness: 5½–6. Specific gravity: 2.7–2.9. Syenite is much scarcer than granite, but nice outcroppings of it occur in California, Maine, and Ontario.

Extrusive Igneous Rocks

Extrusive igneous rocks (also called "volcanic rocks"—named for Vulcan, the Roman god of fire) formed from magma that escaped from volcanic vents or crustal rifts or fissures and cooled and hardened above (or very near to) the Earth's surface, due to rapid heat loss to the much cooler atmosphere. Because extrusive igneous rocks cool so quickly and don't have time to form large crystals, they have fine texture and small mineral grains (if any at all).

Magma is called lava when it reaches the Earth's surface, and it forms four main types of rock textures:

✦ *Compact*—relatively dense rock with fine to very fine mineral grains, which need magnification for positive identification; examples are *andesite*, *basalt*, and *felsite*.

✦ *Porous*—rock containing air pockets, caused by escaping volcanic gases; examples are *pumice* and *scoria*.

✦ *Glassy*—caused by quickly cooling lava flows, with no mineral crystals forming in an amorphous mass; for example, *obsidian*.

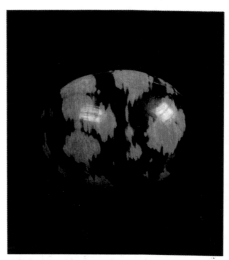

Polished lapidary specimen of "snowflake" obsidian rock. Obsidian is the volcanic glass equivalent of the plutonic rock granite. Photo by Robert Weldon. © GIA.

✦ *Pyroclastic*—irregular fragments of rock, ash, and so forth, that are forcefully ejected from a volcano. Although rocks compacted from such material are sometimes classified as *sedimentary*, I prefer to call them *extrusive igneous* to give credit to their proper origin.

Extrusive Igneous Rock Names

When classifying extrusive igneous rocks, we are torn between categories of *structure/texture* and their *chemical composition*, and it is impossible to reconcile both in an easy classification system. For example, *obsidian* and *pumice* are chemically the same as *rhyolite*, yet all three look radically different from each other in external appearance. *Felsite* is a general field term for light-colored, fine-grained, extrusive igneous rocks, such as *rhyolite* and *trachyte*, that are difficult to identify (as to separate types) in the field, without microscopic examination. Felsite rocks are similar in composition to light-colored intrusive igneous rocks, and they are their "volcanic equivalents." Felsites sometimes show parallel banding caused by lava-flow structure. Rhyolite is light-colored, but it has tiny crystals like *basalt* does; whereas obsidian is dark-colored like basalt, yet it is chemically identical to rhyolite, but it has no crystals like rhyolite does.

Cabochons of cordierite *(also called* dichroite *and* iolite*), a magnesium, aluminum silicate, with spangled inclusions of* magnetite. *Photo by Robert Weldon. © GIA.*

So, instead of chemically or structurally, I've decided to list the extrusive igneous rocks alphabetically so you can find them fast when you're looking for them in this chapter. Realize, also, that extrusive, like intrusive, igneous rocks grade into each other, and a specimen that you stumble upon in the field may seem unlike the "pure" ideal rock types that are neatly described and photographed in a book.

ANDESITE   An extrusive igneous rock, the volcanic equivalent of the plutonic rock *diorite*. Andesite has *biotite, hornblende, plagioclase feldspar*, and *pyroxenes*, with little or no *quartz*. Usually darker than *rhyolite* or *trachyte*, it is intermediate between *basalt* and *rhyolite* in both color and composition. Medium shades of brown, grey, and green. Dull lustre. Hardness: 5–6. Often porphyritic, with phenocrysts of *feldspar* or dark ferromagnesian minerals. Medium-grained.

BASALT   The volcanic equivalent of the plutonic rock *gabbro*. Basalt is a dark grey to black lava rock, sometimes with shades of dark green or dark red. Composed mostly of *plagioclase feldspar* and *pyroxene* (usually *augite*), sometimes with *olivine* phenocrysts. Mineral grains are so small that they cannot be seen with a hand lens. Specific gravity: 2.8–3.3, heavier than *granite*. Hardness: 5–6. The most common lava rock. It underlies the continents and forms the deepest part of the ocean floor. Basalts make up almost all submarine lavas, as well as most of the volume of volcanic islands, such as Hawaii and Iceland. Between one and two cubic miles of basalt is added to the Earth's crust each year by submarine lava flows.

Small 0.5–1.5 cm crystalline quartz geodes with celadonite rims commonly lead miners to the larger, amethyst-filled geodes for which Rio Grande do Sul is known. Photo by Robert Weldon. © GIA.

and brown. Contains *biotite*, *plagioclase feldspar*, *hornblende*, *pyroxenes*, and at least 5 percent *quartz*. Porphyritic with light- and dark-colored phenocrysts.

Malachite rough. A basic copper carbonate mineral, malachite is a popular material for cabochon gemstones and lapidary carvings. © GIA.

The Columbia River Plateau, in Oregon, Washington, and Idaho, was created 10 to 15 million years ago by a massive basaltic lava flow that covered 193,000 square miles. The Columbia and Snake rivers have cut canyons in this plateau, providing spectacular scenery for tourists and residents there today.

Basalt often forms pentagonal or hexagonal columns of rock, often with small mineralized gas pockets. *Geodes* are roundish volcanic rocks where cavities formed by expanding hot gases. These cavities may be completely filled with other minerals, or they may remain partially hollow with linings of *amethyst* crystals, *chalcedony*, or *opal* (for example). So-called "thundereggs" are geode nodules, commonly found in volcanic regions.

Scoria is a type of basalt that is porous from gas bubbles.

DACITE An extrusive igneous rock, the volcanic equivalent of plutonic *quartz diorite*. Light to medium shades of grey

EJECTA Rocks thrown out of volcanoes. Of the chemical composition of lava—which, in fact, these rocks are, often hardening before they hit the Earth. Large ejecta (over 1½ inches in diameter) are called volcanic "bombs." Smaller ejecta (less than 1½ inches) are called lapilli, and even finer material is known as cinders and ash.

Pliny the Younger was 18 years old and living in the Roman city of Pompeii when nearby Mount Vesuvius erupted on August 24, 79 A.D. This eruption buried Pompeii under 20 feet of hot ash and pumice, which rained down on the panic-stricken inhabitants for 48 hours. Pliny's eyewitness account of this eruption, which killed his uncle (Pliny the Elder), includes the following

The sea seemed to roll back upon itself, and to be driven from its banks by the convulsive motion of the earth. . . . On the other side a black and dreadful cloud, bursting with an igneous serpentine vapor, darted out a long train of fire . . . we were immersed in thick darkness, and a heavy shower of ashes rained upon us. . . . Nothing, then, was to be heard but the shrieks of women, the screams of children, and the cries of men . . . some wishing to die, from the very fear of dying; some lifting their hands to the gods; but the greater part imagining that the last and eternal night was come, which was to destroy both the gods and the world together.

Natural obsidian, *back-lighted to show translucency in thin specimens.* © *GIA.*

OBSIDIAN   The volcanic glass equivalent to the plutonic rock *granite*. The same chemical composition as *granite*, *rhyolite*, and *pumice*. High in the silicate minerals *quartz* and *feldspar*. Forms when lava quickly cools. Glassy texture, no crystals, dark-colored (usually black, but sometimes reddish-brown), vitreous lustre, and transparent in thin fragments. Conchoidal fracture. Specific gravity: 2.3–2.6. Hardness: 6–7. Note: Freshly fractured chips are razor-sharp, so never hammer obsidian without wearing wraparound protective eye goggles. Obsidian was often used by Stone Age peoples for making implements. When I taught Earth Science, I always spent one class session teaching my students how to make obsidian arrowheads, which they took home as souvenirs of their day's lesson. "Pitchstone" is a dull, rough type of obsidian. Obsidian is found west of the Mississippi River in the United States.

PUMICE   A porous, spongelike textured, volcanic rock, whose air pockets were formed by hot gases bubbling up through lava. Pumice is actually a frothy *obsidian*, and it has the same chemical content as *obsidian*, *granite*, and *rhyolite*. Some pumice specimens will float in water—but, when crushed, of course, the pumice dust sinks. *Water ice* is the only mineral that is actually lighter in weight than liquid water. Pumice is usually light-colored.

RHYOLITE   A light-colored, fine-grained volcanic equivalent of *granite*, with granite's chemical composition. Usually light shades of grey, yellow, red, or brown, but may darken a bit when weathered. Often porphyritic with tiny phenocrysts of *quartz* and *feldspar*. Hardness: 6–6½. Essentially, black and dark red *obsidian* is a glassy form of rhyolite, and *pumice* is a honeycombed rhyolite, while *pitchstone* is a brownish rhyolite. Rhyolite is often banded, indicating lava flow.

TRACHYTE   An extrusive volcanic rock that is the equivalent of plutonic *syenite*.

A 26-millimetre-long red beryl *crystal on* rhyolite *matrix, from Wah Wah Mountains, Utah. Courtesy of John Barlow, photo by Jeff Scovil.*

Medium-grained, light-colored rock, sometimes with light- or dark-colored phenocrysts. Usually lighter shades of grey, pink, green, or tan. Often without silica, being composed of *biotite* or *hornblende* and *potash feldspar*. Hardness: 5½–6.

TUFF Rock made from compacted volcanic ejecta—for example, rock fragments, cinders, and ash. Tuff is lightly colored shades of whitish, grey, yellow, pink, or brown. It is generally layered, leading some people to classify tuff as a sedimentary rock because it is formed from wind-borne accumulations of dust. Tuff is relatively lightweight, but it may form the "cement" to hold together *breccia* made from large rock fragments (possibly

nonvolcanic ones). So, we can call breccia a type of tuff, or we can give it a separate igneous classification. Many rock experts prefer to use the term "tuff" to mean a volcanic rock compacted from smaller particles of pyroclastic material.

Lazulite rough, also called "blue spar," a basic phosphate of magnesium, iron, and aluminum. Not to be confused with the tectosilicate mineral of lazurite *("lapis lazuli"). Photo by Mike Havstad.* © *GIA.*

SEDIMENTARY ROCKS

Sedimentary rocks are formed from particles of geological matter that have been carried by water, wind, ice, or gravity. Sedimentary rocks make up about 75 percent of the exposed rocks on the Earth's land areas, but they are rather shallow as crustal components. All underlying rocks, and maybe 95 percent of rock in the Earth's crust, are igneous.

The word *sediment* comes from the French *sédiment*, from the Latin *sedimentum*, from *sedere* ("to sit")—and it refers to the broken-up bits of rock that accumulate at the bases of mountains and cliffs, at the bottom of lakes, rivers, and seas, on desert floors, in caverns, and so forth. Sedimentary rocks are produced by erosion of bedrock, transport of the eroded particles to a site of *deposition* (or accumulation), followed by *lithification* (rock-formation) by one of these methods:

+ *Cementation*—whereby a binding material cements the sediments together; examples are *conglomerates* and *sandstones*.

+ *Compaction*—mere pressure from the cumulative weight of overlying sediments causing them to stick together and solidify; for example, volcanic *tuff*.

+ *Compaction with desiccation*—consolidation with the loss of water that is pressed out of the sediments; for example, *shale*.

+ *Evaporation*—precipitation from dissolved aqueous solution, often in desert regions; examples are *halite* and *gypsum*.

Aragonite, *from Saxony, Germany, has the same chemical formula (calcium carbonate) as* calcite, *but aragonite is scarcer and forms orthorhombic crystals. Naturally deposited in hot springs, as stalactites in volcanic rocks, and as the mineral in pearls. Courtesy of Natural History Museum of Los Angeles County.*

+ *Crystallization from subterranean mineral-rich groundwater*—examples are *calcite* formations in *limestone* caverns and crystals lining geodes.

Sediment Types

Sediments are often loosely classified as clay, sand, and gravel, in increasing order of particle size. Or we can classify sediments based on their origins from bedrock weathering:

+ *Clay*—from *feldspars* and *kaolin* minerals.

+ *Sand*—from *quartz*-rich rocks.

+ *Lime*—from the shells and skeletons of sea creatures, and so forth, whose material is ultimately derived from continental rock weathering and transport to the sea.

+ *Precipitates*—from carbonates, phosphates, silicates, and so forth, from solution.

+ *Volcanic sediments*—ash, cinders, and bombs from pyroclastic eruptions; of course, volcanic *tuff* can be considered either an igneous or sedimentary rock.

+ *Magmatic sediments*—from hot spring deposits.

Characteristics of Sedimentary Rocks

Unlike igneous rocks, which are almost universally of uniform texture, sedimentary rocks are typically layered, and individual mineral grains are separated and do not interlock (as they do in igneous and metamorphic rocks). Sedimentary rocks tend to be rough in feel, and with relatively soft "hardness" values (for example, 3–4) so that many can be scratched by a steel knife. But color and chemical composition tend to be extremely variable, due to the random accumulation of eroded rock particles from all over. Some of the most beautiful rock formations visible on the surface of the Earth are color contrasts between the various successive sedimentary rock layers, such as in the Grand Canyon and Painted Desert in Arizona.

Sedimentary rocks can take many centuries to form. When I was a little boy, I read in a child's geology book that some sedimentary rocks build up their depth at about the rate of the thickness of a piece of paper per year. For over 500,000 years, the Mississippi River has been depositing sediments into the Gulf of Mexico. Such deposits are now over four miles thick in places.

Sedimentary Rock Classification

Sedimentary rocks can be classified by how they formed, in two large categories: clastic and nonclastic:

Clastic   Formed by accumulation and lithification of solid pieces of rock, from tiny particles of dust to gigantic boulders; examples are *breccia*, *conglomerate*, *sandstone*, and *shale*.

Nonclastic   Formed by chemical precipitation from solution, evaporation, or organic accumulation; examples are *limestone*, *dolomite*, the evaporites (*anhydrite*, *halite*, and *gypsum*), and geothermal precipitates (if we consider them sedimentary) such as *calcite* and *quartz*-lined geodes. The so-called "rocks of organic origin" are usually classified as sedimen-

tary, although some of them can have metamorphic connotations, such as *amber*, *coal*, *coral*, *dinosaur bone* and *petrified wood*, *oil shale*, *pearl*, and *shell limestone*.

Ivory *with scrimshaw artwork. Although colloquially called an "organic mineral" in the lapidary and jewelry trade, even small weathered fragments of calcareous ivory can be mistaken for true minerals by casual collectors in the field.* © *GIA.*

Most sedimentary rocks show prominent *stratification* (layering), which is evidence of their progressive deposition. Fossil shells and accompanying stratification usually disappear when *limestone* is metamorphosed into *marble*.

Furthermore, we can group certain sedimentary rocks into a category of chemical origin (as opposed to clastic particulate origin), such as *halite* and *limestone*. But halite is an evaporite, while limestone is a precipitate; so, although they both formed from sea water, they formed by different processes.

Understanding that the four most common clastic sedimentary rocks of *breccia*, *conglomerate*, *sandstone*, and *shale*, along with the widespread nonclastic sedimentary rocks of *limestone*, *dolomite*, and the evaporites, are the traditional standard textbook types of sedimentary rocks, I've decided just to list all of them alphabetically, including the organics, to simplify this section and make them easy to find in this chapter.

Common Sedimentary Rocks

AMBER (ALSO CALLED "SUC-CINITE") The fossil resin from pine trees (*Pinus succinifera*) of the Oligocene period, 30 million years ago. An amorphous organic substance of honey-yellow, whitish-yellow, or orangish color, and with greasy lustre. It looks exactly like what it is: hardened tree sap. Chemical composition is variable, but it is a mixture of hydrocarbons, oils, resins, and succinic acid—approximately $C_{10}H_{16}O$ and admixture of H_2S (hydrogen sulfide). Hardness: 2–2½, brittle. Specific gravity: about 1.08, making it just slightly heavier than water. Amber from Sicily often fluoresces. Transparent to translucent, with inclusions of insects, pollen, and leaves, trapped in the pine tree resin as long as 30 million years ago. Common along the Baltic Sea coast. Also from Burma, Domini-

can Republic, and southern Mexico. Amber is used for pendant jewelry, such as earrings and necklace suspensions, although it is extremely soft and easy to scratch. Beware of melted and artificially moulded amber being sold as original fossiliferous amber.

An insect encased in amber. Insects or plant life from millions of years ago can sometimes be found as inclusions in amber. © *GIA.*

ANHYDRITE Calcium sulfate ($CaSO_4$)—an evaporite mineral (see "Sulfates" in Chapter 9), occurring either alone or in conjunction with other evaporites. The same formula as the mineral *gypsum*, but without the water.

BRECCIA A coarse-grained sedimentary rock with sharp, angular rock fragments held together by mineralized "cement." *Breccias* are similar to *conglomerate*, but they do not have rounded pebbles, indicating that breccias generally form near the site of origin of the rock fragments. Breccias form in different ways: volcanic accumulation, in alluvial fans, or at the bases of talus slopes. Breccias may be loosely or tightly consolidated.

COAL An organic sedimentary rock formed by the loss of water and carbonization of compressed plant material. *Peat* is partly decayed plant material with about 80 percent moisture, yellowish-brown in color, and on its way to becoming coal. There are three basic types of coal:

✦ *Lignite* (also called "brown coal")— the least-carbonized coal, with about 25 percent carbon. Brownish-black in color, crumbles easily, and smokes when burned. Lignite forms from peat.

✦ *Bituminous coal* (also called "soft coal")—a black coal with dull lustre and cubic fracture, forms from deeper burial, and has a carbon content of 50 to 65 percent. Forms from further pressure and heat on *lignite*. Bituminous coal is about 90 percent of all coal that is mined for fuel, and is almost smokeless when it burns.

✦ *Anthracite* (also called "hard coal")— metamorphosed *bituminous coal* that has undergone still greater pressures and temperatures deeper in the Earth's crust, driving off more hydrogen and other volatile chemicals—resulting in a hard, dense coal with up to 85- or 95-percent carbon content. Black color,

Tetragonal crystal of apophyllite, *a fluorsilicate common from Poonah, India. Almost always found in crystals, often individuals.* © *GIA.*

shiny lustre, and conchoidal fracture. Burns with a smokeless flame.

Coal is the most common fossil fuel, and over half the known world reserves are in North America. Coal in the eastern and central United States formed during the Pennyslvanian period about 300 million years ago. Coal sometimes contains fossil plant and animal impressions, which make the most desirable collectible specimens. Pennsylvania, West Virginia, and southern Illinois have extensive coal beds, sometimes with coal layers up to 100 feet thick sandwiched between *sandstones* and *shales*.

CONGLOMERATE (SOMETIMES CALLED "PUDDINGSTONE") A clastic sedimentary rock made of rounded pebbles, cobbles, or boulders cemented together with a finer matrix. The rounded

Rough actinolite, *a complex silicate mineral sometimes called "cat's-eye jade" in the jewelry trade.* © *GIA.*

rock materials in conglomerate were water- or glacier-eroded. Conglomerates often form at the mouths of fast rivers, in alluvial fans and deltas, and at the bottom of canyons. *Tillite* is glacially transported conglomerate. *Breccia* is either a type of conglomerate with angular rock fragments or a separate rock type, depending on how we define terms. *Quartz* and *quartzite* make up the pebbles in many conglomerates, and the cement matrix is often calcium carbonate, iron oxide, or silica, and sometimes clay. The so-called "placer gravel" is a conglomerate that bore much of the *gold* in 19th-century mining in Alaska and California. "Puddingstone" is a conglomerate with distinct color contrast between the pebbles and matrix. Pebbles may be of similar, or widely varying, sizes in a conglomerate bed.

DOLOMITE A nonclastic sedimentary rock that is similar to *limestone*, but composed of magnesium, instead of calcium, combined with carbonate: $MgCO_3$. Dolomite is both a rock and a mineral. When dolomite mineral is mixed with *calcite*, the rock is called *calcitic dolomite* if over 50-percent dolomite, and *dolomitic limestone* if less than 50 percent dolomite. Formed on sea bottoms by magnesium-replacement in *limestone* that is forming or has already formed. Some geologists believe that dolomite rock may also precipitate directly out of seawater as a primary rock.

Dolomite is a little harder and more acid-resistant than limestone. Usually greyer or tanner in color than limestone. Fine-grained and hardness 3–4. Unlike limestone, which readily effervesces, dolomite effervesces in hydrochloric acid only when the rock is powdered or tested with hot acid (can be dangerous!).

GYPSUM An evaporite sedimentary rock, formed when seas or salty lakes evaporate. Also believed to form when *anhydrite* hydrates, because gypsum is hy-

Dolomite *crystal cluster from Austrian Tyrol. Dolomite is a calcium, magnesium carbonate mineral that also forms a rock by the same name. Courtesy of Natural History Museum of Los Angeles County.*

Selenite, *the colorless and glassy variety of the hydrous calcium sulfate mineral of* gypsum, *on natural matrix. Courtesy of Natural History Museum of Los Angeles County.*

drated anhydrate: $CaSO_4 \cdot 2H_2O$. Gypsum is both a rock and a mineral. Large gypsum beds in a number of American states, including California, Colorado, New Mexico, and Utah. Color: usually white to grey. Hardness: 2, easily scratched.

The evaporites of *gypsum*, *anhydrite*, and *halite* are precipitated in that order, from evaporating seawater. Gypsum is the least soluble; therefore, it precipitates first from a saturated solution. Halite is the most soluble; therefore, it precipitates last. These evaporite rocks are often found in thick beds above and below each other.

HALITE (ALSO CALLED "ROCK SALT") An evaporite chemical sedimentary rock, often found with *gypsum* beds.

Carved limestone idol head, several centimetres high, from India. Author's collection and photo.

Both a rock and a mineral, usually called "rock salt" when referred to as a rock containing impurities along with the main ingredient of sodium chloride (NaCl). Because halite is very water-soluble, it will not precipitate out of solution, unless a briny lake or piece of sea is cut off and mostly evaporated; hence, rock salt outcrops of recent vintage occur in desert environments. Some rock salt beds are more than a thousand feet thick and cover 100,000 square miles. Rock salt is mostly colorless or white, but it may be grey, yellow, or pink, depending on impurities. It is mined in many localities over the world. Russian criminals were often sentenced to work in the *salt* mines of Siberia.

LIMESTONE The most common non-clastic sedimentary rock, composed mostly of the mineral *calcite*: calcium carbonate ($CaCO_3$). Usually grey, but ranges from white to black. Grains from microscopic to coarse. Made mostly from the remains of marine life (bones, coral, and shells). Limestones tend to be marine chemical precipitates, but some limestones can loosely be termed "clastic" in that they are made up of broken shells or pieces of calcite.

Although all are composed of the same primary chemical, *limestones* can be separated into commonly encountered types—based on their appearance and method of formation—and there is some overlap in types:

✦ *Chalk*—a soft limestone, made from microscopic shells of foraminiferans (a group of Protozoa [one-celled animals] of the order Foraminifera). The chalk used in school classrooms is the rock _chalk_ mixed with _clay_ (derived from clay rocks). So, when you write on a chalkboard with normal chalk, you are using a fossiliferous limestone.

- ✦ _Chemical limestone_—precipitated from water solution in subterranean caverns, hot springs, and seas.
- ✦ _Clastic limestone_—formed from broken shells or limestone fragments.
- ✦ _Coquina_—formed from the consolidation of large shells, usually recently. Common in Florida.
- ✦ _Coral_—an organic lime rock, which is composed of the calcium carbonate ($CaCO_3$) skeletons of tiny invertebrate animals in Phylum Coelenterata, Class Anthozoa. Coral reefs form in warm, shallow seas—and presently cover a half-million square miles on the oceanic surface. The 1,260-mile-long

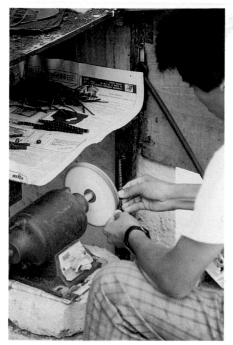

This craftsman in San Miguel de Cozumel, Mexico, uses a lathe-driven cotton buff to polish a piece of Caribbean black coral. Photo by Robert C. Kammerling. © GIA.

Modern pendant with a carved piece of coral, representing Buddha. Composed of calcium carbonate, coral is not a true mineral, but colloquially termed an "organic gemstone" in the jewelry trade. Photo by Mike Havstad. © GIA.

Great Barrier Reef along the northern Australian coast is the largest coral reef on Earth. _Fossil coral_ is often included in invertebrate fossil collections.

So-called "precious coral"— usually some shade of white, pink, or red, sometimes blue or black—is used as a gemstone and lapidary ornament. Hardness: 3–4. Specific gravity: 2.6–2.7 for common types. Crystals: hexagonal, but microcrystalline. No cleavage, uneven fracture, and dissolves effervescently in hydrochloric acid. The western Mediterranean produces the best red coral. Hawaii and the Cameroon coasts yield nice black coral. Japan and Malaysia produce much commercial coral.

✦ *Crystalline limestone*—formed when calcium carbonate recrystallizes in already existing limestone. Looks a lot like *marble*, but is not called marble unless pressure trauma is evident. May be confused with marble by collectors.

✦ *Fossiliferous limestone*—limestone that is rich in observable fossils.

✦ *Marl*—a mixture of clay, sand, and limestone.

✦ *Oölitic limestone*—formed from calcium carbonate, which chemically precipitates out of water, usually around a preexisting nucleus of a sand grain or shell fragment. Looks like stuck-together tiny fish eggs.

✦ *Pearl*—an organic *aragonite* formed in saltwater or freshwater mollusks. Hardness: variable, 2.5–4.5. Specific gravity: 2.6–2.85. Body colors: white to black, often with pinkish overtones. Pearls have been harvested from the seawater of the Persian Gulf for more than 2,000 years. Also commercially found off Australia, Japan, Florida, South Pacific islands, and other localities. Many jewelry pearls sold today are cultured (grown on pearl farms from seeded cores), not natural. Quality is all-important; if you don't know your pearls, know your pearl jeweler.

✦ *Shell limestone*—composed of obvious shells; either more compact than, or used synonymously with, *coquina*.

✦ *Travertine* (sometimes called "flowstone")—the colored, compact crystalline deposit from hot springs or in caverns. *Stalactites* (hanging down from the ceiling) and *stalagmites*

Natural freshwater pearl, 5.43 carats, from the Tennessee River, U.S.A. The mineral aragonite *is the chemical of pearls, which are colloquially termed "organic gemstones," formed by certain freshwater and marine mollusks. Courtesy of J. Caudle, photo by Robert Weldon. © GIA.*

Trio of conch pearl*s from Dominican Republic, showing range of color-flame structure. Photo by Robert Weldon. © GIA.*

Mother of pearl carved cameo. Being relatively soft, pearl is easy to work as lapidary and artistic material. © GIA.

(growing up from the floor) are travertine formations in subterranean caverns, formed as calcium bicarbonate–rich groundwater percolates down through limestone formations, and precipitates out in solidified cavern formations. Not as porous as *tufa* (below).

✦ *Tufa* (not to be confused with volcanic *tuff*)—a porous limestone, often colored with iron, precipitated out at mineral-rich hot springs or in caverns. Tufa is more porous than *travertine* (above), but sometimes both are used interchangeably—or travertine is considered a type of tufa.

SANDSTONE A clastic sedimentary rock that is formed by the solidification of sand into rock. The sand is usually *quartz* grains held together with a binding agent of lime (*calcite*), silica, or iron oxide. Silica cement produces hard sandstones. The color and durability of sandstone is determined by the binding material to a great extent. Reddish-brown sandstone contains iron oxide, but sandstone colors range from white to yellow, tan, grey, and red. Sandstone can form from seas, lakes, rivers, or wind deposits of sand. Sandstone usually forms in shallow seas, often bearing fossil animals that lived just offshore.

Bulky *conglomerate* is usually deposited first in water-carried sediments, then *sandstone*, then *shale*, then *limestone*, as the water flow continues. The sand at the beach is most likely either eroded sandstone or *granite*. Sandstone breaks around its individual grains; *quartzite* (which superficially resembles sandstone) breaks across (through) its grains; this is obvious under magnification.

Sandstone tends to have a rough texture like sandpaper. Fine-grained sandstone grades off into sandy *shale*, whereas coarse-grained sandstones grade into small-pebbled *conglomerate*. Sandstone-walled canyons often have a floor of sand many feet thick from eroded sandstone on the canyon's cliffs, and any streams flowing through such a canyon will have sandy bottoms, frequently littered with rounded pebbles of various sizes.

Sandstone *xenolith, a rock that broke from the wall of a conduit that carried* kimberlite *magma. The geologist's hammer is a vital rock-collecting tool. South Africa. Photo by John Gurney.*

Sedimentary rock particles can be classified by size, whether still in the consolidated rock or in loose sediments. Here are some standard diameters of sedimentary rock fragments:

✦ *Clay*—less than ½₅₆ millimetre; forms shale.
✦ *Silt*—between ½₅₆ and ¹⁄₁₆ mm; forms siltstone.
✦ *Sand*—between ¹⁄₁₆ and 2 mm; forms sandstone.
✦ *Granule*—between 2 and 4 mm; forms granular sandstone or gravel conglomerate.
✦ *Pebble*—between 4 mm and 6.4 centimetres; forms pebble conglomerate.
✦ *Cobble*—between 6.4 and 25.6 cm; forms cobble conglomerate.
✦ *Boulder*—more than 25.6 cm (10 inches); forms boulder conglomerate.

SHALE A clastic sedimentary rock that hardens from clay, mud, or silt. If the rock particles are less than ½₅₆ mm in diameter, it is called *shale*; if between ½₅₆ and ¹⁄₁₆ mm, it is called *siltstone*; particles greater than ¹⁄₁₆ mm would grade into *sandstone*. *Mudstone* is massive and not easily split.

Shale is a fine-grained sedimentary rock of uniform texture; it is thin-layered, easily split, and of individual particles that usually cannot be identified with a hand lens. When sediments are transported by water, conglomerate-sized fragments settle first, then sand, then silt and clay to form shale. When *calcite* is added, shale grades towards *limestone*. When *quartz* is added, shale grades towards *sandstone*. Shale tends to be grey, but it also comes in shades of white, red, green, brown, and black. It is easily scratched by

a knife, and it sometimes contains water ripple marks or mud cracks that have lithified.

Shale often bears deeper water fossil creatures, such as fish. The famous fish-bearing Green River formation shales in Wyoming formed over a time span of 5 million years. Billions of tons of "oil shale" (petroleum-rich) will give us fossil fuel after we deplete the easily extracted petroleum from *sandstone* reserves.

SILICIFIED SEDIMENTARY ROCKS
There are several types, depending on our definitions. *Sandstone* itself could be called "silicified" because it is composed of silica sand. But we usually think of *silicified petrified wood* as the classic silicified sedimentary rock. Such fossil wood has been found in every American state, evidence of prehistoric forests of long ago. Hardness: 7. Found in rocks from Silurian to Recent periods in geologic time. Formed in freshwater sediments as plant material accumulated, then was buried under heavy sediments, and chemically replaced by silica minerals, such as *agate* and *opal*.

Diatomite (also called "diatomaceous earth") is an organic sedimentary rock composed entirely of the silica skeletons of plankton (microscopic floating algae) called *diatoms* (in the plant Phylum Chrysophyta). Diatomite forms in pond and lake deposits, where these plants grow in quantity. Nice specimens from Maryland, as well as Germany and Scotland.

METAMORPHIC ROCKS

Metamorphic rocks are rocks that have been changed by heat, pressure, or fluid (including gases and liquids) permeation, typically resulting in (1) new crystal structure, (2) new minerals created, and/or (3) texture coarsening. The word *metamorphic* comes from the Greek roots *meta* ("change" . . . in this case) and *morphé* ("form" or "shape"); hence, metamorphic rocks are often defined as "rocks that have changed in shape."

Metamorphic rocks come from preexisting igneous, sedimentary, or other metamorphic rocks. They may closely resemble their "parent rocks" (rocks from with they are derived) or may exhibit radically new characteristics. Metamorphic rocks can often be identified in the field because they (1) are usually crystalline, (2) have interlocking mineral particles (unlike sedimentary rocks), and (3) are often foliated—that is, layered or streaked (unlike igneous rocks), often with wavy textures. Metamorphic rocks frequently have alternating bands or streaks of color—light, dark, light, dark, etc.—and they are generally harder and more crystalline than their parent igneous or sedimentary rocks. Certain minerals tend to be found only in metamorphic rocks—such as *chlorite*, *garnet*, and *staurolite*.

By volume, metamorphic rocks comprise very little of the Earth's crust, probably less than 1 percent. However, they happen to be the oldest-known rocks on Earth, not counting meteorites and astronaut-retrieved Moon rocks. Some metamorphic rocks from Greenland have been determined to be 3.8 billion years old, indicating that (1) they must have come from still earlier rocks (ultimately *igneous*) and (2) the processes of rock metamorphism were probably the same in the remote past as they are today on Earth.

A 17.56-carat faceted specimen of andalusite, an aluminum silicate gemstone. Courtesy Pala International. Photo by Robert Weldon. © GIA.

A faceted 7.60-carat benitoite specimen in the collection of the Smithsonian Institution, Washington, D.C. Gemstone-quality benitoite, a barium, titanium silicate mineral, is found only in San Benito County, California. Courtesy of the Smithsonian Institution, photo by Robert Weldon. © GIA.

Types of Metamorphism

Most rock metamorphism probably occurs deep within the Earth's crust, where heat and pressure are both extremely elevated. If the temperature gets too high, however, the rock will completely melt and become igneous. Granite melts at about 800° C (1,500° F), and basalt at 1,200° C (2,200° F). It is thought that most metamorphic rocks form in a temperature range of about 100° to 1,200° C (200° to 2,200° F) and up to 40 miles deep in the Earth's crust, where pressures reach 20,000 times the atmospheric pressure on the Earth's surface.

Geologists recognize five main types of metamorphism in rocks: regional, contact, hydrothermal, dynamic, and retrograde.

Regional metamorphism Occurs over large areas in the Earth's crust, due to large crustal motions and igneous heat. Both heat and pressure are agents of change. May occur deep within mountain ranges.

Contact metamorphism Occurs when hot magma touches cold, already-existing rocks. Limited action due to localized contact zone. Heat is the main agent of change. Quarries and mines are often found along contact metamorphic zones, because much new mineralization takes place here, creating gemstone minerals and ore bodies.

Hydrothermal metamorphism Occurs near the Earth's surface, due to the action of hot groundwater on available minerals; for example, at Yellowstone National Park.

Cataclastic metamorphism (also called "dynamic metamorphism") Occurs where mechanical rock pressure is the main agent of change, such as along fault planes.

Retrograde metamorphism Occurs when heat or pressure are removed from regions of ongoing metamorphism, causing some of the metamorphic rock to revert back towards its original type. Metamorphism tends to be irreversible, so retrograde metamorphism takes place only to a limited extent.

Natural celestite *cluster from Zacatecas, Mexico. Celestite forms orthorhombic crystals of simple strontium sulfate. Courtesy of Natural History Museum of Los Angeles County.*

Cut and polished piece of agate *variety of cryptocrystalline* quartz, *showing the typical varicolored agate bands.* © GIA.

Types of Metamorphic Rocks

Here are some common types of metamorphic rock; you should have no trouble finding choice examples of them in the right locations. Of course, some will inevitably grade into others in the field, so any given specimen must be properly interpreted.

AMPHIBOLITE A metamorphic rock with a high content of *amphibole* minerals (like *hornblende*), with structure schistose to massive, fine- to coarse-grained. Color tends to be dark green to black. Hardness: 5–6. Specific gravity: 2.7–2.8. *Plagioclase feldspars* often present. A tough, tenacious rock. Formed by metamorphosis of *gabbro*, *peridotite*, *dolomite*, or *limestone*. Usually forms by regional metamorphism of basic igneous rocks.

ANTHRACITE COAL Sometimes classified as a metamorphic rock because it is derived from heat and pressure on subterranean deposits of *bituminous coal*. By the same reasoning, *graphite* and *diamond* might be considered to be metamorphosed *coal*, but then we're faced with the prospect of nearly every gemstone in the world being called a single-mineral metamorphic rock. When Superman in the movies and comic books squeezed a lump of coal between his hands to create a diamond, he was merely duplicating nature's slower metamorphism in the Earth's crust.

GNEISS (PRONOUNCED "NICE") A coarse-textured banded metamorphic rock, sometimes called "banded granite" in geological slang. The bands or streaks are alternating light and dark mineral layers, and colors range from white, grey, green, red, brown, to black. The bands are parallel, but they generally are not wavy as in *schist*. Gneiss is named after its parent rock (e.g., "granite gneiss") or its distinguishing mineral (e.g., "garnet gneiss"). Looks similar to granite, but has a parallel arrangement of mica, whereas granite has a random orientation of mica. Looks similar to schist, but lacks the uneven wavy lines of schist. Comes from many different kinds of parent rocks that are subjected to regional metamorphism.

HORNFELS The most common "contact metamorphic" rock, generally surrounding granitic intrusions and volcanic pipes, usually derived from the heating of *shale* without accompanying mechanical deformation pressures. Hornfels is usually darkly colored, but with lighter crystal spots. Hardness 6–7. Unfoliated, and with curved fracture. Dull lustre. Generally fine-grained, and maybe lightly banded, reflecting the recrystallization of shale. Can be confused with *basalt*.

MARBLE A metamorphic rock that is formed by contact or regional metamorphism of *limestone* or *dolomite*. Crystal grains, tiny pieces of *calcite*, are usually visible to the naked eye. Generally whitish, but often colored by impurities, creating colors of grey, pink, green, brown, and black. The patchiness or streaky color patterns so diagnostic of marble are due to these impurities. Usually not with parallel bands, as seen in *gneiss* and *schist*. Hardness: 3. Fine- to coarse-grained. Specific gravity: 2.6–2.8. Often used for statues and orna-

A 32-millimetre-long, 42.20-carat, ornamental marble *cabochon from Utah. Photo by Maha DeMaggio. © GIA.*

mental building stone. The fine white Carrara marble in Tuscany, Italy, has been quarried for centuries. Sometimes compact crystalline limestone is mistaken for marble.

PHYLLITE   A metamorphic rock derived from *shale*, but is more metamorphosed than *slate*. Banded, micaceous, and a coarser texture than slate. Silky lustre due to *mica* grains. Sometimes foliated with uniform composition, grading into *schists*. Hardness: 2.7–2.8. Visible crystals.

QUARTZITE (SOMETIMES CALLED "METAQUARTZITE" TO DISTINGUISH IT FROM SEDIMENTARY QUARTZITE)   A contact or regional metamorphic rock that is derived from recrystallized *sandstone* or *quartz conglomerate*. Granular texture, made of tightly stuck-together *quartz* grains—basically compact and hard (7). Breaks *across* its grains (sandstone breaks *around* its grains). Usually lighter colors from the parent sandstone rock, but can range from white to grey, yellow, pink,

brown, and black, often colored with reddish-brown streaks from iron oxide.

SCHIST   A highly metamorphosed rock, more so than *phyllite*, generally forming by regional metamorphism. Light to dark colors, generally medium to coarse texture with visible grains, but may be finer grained than *gneiss*. Breaks into a wavy surface, a characteristic of this rock called "schistosity." Parallel, wavy bands of minerals, often micaceous. Can be easily split into its foliated layers. Can form from igneous, sedimentary, or metamorphic rocks. Named after its most prominent mineral present; for example, *hornblende schist* or *chlorite schist* ("greenstone"). The most common type is *mica schist*, made mostly of *biotite* or *muscovite mica*, plus *quartz*. Sparkling lustre that can dull with weathering. Hardness and specific gravity vary with the different minerals present. The most advanced stage in the metamorphic series of *shale* to *slate* to *phyllite* to *schist*.

SERPENTINITE   A hydrothermal metamorphic alteration rock that is derived from *peridotite* or *pyroxenite*, sometimes from a sequential metamorphism of *dolomite* into *amphibolite* into *serpentinite*. Yellowish-green, often streaked or mottled with black. Has a smooth and greasy feel. Often waxy lustre.

SKARN   A "metasomatic" metamorphic rock, meaning that it was produced by the addition of mineral-rich hot liquids and gases from an igneous intrusion into *limestone* or *dolomite* beds. The resulting skarn is rich in lime silicates, and sometimes with accompanying ore deposits. *Garnets* and *pyroxenes* often present. Medium- to coarse-grained. Colors range from white to black, depending on minerals present. Usually sparkling lustre.

SLATE A low-grade metamorphic rock that is derived from the regional metamorphism of *shale*. Microscopic grains visible only with magnification. Can be easily split into thin layers. Usually dark grey to black, but may also be yellow, blue, green, red, and brown. Easily scratched with a knife. Used for the blackboards in old schoolrooms.

The lead molybdate mineral wulfenite's *crystals are often thin square plates in large groups and the color of butterscotch candy. Courtesy of Natural History Museum of Los Angeles County.*

chapter three

FIELD COLLECTING OF ROCKS AND MINERALS

"For every man the world is as fresh as it was on the first day . . ."
Thomas H. Huxley (1825–1895), *A Liberal Education*

Nice collectible rocks and minerals are not evenly distributed at the Earth's surface, but they tend to be somewhat concentrated at specific outcrops or buried by nature at certain depths at a given collecting site. Some localities may yield five or six major mineral species, others over a hundred.

Mineral sites are logical, not accidental. The more you understand the local geology, the more likely you are to find the minerals that you seek. Crystals are often found in rock pockets and fissures, gemstones in pegmatite volcanic pipes, native gold in milky quartz veins, and fossils in sandstone and shale.

"Surface guide minerals" are minerals that often indicate other specific minerals to be found underground. For example, greenish *autunite* and *torbernite* are alterations of the mineral *pitchblende* and therefore can be practical "surface guides" to successful pitchblende prospecting in the field, but both autunite and torbernite can be mistaken for *copper* ore by the casual field observer.

The two basic kinds of rock and mineral collections are by type (species) and by locality. You may only want *calcite* and will go anywhere to find it. Or you may start a comprehensive collection of samples of every species of mineral found within a 50-mile radius of your home.

◆

A miner looks inside a pocket in the Himalaya mine in San Diego County, California. Photo by Robert Weldon. © GIA.

Searching for jade in Barn Bay, New Zealand, where jade specimens wash down in streams to collect near the beaches. Photo and © by Fred Ward and GIA.

SAFETY IN THE FIELD

Tell someone about where you will be collecting, when you expect to arrive there, and when you plan to return, and notify that person when you get back. Take companions when exploring remote or dangerous locations.

It's a good idea to take along emergency food and water, a first-aid kit, and a flashlight with extra batteries.

In the field, wear strong clothing for protection against falls or scratches from rocks and thorns. Wear strong leather hiking shoes or boots. Leather gloves are a must when scrambling in the brush or picking up sharp rocks. Wear safety goggles and leather gloves when hammering rocks. Don't toss or swing a geology hammer until you make sure you won't hit anybody.

Wear a hard-hat safety helmet whenever there is a possibility of being hit from falling rocks from above, such as when rock climbing, cliff climbing, and exploring caves and quarries, and in loose rockslide areas.

Active volcanoes, glaciers, and caves should be approached with great caution, and only when accompanied by trained experts as guides. Never go where it is too dark to see without artificial light, and never separate from your companions when exploring caves.

Never pull rocks from cavern walls or hammer inside caves, unless you are absolutely certain that it is safe (and legal) to do so. Vibrations from hammering can cause a rock slide or cave-in.

Never walk around in a quarry or mining district at night—you could step on an explosive or fall into a mine shaft.

DANGERS IN AND AROUND ABANDONED MINES

Abandoned mines should only be entered with an experienced guide who is an expert on the particular mine. Never trust an old ladder, rope, or wooden or metal staircase—years of decay can make them fragile.

The Division of Abandoned Mine Lands of the Nevada Department of Minerals has given permission to quote from its publication, *Dangers in and Around Abandoned Mines*, as follows:

SHAFTS—The collar on top of a mine shaft is especially dangerous. The fall down a deep shaft is just as lethal as the fall from a tall building—with the added disadvantage of bouncing from wall to wall in a shaft and the likelihood of having falling rocks and timbers for company. Even if a person survived such a fall, it may be impossible to climb back out. The rock at the surface is often decomposed. . . . It is dangerous to walk *anywhere* near a shaft opening.

LADDERS—Ladders in most abandoned mines are unsafe . . . ladder rungs are missing or broken. Some will fail under the weight of a child because of dry rot.

TIMBER—The timber in abandoned mines can be weak from decay . . . a well-timbered mine opening can look very solid when in fact the timber can barely support its own weight.

WATER—Many mine tunnels have standing pools of water which could conceal holes in the floor. Pools of water are also common at the bottom of shafts. It is usually impossible to estimate the depth of the water.

CAVE-INS—Areas that are likely to cave often are hard to detect. Minor disturbances, such as vibrations caused by walking or speaking, may cause a cave-in. If a person is caught, he can be crushed to death . . . or [you can] be trapped behind a cave-in without anyone knowing you are there.

BAD AIR—"Bad air" contains poisonous gases or insufficient oxygen. Poisonous gases can accumulate in low areas along the floor. A person may enter such areas breathing the good air above the gases but the motion caused by walking will mix the gases with the good air, producing a lethal mixture for him to breathe on the return trip.

Because little effort is required to go down a ladder, the effects of "bad air" may not be noticed, but when climbing out of a shaft, a person requires more oxygen and breathes more deeply. The result is dizziness, followed by unconsciousness. If the gas doesn't kill, the fall will.

EXPLOSIVES—Many abandoned mines contain old explosives left by previous workers. . . . Explosives should never be handled by anyone not thoroughly familiar with them. . . . Old dynamite sticks and caps can explode if stepped on or just touched.

POISONOUS SNAKES—Old mine tunnels or shafts are among their favorite haunts.

NO INEXPERIENCED PERSON SHOULD ATTEMPT TO RESCUE THE VICTIM OF A MINE ACCIDENT! Call the county sheriff. He is in the best position to organize a rescue operation.

Natural pink sapphire *crystal from Montana. Deep red* corundum *is called "ruby"; any other color of corundum can be termed "sapphire."* © *GIA.*

COLLECTING COURTESIES ON PRIVATE PROPERTY

ᴀen rock collecting on private property,
ᴀt the owner's land as sacred ground.
ny rich rock collecting sites have been
ᴀsed to collectors because the property
ners got tired of having their property
ᴀsed. A few thoughtless and selfish col-
ᴀors can spoil a site for everyone, but
y wouldn't if everyone followed these
ᴀes:

Get permission from the property
ner before entering or collecting on pri-
ᴀ property. Congenial owners will even
ᴀect you to the best collecting sites on
ir property, thus saving you a lot of time
l effort in your rock hunting.

Pay any required collecting fee at com-
ᴀcial sites. Don't sneak in without pay-
, even if no owner seems to be around.
d the owner or his representative, and
' the fee.

Collect only the best specimens that
ᴀ want and need, and maybe a few ex-
ᴀ for trading if the site is unusually
ᴀ. Don't be greedy—leave something
collectors who will follow later. Cover
any holes that you dig on land where
ᴀle might fall in.

Obey all posted signs and orders from
ᴀkmen on the property.

Don't touch any personal property of
land owner, such as tools, equipment,
ᴀicles, buildings, and animals.

Don't litter. Pack out your garbage.
ᴀe nothing but rocks and photographs.
ᴀve nothing but footprints.

7. Don't vandalize: no carving on wooden fences or trees, and don't throw rocks at signs or at anything else.

8. Extinguish your campfires with water, and clean up your campsite.

9. Leave open gates open and closed gates closed, after you pass through. Land owners may or may not want their animals going through those gates.

10. Thank the owner, both verbally when you're there and in a letter after you get home, for letting you collect on his or her property.

"FREE" VERSUS "FEE" COLLECTING

Rock collecting is not necessarily better—or worse—at a site where entrance is free versus a site that requires a fee for admission. Nice specimens can be found everywhere or nowhere, depending on your prospecting skill and luck. Try both types of sites, and judge for yourself.

Check with the appropriate government agency's local office before collecting on government public lands; mineral collecting is forbidden in national parks.

ROCK COLLECTING ENVIRONMENTS

Outcrops are places on the Earth's surface where bedrock is exposed. A *mineral deposit* is a place where minerals are found. An *ore body* is a mineral deposit containing metallic elements. A *vein* is a mineral concentration in bedrock, often referring to ore mineral deposits in mining terminology.

Natural Rock Outcrops

Nature has lifted the veil of mystery off of our Earth's crustal bedrock where natural rock outcrops occur, such as mountains, cliffs, ridges, bluffs, beaches and sea-coasts, canyons and riverbeds, natural caves, storm washes, and landslides.

Fallen rocks at a cliff's base are called *talus*, and they are excellent for sampling the kinds of rocks still on the cliff's face. Be careful that you don't twist an ankle or stumble on the loose boulders and gravel of talus deposits. Expect more rocks to fall from above at any moment.

Float is broken-up pieces of bedrock that have been carried away by water. By following a float trail upstream or up-canyon, you may trace the float to its original bedrock outcrop. *Alluvial* deposits, either still in streambeds or at deltas and floodplains, are sometimes mineral-rich, such as those along the coasts of the Alaskan islands.

Sand dunes and beaches, where collecting is legal, offer endless quantities of sand specimens for your collection.

Moraine (glacial deposits) yield glacier-transported rock specimens. Dry lake-beds, desert floors, and valley floors offer sedimentary float as well as possible outcrops.

Man-Made Rock Exposures

Man-made tunnels, road cuts, railroad beds, canals, construction excavations, mines, and quarries can expose choice rock specimens.

Collecting in Rock Quarries

Quarries often yield nice rock and mineral specimens. Collectors have found over a hundred different minerals in the Crestmore Quarry in Riverside, California. *Limestone* and *marble* quarries often have interesting fossils.

Get permission from the quarry operators before entering and collecting. Don't sneak over fences or crawl under locked gates to get inside inactive quarries, but find out who owns them and ask permission. You may have to sign an accident release form so that you can't sue the owners in case you're injured in a quarry. Obey all company signs and workmen's instructions in a quarry. Collect only where you're told to go, and stay away from workmen and their equipment, especially in blasting areas.

Wear sturdy leather work shoes or boots in a quarry. Carry your own water canteen; don't drink from the pools or streams

Light-colored calcite marble in Kootchinskoye quarry's north wall is representative of material in which ruby occurs in the Ural Mountains of Russia. Photo by A. J. Kissin.

at any quarry or mining site. Always wear a safety hard hat in a quarry, and carry appropriate rock collecting tools: geology hammer and/or crack hammer, chisel, leather gloves, eye goggles, and collecting bag.

You can collect off of the quarry's face—for example, the mineral pockets and veins in the vertical walls. Or you can collect loose rocks and gravel from the quarry floor. Expect loose rocks to fall off the face at any moment, including when you're hammering on the face. Always let someone know when and where you plan to enter and leave a quarry.

Collecting in Mining Districts

Hard rock mines—with tunnels and shafts dug deeply into bedrock—can be extremely dangerous to enter and explore, and should only be entered when you are accompanied by an authorized mine expert who knows the particular mine.

Open-pit mines (also called "strip mines") are surface mines that often yield choice mineral specimens for the collector with official permission to collect on such property.

Mine dumps consist of commercially rejected rocky material that has been brought to the surface from deep underground. Mine dumps (sometimes called "tailings") often contain specimens that a collector couldn't otherwise personally retrieve from the depths of the Earth. For example, choice *beryl, kunzite, topaz,* and especially *tourmaline* gemstones are found in the rough mine dumps in San Diego County, California, situated above mineral-rich pegmatite dikes.

Tourmaline *mine in San Diego County, California.* © *GIA.*

ROCK-COLLECTING TOOLS

Useful rock-collecting tools for serious field work include the following:

Collecting bag Used for holding your rocks, collecting tools, lunch, spare clothing, and incidentals. Should be made of heavyweight canvas or reinforced cotton-duck cloth. Lightweight synthetic cloth can tear easily when loaded with sharp and heavy rocks.

Geologist's hammer An essential field tool of two basic types. *Pick hammers* have a cutting point opposite a square flat striking surface. *Chisel hammers* have their cutting edge opposite the flat face, and at right angles to the hammer's handle. Geologist's hammers these days are usually of one-piece all-steel construction.

A prospector's hammer, also called a hand pick or a long-handled pick hammer, is essentially an elongated geologist's pick hammer, with an extended handle and longer tapered pick point for added leverage and prying power. As with any geologist's hammer, the flat head of the prospector's hammer is often used to hit a cold chisel.

Chipping hammer Has a pick point at one end and a vertical-blade cutting edge at the other striking end. A chipping hammer is similar to a geologist's hammer, but without a flat striking face, and with the chisel head parallel (instead of perpendicular) to the handle. Chipping hammers are useful for fossil collecting from sedimentary rocks, and they are constructed like geologist's hammers.

Crack hammer A short-handled sledge hammer with a heavy head flattened on both striking faces. Crack hammers are used to split or crush big rocks, drive chisels and wedges, test rock strength, and rough-trim a large rock. Except for the hand-grip sleeve, crack hammers should be of one-piece all-metal construction to avoid a loose hammer head breaking off.

Crack hammers are commonly sold in weights of 2, 3, or 4 pounds. Heavier crack hammers deliver more force with less downstroke effort; lighter hammers are easier to lift and carry. Using gloves when hammering protects your hands from flying rock chips, but it reduces your grip on the hammer and rocks.

Do not use carpenter's tools for rock work. Do not use a hammer meant to strike nails or a chisel meant to cut wood!

Chisels There are three main types:
+ *Cold chisels* have long handles of small diameter, with small wedge-bladed cutting edges, and are used to extract crystals from deep pockets and cavities.
+ *Gad-point chisels* are shorter and thicker than cold chisels, and they have a tapered point useful for splitting, prying, and wedging. A gad-point chisel is better than a wedge for general collector use. A gad-pry bar has a gad-point at one end and a pry edge at the other.

+ *Broad-bladed chisels*, also called "pitching tools," are short, thick chisels with a wide-cutting wedge-bladed edge, and they are useful for splitting, trimming, and shaping rocks.

Pry bar (also called a "pocket robber") A long bar that is hexagonal in cross section, with its tapered ends bent in opposite directions. It is used to move heavy rocks. Don't use a crowbar not made specifically for rock use!

Safety goggles Must always be worn to protect your eyes from flying rock chips whenever you are chipping or hammering rocks, or near someone doing so! Goggles are made of clear, hard plastic "windows" in the front, soft, flexible plastic sides, and an elastic headband strap. Avoid goggles that don't have all-around plastic sides, as well as goggles that fit too loosely, because stray rock splinters can fly in and cut your eyes. If you wear glasses, get safety goggles that fit over them.

Shovel Not necessary for all field trips, but useful for digging and removing debris. Tip should be pointed instead of rounded. Blade should be shallow. Shovels are heavy and bulky to carry. The little folding military shovel is adequate for most jobs.

Hand magnifiers (also called "hand lenses") Good for field specimen examination and identification. The lens should swivel into a protective metal or plastic case. Good optics are important: the lenses should be corrected for color and spherical aberration so that you're seeing specimens as they really are.

Magnification lenses that are 5X to 10X (5 power to 10 power, that is, 5 to 10 times natural size) are good for field work. Lenses that are 3X are a bit weak to observe detail. Lenses that are 20X are usually too strong, because they greatly restrict the field of view under magnification. Hand lenses are easy to lose in the field, so keep them strung on a cord around your neck, attached to your belt, or inside your collecting bag.

Examining a cut gemstone with a handheld magnifying loupe and specimen forceps. © GIA.

At Da Ban in Vietnam, most of the mining is done with simple hand tools, like the pick used by these miners to remove the potentially gem-bearing gravel. Photo by R. C. Kammerling. © GIA.

Rough diamond crystals and folding magnifying loupe. © GIA.

Gloves Useful for handling sharp rocks. They should be of strong leather and fit comfortably with freedom of finger movement. Soft leather deerskin gloves are ideal and worth the extra cost.

Compass Necessary for finding directions, map work, and testing minerals for magnetism (magnetic minerals can deflect the compass needle). A hand compass is essential for recording accurate locations in your field notebook. Of course, move away from pieces of iron, steel, or pure nickel when you take compass readings, so that the needle isn't deflected by a metal fence, your car, and so forth.

Magnet Helps to distinguish *magnetite* (strongly magnetic) from *chromite* (weakly magnetic), for example. Be careful that you don't lose your small pocket magnet in the field.

Mineral test kit Containing a comparative hardness set, streak plate, simple chemical reagents (such as dilute hydrochloric acid for testing *calcite* and *dolomite*), magnet, and magnifier. Carry the kit in your field bag.

Optional tools for rock collecting
Some of these may be needed for certain field work:

✦ *Screens* and *sieves*—used for sifting and separating small mineral pieces from dirt, sand, or gravel.

✦ *Gold pan*—black or metallic sheet-iron pan, good for extracting *gold* or other heavy minerals from stream gravel. Patience, experience, and strong arms are required for productive

An Apache Native American miner prospecting for peridot *by shoveling* basalt *rock into a sizing sieve on the San Carlos Reservation, Arizona. © GIA.*

gold panning. For most people, 16-inch-diameter pans are best.

✦ *Camera* and *film*—for photographing collecting sites and specimens *in situ* (that is, as they appear before you attempt to remove them from their surrounding matrix).

✦ *Binoculars*—good for identifying landmarks at a distance, unnecessary for most collecting trips.

✦ *Dental tools*—for sale in lapidary shops, and useful for field trimming and extracting small specimens.

✦ *Geiger counter* (portable)—necessary for radioactive mineral prospecting.

✦ *Hard hat* (also called a safety helmet)—essential when collecting near potentially falling rocks. Both construction-worker helmets and sport rock-climbing helmets are used as hard hats by rock collectors. Get a helmet rated for heavy impacts, with an adjustable chin strap and with net-padding inside so that the top of your head doesn't touch the inside of the helmet.

✦ *Ultraviolet lamp* (also called "UV lamp" or "black light")—necessary for fluorescent mineral prospecting. Get a lamp that is portable and emits both short- and long-wave UV rays, and take extra batteries with portable units into the field.

"Black light" prospecting is done at night or in a dark cave, but it can be dangerous because of the chance of tripping and falling, stepping on nails or broken glass, getting hurt against sharp rocks, and losing or breaking gear in the dark. Take along regular flashlights, but thoroughly explore a collecting site in visible light during the day before prospecting there in the dark that evening.

"Paper" supplies for rock collecting The following are useful in the field:

+ *Guidebooks*—to the local geological formations.
+ *Field notebook*—for recording field data at the specimen collecting site; take spare pens or pencils.
+ *Paper labels*—stick-on type for labelling field specimens.
+ *Wrapping paper*—for wrapping field-collected specimens before placing them in a collecting bag. Common newspaper is adequate for larger rocks, tissue paper for small, delicate specimens.
+ *Maps*—road maps, topographic maps, and geologic maps. A geologic map is a local topographic map with bedrock colors and symbols superimposed.

FIELD-COLLECTING STEPS

Serious rock and mineral collecting in the field can be divided into these sequential steps:

1. Locating a collecting site.

2. Photographing or sketching specimens *in situ* (in their natural rock matrix before extraction).

3. Extraction of specimens from bedrock, ground gravel, and so forth.

4. Field trimming (also called "field dressing") of specimens.

5. Field cleaning of specimens.

6. Field identification of specimens.

7. Field labelling of specimens.

8. Field notes entered in a field notebook. Notes should include the specimen's number, site location, site description (example: "Two miles west of church, along south side of railroad track bed"), rock formation type (example: "Miocene shale"), tentative identification of specimen, date collected, and collector's name. Without these field notes, a rock or mineral specimen is just a curiosity. It is still collectible, of course, but of minimal scientific value for mineralogical research.

9. Packing of specimens for trip home. Be sure the correct labels accompany all specimens packed.

10. Transport home of specimens from collecting site.

A miner is seen sifting through washed gravel at a gem pit in Ratnapura, Sri Lanka. Photo by R. C. Kammerling. © GIA.

chapter four

MINERAL-COLLECTING SPECIALTIES

"It is not the mountain we conquer but ourselves."
Sir Edmund Hillary (1919–　　), New Zealand mountaineer

Gemstones have been admired for their beauty since antiquity, but the first formal mineral collections were assembled by university scholars who were studying the new sciences of crystallography and mineralogy in the 17th and 18th centuries. Mineral collecting, as an intellectual hobby, is about three centuries old, having had its growth and refinement closely paralleling the systematic progress of mineralogical science.

Faceted and rough scapolite, *also termed* wernerite, *a mineral-group series commonly found in metamorphosed* limestones. *Chemically a complex sodium, calcium, aluminum silicate with chlorine, carbonate, and sulfate added. Often fluoresces orange to bright yellow in ultraviolet light.* © *GIA.*

Huge and impressive collections of minerals had been built up in the United States and Europe by the mid-19th century. These were private collections created by amateur geologists for personal satisfaction and aesthetic reasons, and university collections organized by professional scholars for reference and research. The great precious metals and gemstone rushes of the 19th century made people at that time around the world more and more aware of the glories of the subterranean realm beneath the Earth's surface. Even coal miners and petroleum recovery crews sometimes took home interesting rocks as souvenirs of their daily work.

Increasing literacy with universal education, more disposable income, better travel opportunities, and publicity about scientific discoveries encouraged people in the early 20th century to take up mineral collecting.

The proliferation of home lapidary equipment in the 1930s attracted many new rock and mineral collectors. Since World War II, mineral collecting by private citizens has grown still more in popularity due to ready access to gem and mineral magazines and books written for the general public, continued growth in the lapidary crafts and the jewelry business, the founding and growth of local lapidary and mineralogical societies, and investor interest in gemstones.

Rough and polished cabochon feldspar *"moonstone" specimens from Sri Lanka. Cut stone is approximately 5.00 carats in weight. Courtesy of D. Humphrey, photo by Robert Weldon. © GIA.*

Polishing table for gemstone and lapidary work. © GIA.

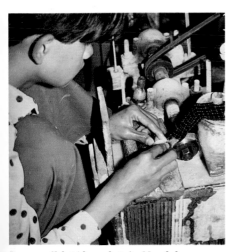

In a small lapidary shop in Mandalay, Myanmar, a worker saws a double ring blank in half to produce ring "preforms." Photo by R. C. Kammerling. © GIA.

MINERAL SPECIMEN SIZES

Most collectors begin by acquiring specimens of any size available; then they gradually concentrate on one or two size ranges, due to personal interests, budget limits, and home storage-space limitations. Uniformity in specimen size makes a collection more visually appealing when shown in a group exhibition, easier to handle and store, and easier to plan because you can predict the approximate price range or difficulty in field collecting of any given mineral species.

What follow are the rock and mineral specimen sizes, along with descriptive in-

Mineral specimens for sale on table display of mineral dealer Steven Bookbinder of Gleneden Beach, Oregon. Author's photo, used with Mr. Bookbinder's permission.

formation, as they are commonly understood and accepted by collectors today:

Micromounts Very tiny specimens, must be viewed with magnification, preferably with a binocular stereomicroscope. Micromounts are usually collected in little plastic boxes no bigger than ⅞ inch by ⅞ inch square. Some collectors mount them on plastic or Styrofoam platforms. Advantages of micromounts are that they are cheap to buy and store (hundreds can fit in a large drawer), they are easy to handle, and small crystals tend to be more perfectly formed than larger crystals of the same species. Disadvantages of micromounts are that they are easily broken and

their beauty must be magnified to be appreciated. A quality stereomicroscope costs hundreds of dollars, but it is a one-time expense and will last for a lifetime of viewing a micromount mineral collection.

Thumbnail size These are 1 inch by 1 inch specimens. They are still reasonably cheap, but thumbnails have the advantage over micromounts in that they can be seen without magnification. Crystal perfection is easier to obtain in thumbnails than in larger specimens, and they are easy to store, display, and handle. They are good for beginning collectors and are commonly used in school Earth Science courses, including the Dana Collection mineral reference set. Thumbnails are big enough to show diagnostic mineral features.

Miniature size These are 1½ by 2 inches; some collectors go as far as 2 by 3 inches and still call them miniatures. Miniatures have the advantages of thumbnails but are larger and more attractive (and a little more costly). Miniatures are good for beginning mineral collectors and for home collections, because they are big enough to see, test, and handle but small enough to afford, store conveniently, and display.

Standard size Standards are 3 by 4 inches. They are commonly used in university and museum reference collections. A nice size for the collector with a liberal budget and adequate storage/display space. Standards are more expensive than miniatures and less expensive than hand size. Standards are a good size for *ores*, rock (as opposed to pure mineral) collections, and regional collections. They start to weigh heavily, though, when grouped on glass display shelves!

Hand size Hand-size specimens are 4 by 5 inches. Good for showy cabinet displays. Quality specimens are usually expensive, however. Easy to sell if of top quality. Need adequate storage/display space, and can be very heavy on shelves. Some collectors get cheap rocks in hand size; then they work their way down in size as the price goes up, with their gemstone specimens being micromounts.

Museum size (also called "cabinet size") This refers to any very large specimen, weighing up to hundreds of pounds. "Museum size" doesn't necessarily mean "museum quality"—as a large specimen may be of very poor quality.

Museum-size specimens look great in museums, but they are impractical for most home collections, due to their large volume and weight. Also, museum-size specimens make small specimens look insignificant when displayed with them, are hard to handle and store, and are often prohibitively expensive to purchase.

COLLECTING FOR STUDY, EXHIBITION, AND INVESTMENT

If you collect minerals for the purpose of studying their physical and chemical properties, you might be satisfied with smaller and cheaper specimens that you can run through tests without fear of damaging them. An exhibition collection should always be chosen for quality over quantity or size considerations. Collecting for the potential investment value of min-

erals is the most difficult type of collecting to do successfully, as you must not only judge the quality of a specimen, but you also need to estimate its true wholesale and retail market values both now and projected into the future.

A carving of chalcedony, *a general term for any variety of cryptocrystalline* quartz. © *GIA.*

GENERAL AND SPECIALIZED MINERAL COLLECTIONS

Many rock and mineral collectors start with a general collection, which includes all sizes, qualities, and varieties of any interesting specimens of rocks, minerals, fossils, and meteorites that they can find or afford. The general collection is best for

Gold cuff link inlaid with a Gibeon-class iron-nickel meteorite *from Namibia, where this meteorite site has been known by native residents before 1836. Displays the Widmanstatten lines that positively identify* octahedrite meteorites, *because such markings are unknown on rocks that originated on Earth. Photo by Maha DeMaggio. © GIA.*

beginners who will learn much by seeing and handling many different kinds of rocks and minerals, comparing and contrasting the physical properties of minerals especially, from species to species.

The general mineral collection is the most common type of private mineral collection. Many advanced mineral collectors keep the core of their original general collection, and develop several specialized collections within it.

As more than 3,000 different mineral species have been discovered and classified by mineralogists, no private collector can hope to own choice specimens of most of them. Therefore, collectors sensibly limit their range of collecting to certain specialized collections that intrigue them. Specialized mineral collections can categorically overlap each other, as can be seen from examining the following list:

Single mineral species Specializing in one mineral species from many different localities in all known forms, colors, and so forth. Some popular one-mineral-species collections are *barite, beryl, calcite, fluorite, native gold, quartz,* or *tourmaline.*

Natural greenish-blue fluorite, *a popular mineral with collectors. © GIA.*

Single mineral class Collecting all minerals in a given mineralogical chemical class, such as sulfides (*chalcopyrite, cinnabar, galena, pyrite,* and so on) or carbonates (*azurite, calcite, dolomite, malachite,* etc.). Also called "single mineral families" by collectors.

Single chemical elements Either native elements (monoelemental minerals, such as *native copper* and *native silver*) or chemical compounds containing a specific element (such as *iron*-bearing minerals). As in "single mineral class" above, the collecting category of "single chemical elements" is also called "single mineral families" by some collectors.

Crystal system Collecting minerals within a single crystal system, such as the tetragonal crystals (*cassiterite*, *wulfenite*, *zircon*, and so on) or monoclinic system (*augite*, *epidote*, *gypsum*, etc.).

Pseudomorphs Minerals having the crystal form of another species, due to chemical replacement or alteration, such as *limonite after pyrite*.

Single crystals Collecting a single crystal per specimen; crystals can be of any size range, with emphasis on quality and perfection of form.

Dana collection Striving to get as many as possible of the listed mineral species described in Dana's *Manual of Mineralogy*.

Faceted 2.89-carat specimen of clinohumite, *a basic magnesium fluosilicate in the* humite *group of minerals. Courtesy of Bill Pinch, photo by Maha DeMaggio. © GIA.*

Ores Specializing in metal-bearing minerals, such as zinc ores (*hemimorphite*, *smithsonite*, *sphalerite*, and so on); because ores can be relatively cheap to buy, the astute collector can get big specimens inexpensively.

Gemstone minerals Collected in both rough and cut specimens. A gemstone is a mineral that is prized for its beauty, due to its color, hardness, lustre, and transparency. In the commercial gemstone trade, the two general gemstone categories are precious stones (*diamonds*, *emeralds*, *rubies*, and *sapphires*) and semiprecious stones (all others).

Quality is all-important in determining the market value of precious gemstones —which can range from a few cents a carat for junk stones to many thousands of dollars per carat for top quality. In the jewelry business, they say, "If you don't know your jewels, know your jeweler." What follows is a description of the four precious gemstones.

Native miners wash gemstone concentrates in the waters of the Umba River, Tanga province, Tanzania. Photo by Eduard Gubelin.

DIAMOND   Found rough in *kimberlite* (a variety of *peridotite*) and in the sand and gravel of streambeds. Used as a gemstone when gem quality, as an abrasive otherwise. The hardest natural substance, a form of crystallized pure carbon. Diamonds are found colorless to black, with yellow and brown being common shades. Red and green diamonds are called "fancy" colors. Blue or blue-white are prized among many diamond connoisseurs; the Hope Diamond at the Smithsonian is a deep blue. The most valuable are generally the colorless diamonds. Jewelry-store markups on diamonds can reach extortionist proportions for smaller stones. The best diamonds come from Africa and the former Soviet Union.

Rough natural sapphires, from Rock Creek mine in Montana, show their size and color range. Pictured stones weigh from 0.50 to 15.00 carats each. Photo by Tino Hammid. © GIA & Tino Hammid.

A 1.02 ct oval cut Burmese ruby. Photo by Robert Weldon. © GIA.

Brown diamonds, 1.20-carat rough, 0.69-carat cut. © GIA.

EMERALD The rich green variety of the mineral *beryl*. Beryl is called aquamarine when blue or bluish-green, *golden beryl* when golden yellow, and *morganite* when pink. Top-quality emeralds come from Colombia and are the most costly type of beryl gems.

Natural beryl, *variety* emerald, *crystal more than 100 carats in weight. Photo by Robert Weldon. © GIA.*

Sandawana emerald *mine operated by Rio Tinto, a British firm in Zimbabwe. Emeralds are extracted from the* schist's *face. Photo by Fred Ward. © Fred Ward & GIA.*

RUBY The deep red variety of the mineral *corundum*. When corundum is any other color, it is called *sapphire*. A pink sapphire is worth less than the same quality and same-sized red ruby. The finest rubies are "pigeon blood" rubies from Burma. The second finest come from Thailand and Sri Lanka.

SAPPHIRE The nonred shade of the mineral *corundum* (see "ruby" above). The best sapphires are cashmir-blue, but sapphires come in many different colors. The old term "oriental" was used as a prefix to indicate *corundum* (that is, "sapphire")—so, "oriental amethyst" is actually purple corundum, for example.

Rough natural sapphires *with their faceted counterparts, from the Umba Valley of Tanzania.* © GIA.

Semiprecious gemstones (all gemstones *except* diamond, emerald, ruby, and sapphire) include *beryl* (*nonemerald* varieties), *chrysoberyl* (including *alexandrite*), *cordierite* (*iolite*), *garnet*, *jadeite*, *labradorite* (*plagioclase*), *lazurite* (*lapis lazuli*), *nephrite* (*tremolite*), *periodot*, *rhodochrosite*, *smithsonite*, *spodumene* (*kunzite* and *hiddenite*), *topaz*, *tourmaline*, *turquoise*, *zircon*, *zoisite* (*tanzanite*), the so-called "organic gemstones" of *amber*, *coral*, and *pearl*, the transparent *quartz* stones (*amethyst*, *citrine*, *rock crystal*, and so forth), the cryptocrystalline *quartz* stones (*chalcedony*, *jasper*, etc.), and *opal*. Many softer minerals, such as *calcite* and *fluorite*, are collected as cut-gemstone art, but not worn in jewelry because they're not durable.

Faceted heliodor, *the yellow-color variety of the mineral* beryl, *from Brazil. Yellow beryl has more gemstone "fire" than quartz* citrine *of similar color, and yellow* sapphire *has more than beryl.* © GIA.

Beryl, *variety* aquamarine, *crystal more than 100 carats in weight, Afghanistan. Courtesy Gary Bowersox, photo by Robert Weldon.* © GIA.

A GIA GEM shortwave/longwave ultraviolet lamp and viewing cabinet used to check for fluorescence in gems and minerals. © GIA.

Fluorescent minerals Those that fluoresce under ultraviolet light, such as *calcite*, common *opal*, *fluorite*, *scheelite*, and *willemite*.

Radioactive minerals Those that emit invisible radiation from nuclear decay, detectable by a Geiger counter, such as *autunite*, *carnotite*, *thorite*, and *uraninite*. Note: Beginners should seek expert guidance before keeping collections of radioactive minerals.

Localities Collecting minerals based on their geographical origin, such as specimens from a single country, state or province, or county. Single mining disrict collections were popular in old-time European mineral collections—for example, the minerals of the Tsumeb mining district in Namibia. Some collectors seek specimens from a single mine site. A 'locality collection' is also called a "regional collection."

Montana agate carved in Thailand in the shape of a fish. Photo by Robert Weldon. © GIA.

Two blue pectolite carvings from Thailand. The elephant is approximately 5 centimetres high. Photo by Robert Weldon. © GIA.

Birthstones

According to legend and superstition, certain stones bring good luck to their human wearers who were born in the month associated with given stones. Science dismisses any magical or supernatural powers attributed to stones, but many rock collectors enjoy collecting the different varieties of all the birthstones, or just the stone(s) of their own birth month. At its convention in Kansas City in 1912, the American National Association of Jewelers officially declared that the birthstones are as follows:

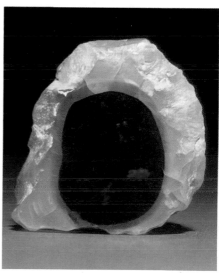

An interesting specimen of rough "black" opal, from Lightning Ridge, Australia. © GIA.

Month	Stone	Legendary Fortune Imparted by Stone
January	Garnet	Constancy
February	Amethyst	Sincerity
March	Aquamarine or Bloodstone	Courage
April	Diamond	Innocence
May	Emerald	Love
June	Pearl, Moonstone, or Alexandrite	Health
July	Ruby	Contentment
August	Peridot or Sardonyx	Married happiness
September	Sapphire	Clear thinking
October	Opal or Tourmaline	Hope
November	Topaz	Fidelity
December	Turquoise or Zircon	Prosperity

A pear-shaped faceted tsavorite garnet *from Kenya, East Africa. Photo by Mike Havstad. © GIA.*

HANDLING AND HOUSING A COLLECTION

"A rolling stone gathers no moss."
Publilius Syrus (first century B.C.), *Maxims*

Most minerals theoretically have somewhat lengthy and indefinite lifespans (measured in thousands or millions of years). In reality, however, as a result of our collecting, handling, testing, and storing them, we inescapably expose them to accelerated alteration and degradation. This takes place by means of oxidation, hydration, dehydration, light- and chemical-induced fading of color, vibration-shock damage, and so forth. Minerals are chemicals, and they react to contact with other chemicals—in the air, on your fingertips, on their display shelves, and in storage boxes.

A 348.7-gram rough specimen of morganite *with faint pink color. Morganite is the pink to violet color variety of the mineral* beryl. *Photo by Tino Hammid.* © *GIA & Tino Hammid.*

ROCK AND MINERAL SPECIMEN CLEANING

After completing your home trimming (dressing) of rock and mineral specimens that you field-trimmed, they're ready for their first cleaning. Use small forceps to pick away final bits of distracting material; then brush or blow off remaining dust.

Mild soap and plain tap water are suitable for washing many rocks and minerals. Very hot or cold water might crack some specimens. Avoid strong cleansers that can bleach or abrade. Use a toothbrush for routine scrubbing. Don't wash delicate or water-soluble minerals with water (100 percent pure alcohol might work on *halite*).

Cleaning with acids is sometimes nec-

Rock crystal quartz specimen weighing 20 to 30 lbs. © GIA & Tino Hammid.

tilled water after cleaning is done, then allowed to air-dry on newspapers or paper towels away from the direct rays of the sun.

Dust accumulation is a problem in many home-stored mineral collections, particularly when displayed unprotected on open shelves. Blow dust off your specimens with a syringe, or use a soft camel's-hair brush.

Rough and faceted specimens of tanzanite, *which is actually blue* zoisite, *a basic calcium, aluminum silicate mineral. Photo by Mike Havstad. © GIA.*

essary but often risky. The reddish-brown iron stains on *quartz* crystal clusters can often be removed with oxalic acid or acetic acid. Hydrochloric acid is effective on some matrices, but it can dissolve certain desirable minerals. Use diluted acids, clean for short periods, and get advice before experimenting with acids.

It's important to remember that all acids should be handled with great care. Always wear protective eye goggles, and always have a bucket of cold water nearby for first-aid splashing (acid spills should be washed off with plenty of cold water). Keep acids away from small children or household pets.

Specimens that can be washed with water should be given a final bath in dis-

SPECIMEN STORAGE

Store rock and mineral specimens in moderate physical conditions, ideally in a cool, dry, and dark box, cabinet, or drawer, to keep strong light away and extreme temperature and humidity fluctuations to a minimum. Proper storage should inhibit dust accumulation.

Delicate specimens can be damaged by frequent handling, moving them around, drawer vibrations, and so forth. Don't store alien species in direct contact with each other. Rocks and minerals "breathe"—they absorb and emit gases over time—and may undergo surface molecular changes correspondingly. Keep collections away from open windows, direct sunlight, room heaters and air conditioners, kitchen and bathroom humidity, automobile exhaust, and anywhere that people or pets may bump into them.

Many minerals oxidize and tarnish when exposed over time to sulfur in city smog; examples are *native copper*, *native silver*, *marcasite*, and *pyrite*. *Borax* min-

of water to keep it from drying out and changing color or cracking. Some collectors coat certain minerals with a transparent lacquer, such as clear fingernail polish, to form a chemical barrier between the air in the storage room and the surfaces of the specimens.

The hydrous sodium borate mineral kernite *changing to the unpurified* tincalconite *variety of the more hydrated borate mineral* borax. *Photo by Kurt Nassau. © Kurt Nassau & GIA.*

Pyrite *disintegrating into dust. Photo by Kurt Nassau. © Kurt Nassau & GIA.*

erals can dessicate (dry out) and crumble to dust, and these should be stored in airtight containers in dry rooms. *Halite* can hydrate (absorb water from air) and gradually dissolve, so it should be kept in low humidity with silica-gel packets to absorb air moisture if necessary. *Opal*, both rough and polished, is often stored in vials

Rough Australian opal *on matrix. Opal is hydrous noncrystalline quartz. Courtesy of B. Daveport, photo by Robert Weldon. © GIA.*

CATALOGING A COLLECTION

Your rock and mineral collection should be cataloged at home on index-card files or in computer software. Most collectors organize their collections either alphabetically by rock or mineral name or numerically by personal catalog number and/or Dana number. It makes sense to use all three: specimen name, personal number, and Dana number—cross-referenced to each other, so that you can locate information about a specimen from all three perspectives. Some collectors even prepare a separate file that lists specimens by localities. For each mineral specimen listed in your collection catalog, it is useful to enter these items:

1. Personal catalog number

2. Dana number

3. Mineral name

4. Chemical composition

5. Mineral class or group

6. Locality (where collected in the field)

7. Matrix name and geologic age (if known)

8. Date acquired (including date field-collected)

9. Collector's name (person who field-collected it)

10. Miscellaneous data (its ownership history, its purchase price, how it was obtained, and unusual characteristics of the specimen)

PERMANENT SPECIMEN LABELS

Permanent specimen labels are made at home after positive identification is made. At home, replace the adhesive tape *field number* with a spot of white enamel and India ink *specimen number* for each specimen's permanent number.

Permanent specimen labels will be placed next to the specimens on display, in their storage boxes, and accompany specimens whenever they "travel" away from home (to exhibitions, for potential sale, and so forth). Permanent specimen labels should include the mineral's species name, chemical formula, locality of origin, personal catalog number, and collector's name (not included for many competitive exhibitions).

COLLECTION HOUSING AND DISPLAY

The four basic methods of mineral-collection housing and display are open shelves, enclosed glass display cabinets, specimen boxes, and drawer cabinets. Because rocks and minerals tend to be bulky, much of your collection will of necessity not be on constant home display. Most collectors rotate their specimens from stored stock in boxes or cabinet drawers to visible displays on open shelves or in glass-windowed cabinets.

Open shelving A good method if your collection has few and relatively large specimens, a poor one if you have a thousand thumbnail sizes sliding around or a hundred lapidary "eggs" rolling off. While open shelving can be the cheapest and most "specimen-accessible" method of display because specimens are completely exposed to view and touch, it is also the most dust-prone. In addition, specimens are vulnerable to children and pets.

Glass shelves are easy to clean, but also easily scratched or chipped by the specimens. Keep heavy specimens off glass shelves, and on wooden or metal shelves instead.

Natural crystal cluster of hemimorphite, *a hydrous zinc silicate mineral from the mines at Mapimí, Durango, Mexico. Courtesy of Natural History Museum of Los Angeles County.*

Display of mineral and gemstone specimens. © *GIA.*

Enclosed glass display cabinets An expensive, but handsome, method of displaying rocks and minerals. China or curio cabinets, as well as retail-store glass showcases, make excellent mineral cabinets. Enclosed display cabinets keep most dust off specimens.

Mineral display cabinets need to be positioned away from direct sunlight, and you should only turn on artificial illumination for your specimens when you are viewing them. All light sources can fade specimen colors, and hot light may dry out certain hydrated minerals.

Specimen boxes Any boxes into which your specimens fit; can be plastic, glass, cardboard, or wood. Be careful that metal boxes don't react chemically with your minerals. Boxes are good for small specimens, many specimens, and delicate specimens. Lapidary-supply dealers sell a variety of cheap, clear plastic boxes with snap-top lids that are ideal for small mineral specimens. A group of clear plastic specimen boxes can be displayed together on shelves.

Drawer cabinets Excellent for long-term storage. Drawer cabinets are easy to organize, occupy minimum space for a given collection size, are the most dust-resistant storage method, and facilitate logical divisions in a collection—for example, all iron minerals in one drawer, all barite specimens in another. Any cabinet with drawers can be used, or you can buy cabinets made specifically for mineral storage. Wooden and metal cabinets are the most common types.

The inside of each drawer must be subdivided with vertical dividers that partition the drawer into appropriate small sections, so that the specimens won't roll around and get mixed up or break each other. Cardboard and wooden dividers are good to use in each drawer, as are individual plastic boxes or partitioned plastic trays.

SPECIMEN MOUNTS

Rocks and minerals look handsome when mounted on bases that fit specimen sizes.

Specimens can rest loosely on mounts or be glued on with harmless adhesive. Mounts should be lightweight but sturdy. The most accepted colors for mineral mounts are black, white, and clear (transparent plastic). Popular mount bases include cork, plastic, Styrofoam, wax slabs, wood, or another mineral (such as a thin slab of *onyx* or *marble*).

A 128.98-carat rough turquoise *specimen from Kingman mine in Arizona. The mineral turquoise is a complex copper, aluminum phosphate that is popular in jewelry. Courtesy of Loretta Loeb, photo by Robert Weldon.* © GIA.

A cut slab of the mineral variscite, *a hydrous aluminum phosphate that resembles* turquoise *but is greener than turquoise and contains no copper.* © GIA.

MINERAL CRYSTALLOGRAPHY

"The universe . . . is written in the language of mathematics, and its characters are triangles, circles, and other geometrical figures . . ."
Galileo Galilei (1564–1642), *Il Saggiatore*

Three states of matter exist on Earth: *solids*, *liquids*, and *gases*—and, of course, transitional phases between those pure states. A solid is a material substance that has definite volume and definite shape. On the Earth's surface, all minerals are solid at "room temperature," except elemental (pure) *mercury* and the liquid/gaseous stages of the mineral *water*.

Solids can be subdivided into *crystalline* and *amorphous* substances. A true mineral is crystalline—that is, capable of forming regular geometrical crystals with internal atomic order (such as *calcite*, *quartz*, or *tourmaline*). A *mineraloid* is an amorphous (without definite form—that is, noncrystalline) substance, incapable of forming crystals because it doesn't have a symmetrical, repetitive internal atomic/molecular arrangement (such as *opal*, *obsidian*, and *tecktites*). In loose terminology, some collectors call mineraloids "amorphous minerals"—so, we often hear a statement like "Amorphous minerals are those that never crystallize, and are much rarer in nature than minerals known with crystal forms."

Cryptocrystalline minerals superficially appear to be amorphous, but they actually have an internal crystal structure (such as *chalcedony*, *chert*, *flint*, and *jasper*, some *cryptocrystalline quartz* varieties).

Glass, both natural (such as *obsidian* or *tektites*) and artificial (such as your windowpane), is an amorphous solid for practical purposes, but it may actually be classified as a highly viscous liquid, because glass has no definite shape or melting point as true crystalline solids have. Just remember that amorphous mineraloids (minerals?) have no regular geometrical shape in the solid state of matter.

The five main branches of the science of crystallography are chemical, geometrical, optical, physical, and structural. The mineral collector is usually most interested in crystal morphology—the study of crystal shapes, and the major topic of discussion in this chapter.

◆

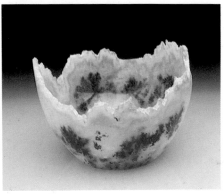

"Angel wing" agate *variety of cryptocrystalline* quartz, *5.3 × 7.9 centimetres. Courtesy of Arizona Mining and Mineral Museum, Neavitt Collection. Photo by Jeff Scovil.*

WHAT ARE CRYSTALS?

As used in this book, a mineral crystal is a symmetrical, geometrical solid. Its *faces* (external, smooth, flat surfaces) are arranged at definite *angles* along the *edges* (external intersections of two adjacent faces)—with these interfacial angles corresponding to the internal atomic/molecular arrangement of the mineral's component elements. Common abbreviations are "xl = crystal," "xls = crystals," and "xlized = crystallized." A *termination* is the end point of a crystal. A *doubly terminated* crystal has two end points. The faces are sometimes called the "sides" of a crystal, in everyday speech, and the termination the "end."

Mineral crystals can be natural (made in nature) or synthetic (artificially made in laboratories), and some collectors seek both, others prefer only naturally made specimens.

Libyan tektite, *also termed "Libyan desert glass," a natural glass tektite with a light golden color, from the Egyptian-Libyan border. Tektites are possibly related to the fall of extraterrestrial objects.* © GIA.

Synthetic beryls *made in Russia. The gemstone and jewelry business is plagued more by synthetics than the hobby of collecting rough natural mineral specimens.* © GIA.

Some minerals are common in the Earth's crust, but rare in crystal form, such as *lead* and *turquoise*. A mineral may often be found in crystalline form, but large, "perfect," transparent crystals of it may be rare, such as *beryl*/variety *emerald*, *realgar*, and *rose quartz*.

Crystals range in size from microscopic to enormous giants. At the Etta Mine in South Dakota, a crystal of *spodumene* was found that measured 47 feet long, 5 feet in diameter, and weighed almost 90 tons.

CRYSTALLIZATION IN NATURE

Mineral *crystallization* (crystal formation) occurs naturally by precipitation from hot or cold chemical solutions, condensation from hot gases, solidification from molten material (magma), and evaporation. Evaporites include such minerals as hydrous *borates*, *gypsum*, and *halite*, and they form from simple evaporation of mineral-rich aqueous (usually) solution. Metamorphic processes often transform crystals from one mineral species to another.

A mineral's crystal shape is never accidental; rather, it results from specific natural laws acting on the fluid material undergoing crystallization. Because crystallization is an *interatomic* (between-the-atoms) process whereby the external form of the resulting solid corresponds directly to its internal atomic/molecular structure, we can say that the diversity of external morphology of crystals has its origins in nature's laws of chemistry and physics.

Crystal growth is affected by four main factors:

A 106.25-carat natural tourmaline crystal with adhering mica platelets as crystal surface growth, from California. Specimen in the GIA stone collection. Photo by Robert Weldon. © GIA.

◆ Chemical composition of the depositing solutions or gases.
◆ Temperature.
◆ Pressure.
◆ Speed of formation—the rate of heating and cooling of crystal ingredients in variable mineral deposition processes, for example. Crystal growth is generally slow.

Paragenesis is mineral formation in relation to specific environments. The above four factors of crystal growth decide which crystal *forms* and *habits* will result.

Natural diopside *crystals from Diana, New York state. Courtesy of Natural History Museum of Los Angeles County.*

An etched natural spessartite garnet *crystal. The spessartite garnet species is a manganese, aluminum silicate, and rather scarce. Photo by Robert Weldon.* © *GIA.*

CRYSTAL FLAWS

Mineral crystals in nature usually do not appear in ideal forms with faces and dimensions perfectly developed. Crystals are usually distorted—that is, exhibit various defects or deformations, due to imperfect growing conditions, such as an irregular mineral supply, mechanical pressure limits, or impurities in chemistry. Crystal defects are classified as follows:

External crystal defects For example, unequal face growth, striations (parallel streaks on a face), grooves, ridges, incomplete face development, parallel overgrowths, and color blemishes.

Internal crystal defects For example, cracks, chemical impurities incorporated into the crystal's chemistry, phantom crystals, and *inclusions* of gases, liquids, or solids (see below).

Crystal Inclusions

Defined broadly, an inclusion is a foreign chemical that appears as a visible solid, liquid, or gas contaminant inside of a mineral crystal. Under this definition of inclusion, *water* is the most common one to be found in crystals, often having bubbles of gases (such as carbon dioxide) in it. Sometimes suspended crystal inclusions are floating in water inclusions: solid inclusions within liquid inclusions within the host mineral. Air or carbon dioxide bubbles are found in liquid inclusions (mostly water) in *calcite*, *fluorite*, *halite*, and *quartz* crystals, for example.

Defined narrowly, an inclusion is a solid mineral occurring within another, usually transparent or translucent, mineral. The inclusion is the inside mineral, the impurity in the external host mineral. The host mineral is the outside mineral that surrounds the included mineral. Solid mineral inclusions may be dustlike, single crystals, or crystal aggregates. Which came first—the included mineral or the host mineral? One theory holds that they grew simultaneously, slowly solidifying together out of a solution containing fluid minerals of varying solubility.

Color-change garnet *inclusion in a* diamond, *greatly magnified and photographed with fluorescent light.* © GIA.

Detection of gas bubble inclusions in a mineral specimen by using a handheld penlight. © GIA.

Quartz is the most common mineral bearing inclusions. Some quartz inclusions are crystals of *azurite, garnet, gold, hematite, malachite,* and *rutile.* Mineral inclusions found in *calcite* include *adamite, arborescent copper, hematite, wire-silver,* and *wulfenite.* While inclusions may increase the market value of collectible minerals such as common *calcite* or *quartz,* inclusions usually decrease the market value of gemstones such as *diamond* or *sapphire* (*corundum* variety).

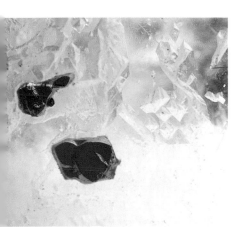

Red cinnabar *inclusions in a* barite *crystal, greatly magnified. Cinnabar is the chief ore of mercury.* © GIA.

Polished lapidary specimen of tourmalinated quartz, *showing typical elongated inclusions of the silicate mineral* tourmaline. *Such specimens are popular with gemstone collectors.* © GIA.

Phantom crystals are ghostlike, solid crystal inclusions, indicating an early growth period of the crystal. For example, *kaolinite* impurity can form phantoms inside *quartz* crystals, showing various stages in the quartz crystal growth. Usually, just part of the crystal becomes phantomed; a whole phantom inclusion is scarce. Multiple phantoms, up to a couple of dozen, are known within a single crystal.

"Phantom" quartz crystal, formed when solid crystal inclusion impurities outline crystal growth at an early period of development. Up to a couple of dozen multiple phantoms are known within a single crystal. Photo by Robert Weldon. © GIA.

MINERAL CRYSTAL FORMATION FROM MAGMA

As magma (hot molten rock) rises near the surface of the Earth's crust, it begins to cool due to heat loss to the colder matter above and around it. The homogeneous magma mixture begins to separate out as individual minerals, with lighter-weight species (such as *feldspar* and *quartz*) forming above the heavier species (such as *chromite* and *magnetite*). This process of mineral crystal formation from magma is called *magmatic differentiation*.

Pegmatites (magmatic offshoots from the original mass) form gemstone minerals (for example, *diamond*, *beryl*, and *tourmaline*) as well as metal ores (e.g., *tin* and *tungsten* ores).

Then, magmatic gases begin to form cavities inside the cooling magma masses, into which *hydrothermal minerals* (such as *calcite* and *quartz*) crystallize out of hot liquids and deposit as crystal linings on the insides of cavity walls. *Ore veins* can form as *pneumatolytic minerals* (that is, minerals resulting from metal-rich magmatic gases) in spaces between rock formations underground.

Finally, the underground steam cools to mineral-rich liquid water as it reaches the Earth's surface as mineralized hot springs, where mineral species such as *aragonite* and *geyserite* form. And where hot subterranean gases and liquids enter cracks in sedimentary bedrock, the sedimentary rocks are metamorphosed into new minerals, called *metasomatic* minerals.

Heated minerals crystallize from the

molten state at various specific temperatures, producing characteristic mineral species and structures. For example, above 870° C, *quartz* becomes *tridymite* (same chemical formula, but different structure). Above 1,470° C, *tridymite* becomes *cristobalite*, which, in turn, melts at 1,710° C.

Crystal grains in rocks are typically irregular, rather than ideal, in form, because of restraining forces on them when they are growing. For instance, a developing crystal may be fed raw material in one direction only, resulting in an abnormally elongated crystal relative to its ideal symmetry.

CRYSTAL DEVELOPMENT IN ROCK CAVITIES

Crystals can grow in rock cavities and cracks by precipitation (forming the solid state) from aqueous solution or the gaseous state. Instead of being *embedded* in rocks (for example, *quartz* in *sandstone*), minerals can also be *attached* to rocks in cavities, cracks, and veins as aggregates, druses, and geodes:

Aggregates Groups of crystals, of one or more minerals, growing adjacent to each other; also defined as irregular clusters of crystals growing on a rock surface. Not to be confused with crystal *twinning*.

Druses Clusters of individual crystals growing somewhat parallel to each other out of a relatively flat substratum rocky base; sometimes called a "parallel group" of crystals. Not to be confused with crystal *twins*, which have inclined—that is, not parallel—crystal axes. *Barite*, *calcite*, *fluorite*, and *quartz* often form drusy crystals. Druses are parallel growths of crystals, in contradistinction to geodes (below).

Geodes Globular cavities filled with crystals growing on their inside walls, with the crystals' terminations (free ends) pointing more or less towards the middle of the cavity. *Calcite, quartz,* and *zeolite* are common geode minerals. *Enhydros* are water-filled geodes, some of the most interesting ones coming from Brazil and Uruguay as water-filled agate geodes. "Rattle stones" are loose crystals inside the cavity of a geode; they bounce and rattle when the unopened geode is shaken.

MINERAL IDENTIFICATION BY X-RAY DIFFRACTION

Max von Laue and William H. and his son William L. Bragg discovered in around 1912 that X-ray diffraction can determine the atomic crystal structure of minerals. *X-ray powder diffraction analysis* produces a positive identification of a sample of mineral powder, based on the principle that, when X rays linearly enter an atom, some of their energy is absorbed by the atom's orbiting electrons, which reemit X rays of their own in specific patterns due to their atomic structure. These patterns of emitted rays are recorded and enhanced on film and compared against known X-ray diffraction analyses for the various chemical elements; when a match is made, an element is identified.

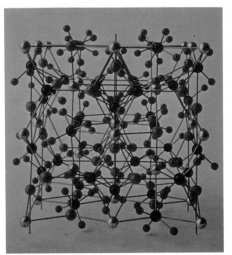

Molecular structure model of the mineral garnet, *with colored spheres representing atoms. Photo by Kurt Nassau. © Kurt Nassau & GIA.*

bonded to each other at right angles (90°); hence, natural halite crystals are cubic. Here is schematic (diagrammatical) representation of a lattice of halite, with positively charged sodium ions (Na⁺) ionically bonded to negatively charged chloride ions (Cl⁻):

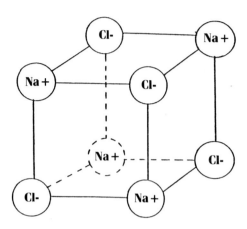

X-ray diffraction equipment is not available for use by the average mineral collector, but jewelers and university science departments (who have access to such equipment) can analyze a small sample of mineral powder by X-ray diffraction and identify the mineral. Sometimes a tiny amount of powder is scraped from the girdle (hidden rough area of a gemstone's cut diameter) of a gemstone and identified by X-ray diffraction.

CRYSTAL LATTICE

A *crystal lattice* (also called a space lattice) is the three-dimensional geometrical pattern in which atoms are arranged inside a crystal.

For example, the mineral *halite* (*rock salt*) has alternating ions (electrically charged atoms) of sodium and chlorine

MORPHOLOGICAL CRYSTALLOGRAPHY

Morphological crystallography (the study of crystal shapes) concerns the visible appearance of crystals: their faces, angles, edges, axes, symmetry, the six crystal systems, and their classes and habits (forms). Mineral collectors are vitally interested in crystal morphology, as the most applicable branch of crystallography to the collecting hobby.

Crystal Axes

Crystal axes are imaginary lines through the middle of a crystal and parallel to the main faces' intersecting edges. The *axial*

cross is the common point within a crystal, where its axes internally intersect. The length of the axes within a given mineral crystal species may be of equal or unequal length. The hexagonal crystal system has four crystallographic axes. All the rest have three.

Law of Constancy of Angle

The *Law of Constancy of Interfacial Angles* states that the *interfacial angles* (also called "space angles") at which a crystal's faces intersect are constant in all crystals of a given mineral species. This crystallographic law was proposed by the Danish scientist Nicolaus Steno (Niels Stensen), in 1669, and is often called *Steno's Law*.

The Law of Constancy of Angle is the single most important physical diagnostic test of a mineral. The colors, shapes, and sizes of crystals (including the shapes and relative sizes of crystal faces) are highly variable within a given mineral species, but not their angles between adjacent faces of a crystal of a certain species.

Goniometers are instruments used by professional mineralogists to measure crystal interfacial angles. Owning a goniometer is unnecessary for most beginning mineral collectors, although you can fashion one yourself from a protractor and transparent straightedge or buy one inexpensively from a lapidary-supply shop.

Crystal Symmetry

A crystal may be geometrically organized with its faces and angles symmetrically balanced around a central point, axis, or plane:

Central-point symmetry An imaginary point divides in two equal halves a crystal's faces, edges, and intersecting angles. A crystal has a central point of symmetry if every face has a face parallel to it on the opposite side.

Axial symmetry An imaginary line passes through a crystal's ideal center, such that when the crystal is rotated about this axis of symmetry, identical faces come into identical positions. Symmetrical axes are subdivided into diad, triad, tetrad, and hexad axes—and, depending on how many crystal faces come into identical positions upon rotation, the axial symmetry is called twofold, threefold, fourfold, and sixfold.

Plane symmetry An imaginary plane divides a crystal into two symmetrical halves, each half being a mirror image of the other. For example, in the cubic (isometric) system of crystals, a perfect cube has nine planes of symmetry; that is, there are nine ways that the cube can be cut to produce two equal half mirror images.

Crystal Systems

Based on the positions and lengths of their crystal axes, all minerals can be classified into just six *crystal systems:* the isometric (also called cubic), tetragonal, hexagonal, orthorhombic, monoclinic, and triclinic. These six crystal systems are further broken down into 32 *crystal classes*, as demonstrated in 1830 by the German crystallographer Johann Hessel. Each of these crystal classes can have many *forms* (the assemblage of all crystal faces) and *habits* (the arrangements and relative proportions of faces on a crystal).

Many collectors use the words "form" and "habit" very loosely and interchangeably. Forms are sometimes defined as "shapes that appear in the various crystal systems." Some forms are typical of each crystal system. For example, the isometric (cubic) crystal system has forms of the cube (six equal sides), hexahedron (six sides), octahedron (eight sides), tetrahedron (four triangular faces), and their combinations. Triclinic, monoclinic, and orthorhombic minerals have forms of pedions, pinacoids, prisms, and pyramids, and their combinations. Trigonal minerals show the rhombohedral form (see "Hexagonal crystal system" below).

A natural, weathered, octahedron diamond crystal. Yellow shades are common in diamonds, but not as desirable as colorless specimens. © GIA.

Thus, all minerals that crystallize can be classified by system, class, and habit. The atomic and molecular forces within a crystal determine its crystal system:

Isometric (cubic) crystal system Three equal-length axes that intersect at right angles to each other. Mineral examples: *almandine* (*garnet*), *fluorite*, *galena*, *halite*, *magnetite*, *pyrite*, and *tetrahedrite*.

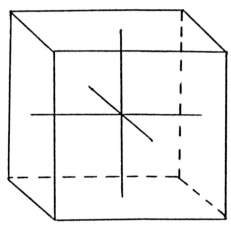

Isometric crystal.

Tetragonal crystal system Two equal-length horizontal axes—and a third (vertical) axis, longer or shorter than each horizontal axis—all at right angles to each other. Mineral examples: *apophyllite*, *cassiterite*, *chalcopyrite*, *rutile*, *scapolite*, *scheelite*, *vesuvianite* (*idocrase*), and *zircon*.

A violet fluorite crystal in matrix. Fluorite is a simple calcium fluoride mineral that often fluoresces in ultraviolet light. GIA stone collection, photo by Robert Weldon. © GIA.

Hexagonal crystal system Three equal-length horizontal axes that intersect each other at 60° (sometimes called "120 degrees")—and a shorter or longer vertical axis that is perpendicular to all of the horizontal axes. The so-called "trigonal crystal system" is actually a subclass of the hexagonal crystal system, though sometimes erroneously classified as the seventh crystal system. Mineral examples of the hexagonal system are *apatite*, *beryl*, *calcite*, *cinnabar*, *corundum*, *dolomite*, *hematite*, *quartz*, *tourmaline*, *vanadinite*, and *zincite*. *Calcite* forms rhombohedral class crystals in the hexagonal system and has more known habits (20 +) than any other mineral. In some older mineralogical books, you might see the hexagonal crystal system termed the "rhombohedral system" for the many rhombohedral minerals in the hexagonal system.

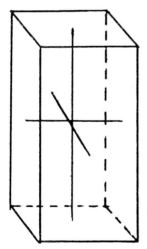

Tetragonal crystal.

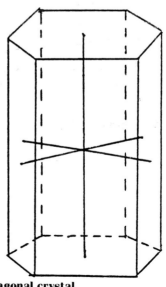

Hexagonal crystal.

Natural trigonal crystals of calcite, *a simple calcium carbonate, which is the most common mineral in the Earth's crust, after* quartz. *Calcite is the principal mineral in* limestone *and* marble. © GIA.

Faceted gemstone and natural crystal specimens of smoky quartz, *the yellowish-grey to brownish-black color variety of crystalline quartz. If there's any grey at all in the color of yellowish quartz, it is termed "smoky quartz" instead of "citrine." Photo by Robert Weldon.* © GIA.

Orthorhombic crystal system Three unequal-length axes, all perpendicular to each other. Mineral examples: *aragonite, barite, celestite, cerussite, hemimorphite, marcasite, olivine, sulfur,* and *topaz.* Sometimes a mineral species mimics a crystal system that it actually isn't; for example, *pyrrhotite* is a true orthorhombic crystal, but it sometimes appears to be hexagonal and therefore is properly identified as "orthorhombic (pseudohexagonal)." Reference books with a cavalier attitude towards scientific accuracy might erroneously classify pyrrhotite as a hexagonal mineral, so be watchful when reading mineral books written for the general public.

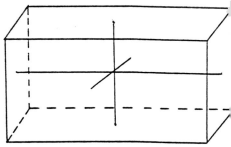

Orthorhombic crystal.

Monoclinic crystal system Three unequal-length axes, two of which intersect each other at oblique angles (not perpendicularly), with the third axis perpendicular to the other two. Mineral examples: *augite, chrysocolla, diopside, epidote, gypsum, hornblende, jadeite, melanterite, mica, orthoclase* (that is, the monoclinic feldspars of *orthoclase* proper and *sanidine,* in contradistinction to the *orthoclase* feldspar *microcline,* which is triclinic), *realgar, spodumene,* *titanite* (*sphene*), and *wolframite*. The mineral *staurolite* is monoclinic, but it may present a pseudoorthorhombic appearance—an example of how a specimen's crystal system can be misidentified by the casual observer.

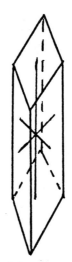

Triclinic crystal.

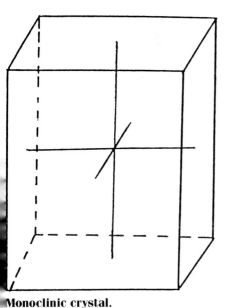

Monoclinic crystal.

Triclinic crystal system Three unequal-length axes, none of which are perpendicular to each other. Mineral examples: *ambligonite, axinite, babingtonite, chalcanthite, inestite, kyanite, microcline* (triclinic *orthoclase* feldspar), *pectolite, plagioclase* (that is, the triclinic feldspars such as *albite*), *rhodonite, turquoise,* and *wollastonite*. The mineral *wulfenite* is triclinic, but it can appear pseudotetragonal due to crystal twinning and therefore be misidentified as tetragonal.

A 36.6-millimetre-long axinite *crystal from Russia. Axinite is a complex silicate mineral whose triclinic crystals often show intergrowth and surface growth of other minerals. Courtesy of William W. Pinch, photo by Maha DeMaggio. © GIA.*

Wulfenite *actually has triclinic crystals, but false twinning produces a pseudotetragonal appearance. This "false twin" specimen is from the Nammoth mine in Tiger, Arizona. Courtesy of Smithsonian Institution, photo by Robert Weldon. © GIA.*

CRYSTAL "PERFECTION"

In the preceding crystal-system diagrams, the crystals are idealized. In reality, few naturally perfect crystals exist. A perfect crystal has exact angles, equal faces, and undistorted proportions. A perfect crystal is also complete and undamaged. Most natural crystals, on the other hand, are distorted, incomplete, and/or damaged. Here are some terms commonly used to describe various states of crystal "perfection":

+ *Anhedral*—crystals that completely lack faces; sometimes defined as "minerals with irregularly terminated grains."
+ *Euhedral*—crystals with regular intact faces all over; that is, crystals consisting only of crystal face boundaries.

Also called *idiomorphic*.
+ *Subeuhedral*—crystals with distinct faces. Also called *hypidiomorphic*.
+ *Subhedral*—crystals with partly developed faces or defective faces.
+ *Xenomorphic*—deformed crystals, caused by lack of space for full crystal growth.

ISOMORPHS

Isomorphs are minerals of constant crystal structure (similar crystal lattice), but different chemical composition. Mineral examples include *albite*, *anorthite*, *calcite*, *magnetite*, *rhodochrosite*, and *siderite*.

PSEUDOMORPHS

Pseudomorphs (literally meaning "false shape") are crystals in which a mineral gets the crystal shape and form of another mineral. Pseudomorphism may be either complete in which the entire original mineral is replaced with a new mineral, or incomplete (also called "partial"), whereby there is incomplete mineral chemical exchange—that is, part of the original mineral's chemicals coexist with the new mineral. Pseudomorphs can make mineral identification tricky, although they are avidly sought by serious mineral collectors.

There are four basic pseudomorphic types: *alteration*, *encrustation* (sometimes spelled *incrustation*), *paramorphs*, and *replacement* (also called *substitution*). We also can't forget *skulls* and *fossils*.

Alteration pseudomorphs The chemical composition of a mineral is changed to that of another mineral, but the crystal form of the original mineral remains. This is the most common pseudomorphic type. By custom, the newer mineral is named first when naming pseudomorphs. For example, if *limonite* replaces *pyrite*, the pseudomorph is termed *limonite after pyrite*, which happens to be an alteration pseudomorph. Others are *kaolinite after orthoclase* and *malachite after azurite*.

Rough pieces and a cabochon of petrified wood. Petrified wood is fossilized wood that has been entirely replaced by chalcedony. © GIA.

Encrustation (or incrustation) pseudomorphs These are formed when a mineral gets coated by another mineral— that is a new mineral is deposited over an already existing mineral, thereby assuming the crystal form of the older mineral. The original underlying mineral may later disappear, leaving a mould (hollow pseudomorphic cast) made entirely of the newer mineral. Examples are *calcite after quartz* and *pyrite after fluorite*.

For the purists, we might say that en-

crustation pseudomorphs are not true pseudomorphs if the word is strictly defined, but we won't strictly define it here.

Paramorphs Pseudomorphs with the same chemical composition, but different atomic/molecular arrangement. A paramorph is a crystal whose chemistry has been rearranged using the same chemicals in the original specimen, but without changing its external shape. Paramorphs exist only in polymorphous minerals, such as *calcite after aragonite* or *rutile after brookite*.

Replacement (substitution) pseudomorphs The new mineral completely replaces the old mineral, which is gradually removed as the new mineral is deposited. The new mineral thus fills a cavity and forms a cast of the original mineral. An example is the semiprecious gemstone "tiger-eye" (*crocidolite*), which is a *quartz*-composition replacement pseudomorph for *crocidolite* asbestos.

Natural rough specimen of staurolite with its typical twinned (intergrown) monoclinic crystals. Staurolite is an iron, aluminum silicate mineral found in regionally metamorphosed schists and gneisses. Photo by Robert Weldon. © GIA.

Skulls Hollow pseudomorphs, which form around a curved mineral piece shaped like a conglomerate pebble, for instance. A prime example is the *copper* "skulls" from the Keweenaw Peninsula in Michigan.

Fossils Fossils are usually pseudomorphs. Most are complete replacement pseudomorphs, typically with silica minerals replacing the original bone, teeth, shell, and so forth.

Some fossils, however, are the actual preserved remains of prehistoric creatures, such as animals in tar, insects in amber, mammoths in permafrost, carbonized residues of plants or fish fins, and original shell carbonates.

A 55-millimetre-high fossilized pinecone from Patagonia, Argentina. Fossils are usually found in sedimentary rocks. © GIA.

POLYMORPHS

Most minerals are in a single-crystal-system class. Some minerals, however, appear in two or more classes and are called *polymorphs* ("many shapes"). Polymorphic examples are *anatase/brookite*, *aragonite/calcite*, *cristobalite/quartz*, *diamond/graphite*, *marcasite/pyrite*, and *rutile/tridymite*. Each member of these mineral pairs has identical chemical composition but is of a different crystal class.

CRYSTAL TWINNING

Crystal *twins* are two intergrown crystals with some common points or axes. Crystal twins of the same mineral species are more common than twins of different minerals—which may be of the same chemical composition (for example, *marcasite twinned with pyrite*) or different chemical composition (for example, *hematite twinned with rutile*). Not only twins, but also higher crystal intergrown multiples exist—for example, three, four, and five intergrown crystals are called, respectively, threelings, fourlings, and fivelings.

Twinned crystals are of three types:

Contact twins These result when two crystals stick to each other during growth, being united by the composition plane. Each half is in reverse orientation to the other, as though one-half was revolved 180° from the other. *Aragonite* and *gypsum* exhibit contact twinning. Contact twins are more common than penetration twins (below).

This 114 ct. twinned chrysoberyl crystal is reportedly the largest recovered in Sri Lanka in recent years. Photo by Maha DeMaggio. © GIA.

An 8.2-centimetre-long brecciated "tiger eye" quartz slab from South Africa. "Tiger's Eye" is a pseudomorph of quartz formed from the weathered fibrous silicate mineral crocidolite. Photo courtesy S. McClure. © GIA.

Penetration twins (sometimes called "interpenetrated twins") These are formed when two crystals actually grow through each other, with their corners emerging from each other's faces. Penetration twins are not only revolved 180°, but they also merge. The classical example of a popularly collected penetration twin mineral is *fluorite*.

Repeated twins Parallel groups of successive crystals; for example, *plagioclase* feldspars, which exhibit parallel striations on their crystal cleavage surfaces.

MINERAL HABITS (FORMS, OR AGGREGATES)

A mineral *habit* is its outward appearance of crystal shape, also called *structural form* or (sometimes) *crystalline aggregate*. Here are some standard terms used to describe mineral crystal habits:

Acicular Needlelike; examples are *scolecite* and *natrolite*.

Aggregate Crystal cluster (group, or mass) of one or more minerals.

Arborescent Treelike, branching aggregates; examples are *native copper* and *native silver*.

Bladed Flat, elongated crystals; for example, *barite*.

Botryoidal Small and rounded, like grapes; for example, *azurite*. Smaller than mammillary or reniform habits.

Capillary Hairlike; finer than acicular.

Columnar Columns or rods, usually parallel, but can be irregular or radiating; for example, *aragonite*.

Concentric Banded, shell-like, spherical.

Coralloidal Branching, like coral; for example, *aragonite*.

Concretionary Rounded, as in geodes.

Crusty and colloidal For example, *aragonite, limonite, marcasite,* and *pyrite*.

Cryptocrystalline Crystals so small that they need magnification to be seen.

Crystalline Compact mass of crystals.

Dendritic Fernlike branching; a delicate type of arborescent. Examples: *copper, gold,* and *psilomelane*, as well as *man-*

ganese dendrites in shale. Often confused with fossils.

Drusy (or druse)   Thin layer of crystals coating a rocky surface.

Etched   Crystal faces altered, pitted, scratched, and so forth.

Fibrous   Threadlike, fibrelike. The fibres can be irregular, parallel, or radiating. Examples: *asbestos* and *sillimanite*.

Filiform   Thread or wirelike, often twisted; examples are *native gold* and *silver wires*.

Foliated   Leaflike, in thin, easily separated leaves (laminae).

Geniculated   Kneelike bend.

Geode, or geodal   Rounded, spherical, with a crystal-lined cavity; examples are *calcite* or *quartz* crystal geodes.

Globular (or spherical)   Spherelike; for example, *prehnite*.

Granular   An aggregate of coarse to fine grains.

Helictite   Branching protrusions from cavern formations; for example, *aragonite*.

Lamellar   Thin, flat plates that are easily separated; examples are *chlorite* and *mica*.

Lenticular   Lens-shaped.

Mammillary, or mammillated   Large and rounded; larger than either botryoidal or reniform.

Massive   Solid mass, without obvious structure.

Matrix   Rock host upon which the crystals are grown.

Micaceous   Thin and easily separated into sheets, like *mica*.

Nodule, or Nodular   Spherical (either regular or irregular); sometimes called "concretions" or "tuberous." Examples: *chalcedony*, *chert*, *opal*, and *serpentines*.

Oolitic   Egglike, that is, resembling fish eggs that are very tiny. Smaller than pisolitic. Example: *chamosite*.

Pisolitic   Pea-sized spherical grains, resembling peas, larger than oolitic.

Porous   For example, *calcite* and *limonite*.

Radiated, or radial   Spreading outward from a common central point; examples are circular disklike forms such as *marcasite* or crystal aggregates such as *stibnite*, *stilbite*, and *black tourmaline*.

Reniform   Kidney-shaped; larger than botryoidal, but smaller than mammillary. For example, some *hematite*.

Reticulated   Net or latticelike intersecting crystals; for example, *cerussite*.

Rosette   Roselike; examples are some *barite*, *gypsum*, and *hematite*.

Barite *"rose"* (also termed the *"desert rose"*) crystal aggregates, a common reddish-brown form of barite. Courtesy of Natural History Museum of Los Angeles County.

Faceted rutilated quartz *showing the needle inclusions of the simple titanium dioxide mineral* rutile. *Quartz is the most common mineral frequently bearing inclusions.* © *GIA.*

Rutilated　Rutile needle inclusions; for example, *rutilated quartz*.

Sheaflike　Resembles a wheat sheaf; for example, *stilbite*.

Stalactitic　Hanging, iciclelike; for example, *stalactites* in caverns.

Stalagmitic　Rising from a cavern floor, for example, *stalagmites*.

Stellated　Starlike radiations; for example, *water* in snowflake crystals.

Striated　Tiny, straight ridges and grooves; examples are *pyrite* and *tourmaline*.

Tabular　Flat plates; thicker than lamellar.

MINERAL PHYSICAL PROPERTIES AND TESTS

"Nothing has such power to broaden the mind as the ability to investigate systematically . . ."
Marcus Aurelius (121–180 A.D.), *Meditations*

Minerals are identified by observations and tests of their physical and chemical properties, which are mostly covered in this chapter. Technically, however, physical properties include crystal morphology, discussed separately in Chapter 6, and optical properties, summarized in Chapter 8. Each mineral species presents traits that may lend themselves more to certain diagnostic tests than others; tentative guesses as to a given mineral's species help us choose the tests most likely to confirm our identification.

◆

THE PROCESS OF MINERAL IDENTIFICATION

Mineral identification is often possible by following these general procedural steps:
1. First, observe the mineral's *morphological* characteristics, including:
  ◆ *Crystal shape*—a mineral species may exhibit many different forms, particularly from different localities.
  ◆ *Crystal habit*—the manner in which minerals typically occur in homogeneous groups (same species) and associations (with other species—for example, *cassiterite* and *sphalerite* often look similar, but cassiterite associates with *mica* and *quartz*, while

sphalerite is often associated with other sulfides).
2. Secondly, the *physical* tests for these properties may be necessary:
  ◆ *cleavage*
  ◆ *fracture*   in this chapter
  ◆ *color*
  ◆ *lustre*   in next chapter
  ◆ *diaphaneity*
3. It may also be necessary for these *physical* tests:
  ◆ *hardness*
  ◆ *tenacity*
  ◆ *specific gravity*   in this chapter
  ◆ *magnetism*
  ◆ *streak*   in next chapter
4. *Chemical* tests, either at home or in the laboratory, may be required to confirm or

deny a mineral's name:

+ *solubility* in water, acids, or other liquids
+ *taste* test (be careful!)
+ *odor* test

5. *Heating* tests—including in candle or Bunsen flames, blowpipe tests, and melting-point determinations.

6. *Electrical* tests, such as pyroelectric and piezoelectric phenomena.

7. *Radioactivity* measurements with a Geiger counter.

8. Lastly, *X-ray diffraction crystallographic analysis* in a laboratory equipped for such.

Some minerals will be difficult to identify due to their alterations, impurities present, small size that is hard to test and observe, atypical (unusual) morphology, absence from your handbooks, and variable properties.

What follow are separate sections explaining these mineral physical properties and their tests: (1) hardness, (2) breakage (including cleavage, fracture, and parting), (3) specific gravity, (4) tenacity, (5) magnetism, (6) chemical properties, (7) heat conductivity, (8) electrical conductivity, and (9) radioactivity. The chapter concludes with a section on miscellaneous tests—including touch, temperature, taste, and smell.

HARDNESS

Hardness is a mineral's resistance to scratching (mechanical abrasion). Do not confuse hardness with tenacity (resistance to breakage).

Hardness is dependent on the atomic/molecular bonds that hold a specimen together, as well as the spatial arrangements of atoms and their sizes. Minerals with large atoms tend to be soft, while minerals with small atoms tend to be hard.

Hardness is particularly useful in field collecting, because the hardness test can be done without elaborate testing equipment for many specimens *in situ* (that is, in the bedrock matrix before the specimen is even removed), and hardness determination often narrows the species possibilities for unknown minerals. While hardness alone may not positively identify a mineral, it can rule out many look-alike species.

Rough apatite, *a popularly collected phosphate mineral whose crystals may resemble, but are softer than,* beryl's. © *GIA.*

For example, *amethyst, apatite,* and *fluorite* are often of a similar violet color, but amethyst (Hardness 7) is harder than apatite (Hardness 5), which, in turn, is harder than fluorite (Hardness 4) by one degree. *Pyrite's* isometric crystals look similar to *chalcopyrite's* tetragonal crystals if the crystal boundaries are indistinct, but pyrite (Hardness 6–6½) is several degrees harder than chalcopyrite (Hardness 3½–4). *Black cassiterite* and *black sphalerite* both may show an adamantine or submetallic lustre, but cassiterite is Hardness 6–7 while sphalerite is Hardness 3½–4.

Mohs' Hardness Scale

The *Mohs' Hardness Scale* was proposed in 1822 by the German mineralogist Friedrich Mohs (1773–1839), and it is used to this day by mineral collectors and geologists everywhere for measuring the relative hardnesses of minerals. By custom, the word "hardness" is abbreviated "H." This is followed by the numerical hardness value, such as "H. 4" for "Hardness 4."

The Mohs' Scale lists 10 minerals by their hardness numbers, from softest to hardest, 1 to 10: 1. talc, 2. gypsum, 3. calcite, 4. fluorite, 5. apatite, 6. feldspar, 7. quartz, 8. topaz, 9. corundum, and 10. diamond.

Natural rough specimen of the mineral talc, *a basic magnesium silicate with Hardness 1, from Winston County, Vermont. Courtesy of Natural History Museum of Los Angeles County.*

A mineral is harder than minerals with lower numbers on the Mohs' Scale, but softer than minerals with higher numbers. Thus, *feldspar* will scratch *apatite*, but it will itself be scratched by *quartz*, which it cannot scratch; hence, feldspar is harder than apatite but softer than quartz.

Individual mineral species can vary in hardness—for example, *chalcocite* (H. 2½–3), *hematite* (H. 5–6), and *sulfur* (H. 1½–2½). The mineral *kyanite* has a hardness of 4 to 7 that varies within a single crystal! Many common minerals, though, such as *calcite* (H. 3) and *quartz* (H. 7), have fixed, unvariable hardness numbers for pure specimens tested properly.

Mohs' Hardness Scale is not incrementally proportional. It is a scale of relative hardness; in other words, higher numbers will scratch lower numbers, but not necessarily of proportional hardness increases. Thus, the difference between *corundum* (H. 9) and *diamond* (H. 10) is much greater in actual hardness than the

A faceted calcite *specimen. Being Hardness 3 and brittle, calcite gemstones are collectible, but not wearable in jewelry. Photo by Mike Havstad. © GIA.*

difference between feldspar (H. 6) and quartz (H. 7), even though such pairs are both separated by one hardness point. Furthermore, hardness numbers are not exact measurements, but relative values.

Professional mineralogists use a *sclerometer*, an instrument that measures exact hardnesses of minerals by employing a diamond or steel scratch point with variable weights.

Hardness Test

The hardness test is done by scratching an unknown mineral with a mineral of known hardness. A hardness set (also called "hardness points") is made up of samples of each of the 10 hardness numbers on the Mohs' Scale (sometimes diamond is left out), and a known mineral from the set is used to scratch a test specimen. By process of elimination, the unknown mineral will soon be between a known mineral that scratches it and another mineral that will be scratched by the unknown mineral, hence determining its approximate hardness number.

Test scratches should be done on a fresh, unweathered, flat surface of a specimen. A weathered surface may be softer than a freshly exposed surface on a mineral. The edges and corners of a crystal are sometimes harder than its faces or cleavage planes, so always scratch a flat surface of a specimen.

Be sure to wipe away the mineral dust that is produced by scratching, to see if the test specimen (unknown mineral) is indeed being scratched by the scale sample (known mineral/hardness), and not the other way around! A scratch will be a permanent shallow groove in the softer mineral. The Mohs' Scale minerals all have a white streak, so they should leave no colored powder themselves. Native metals produce no powder when scratched.

Two mineral samples have the same hardness if *neither* scratches the other—or if *both* scratch each other.

Don't unnecessarily disfigure a nice mineral specimen by scratching it across a displayable crystal face. Scratch tests, like all tests, should be done on the underside, or least-interesting side, of a specimen. Hardness scratch tests are sometimes done on the rough girdles of cut gemstones, not on their polished facets. Scratch tests are done on the back or bottom of statues—for example, to distinguish *jadeite* (H. 6½–7) from *nephrite* (H. 5–6) from *serpentine* (H. 3–5).

A "positive" hardness-test scratching usually emits a scraping sound, as the softer sample is cut into. "Negative" results from scratch tests sound squeaky or slippery, as the softer known mineral slides harmlessly over the harder test mineral.

Don't confuse hardness with brittleness. *Diamond* is the hardest substance known, but it is very brittle and will shatter to pieces when struck with a metal hammer head whose metallic alloy is much softer, but much less brittle, than diamond. A diamond will scratch steel, but steel will crush a diamond into dust.

Besides mineral scale samples in a field hardness-test kit, many mineral collectors like to carry along some common objects of known hardnesses for performing scratch tests at specimen collecting sites. Popular objects include the following:

- ✦ Fingernail—Hardness 2.5
- ✦ Copper coin—H. 3
- ✦ Window glass—H. 5.0 to 5.5
- ✦ Steel knife blade—H. 5.5 to 6.0
- ✦ Steel file—H. 6.5 to 7.5

So, a steel pocketknife will scratch *calcite*, but not *quartz*. A copper coin will scratch *gypsum*, but not *apatite*. The hardness test for a *diamond* is whether or not it will scratch *corundum*, not glass; glass will sometimes scratch glass, and quartz will always scratch common window glass, so a *rock crystal* (clear *quartz*) gemstone cannot be identified as a diamond just because it scratches glass! *Opal* is not a good ring stone because it will scratch easily due to its relative softness (H. 5.5–6.5), which makes it readily scratched by quartz sand dust (H. 7.0). A better gemstone, hardnesswise, is *sapphire* (H. 9.0), which is harder than anything it is liable to bump into, except other corundum or diamond.

Minerals softer than 5.5 will be scratched by a good steel knife. Minerals harder than 5.5 will scratch glass.

Reddish corundum *in green* muscovite mica, *from Pakistan near the Afghanistan border. Corundum is the aluminum oxide mineral of* ruby *and* sapphire. *Photo by Robert Weldon.* © *GIA.*

False Hardness-Test Results

Scratch tests may yield false results due to various factors, such as:

- ✦ *Weathered surfaces* being scratched— may be softer than fresh, unweathered surfaces of a sample mineral.
- ✦ *Impure sample*—if the specimen has chemical impurities in it, you may get a composite value somewhere between the pure hardnesses of all the ingredients averaged together.
- ✦ *Edges, instead of planes, tested*—a mineral's planar (flat) surfaces tend to be softer and more indicative of its textbook hardness value than crystal edges and corners. With a weathered or broken specimen, you may be testing a harder region of a sample and not realize it. So, it is always sensible to make several scratch tests on different parts of a sample if you don't mind getting it scratched all over.
- ✦ *Hardness is different in different directions*—for example, the mineral *kyanite's* hardness varies from 4 to 4.5 when scratched *against* its crystal grain and from 6 to 7 when scratched *with* the grain.
- ✦ *Crystal clusters tend to be softer than single crystals* of a given species.
- ✦ *Very soft, porous, and delicate specimens may be difficult to scratch-test because of their flimsy substance.*

MINERAL BREAKAGE

A mineral can break in three ways: it can *cleave* along natural, flat, atomically determined planes, it can *fracture* into irregular, rough surfaces, without a definite directional plane of breakage, and it can *part* along planes unrelated to the mineral's crystal structure. Cleavage, fracture, and parting should not be confused with each other (see below).

Cleavage

Cleavage is mineral breakage along natural planes of weakness that are parallel to theoretical crystal faces of a mineral and follow the internal atomic/molecular structure of the mineral species. Cleavage is the natural tendency of a given mineral species to split in specific directions. Crystals cleave in the direction of weakest cohesion (that is, weakest intermolecular forces). Cleavage potential is always present in all specimens of a given mineral species that cleaves.

Not all minerals cleave. Not all crystals cleave. Some minerals just fracture. *Quartz* doesn't cleave, even though it has a regular hexagonal crystal system. *Obsidian* (volcanic glass) never cleaves because it is amorphous (without crystal structure). Glass is not only not a crystal, but not a true solid either, because it has no definite melting point. Chemists consider glass to be a highly viscous supercooled liquid. On the stained glass windows of Medieval European churches, you can sometimes measure the thickness of the glass panels to be greater at their bottom than at the top of the panes, because the "liquid" glass has been slowly flowing down due to gravity over the centuries.

Cleavage Planes

Cleavage planes (the flat surfaces into which minerals cleave) are always parallel to a possible or actual crystal face. A crystal face is the highly reflective flat surface of a crystal, with geometrical orientation coincident to the crystal's internal atomic/molecular structure. Some minerals have more than one cleavage plane (direction of natural cleavage): *mica* cleaves in one direction, *feldspar* in two directions, *galena* and *halite* in three directions. *Calcite* and *halite* cleave along their crystallographic planes. *Aragonite* cleaves along specific cleavage planes.

Cleavage may not be equally "perfect" in all directions in a multidirectional cleaving mineral. *Gypsum* has perfect cleavage along one plane, but it has poor cleavages along its other two planes.

Cleavage Quality

Different mineralogical reference books give different terms and different definitions of them for cleavage qualities—which can be confusing. Some references use the terms "distinct" and "indistinct" to mean "good" and "fair" cleavages, respectively; others just use a scale in descending order, such as the following:

1. *Eminent* cleavage—unidirectional and perfect; examples are *chlorite* and *mica*.

2. *Perfect* cleavage—sometimes refers to *mica* and *chlorite*; other authorities use "perfect" to mean easily formed multidirectional cleavages, such as in *calcite*, *fluorite*, *galena*, and *halite*. Gemstones with perfect cleavage must be cut, set, and worn with great care, because they can cleave and split if hit hard enough (examples are *rhodonite* and *spodumene*).

3. *Good* cleavage—slightly uneven cleavage planes; examples are *azurite*, *feldspar*, and *realgar*.

4. *Fair* cleavage ⎫ very
5. *Poor* cleavage ⎬ irregular ⎰ e.g., *apatite*
　　　　　　　　　 ⎭ cleavage ⎱ and *sulfur*

6. *None* (no cleavage)—*bornite*, *garnet*, native metals, and *quartz*. *Amethyst* (purple *quartz*) and *fluorite* often have a similar violet color, but amethyst never cleaves, while fluorite shows perfect cleavage, a diagnostic test to distinguish the two (along with hardness, and so forth).

Cleavage Bodies

Cleavage bodies (also called "cleavages") are the three-dimensional geometrical shapes that minerals naturally assume by cleaving. Cleavage bodies are not crystals; they are regularly shaped geometrical solids, such as cubes, octahedra, and rhombohedra. *Halite* and *galena* cleave into cubes. *Fluorite* cleaves into octahedral cleavage bodies, but it rarely forms octahedral crystals; fluorite usually forms cubic crystals. The octahedral fluorite cleavages sold in rock shops and at mineral shows result from breakage, not natural crystal growth. *Calcite* cleaves into rhombohedra.

Cleavage forms are cleavage bodies bounded by natural cleavage planes on all sides. Examples are *calcite*, *fluorite*, and *halite*. Cleavage of any kind is best demonstrated when a mineral specimen is struck by a metallic hammer head.

Fracture

Fracture is mineral breakage in directions different from cleavage planes. Fracture is not completely random, because it does result in definable fracture types (see below), but fracture doesn't produce regular planar surfaces as cleavage does.

Fracture Types

✦ *Conchoidal*—shell-like, with gently curving, concave and convex, smooth surfaces; mineral examples are *obsidian* and most silicates, such as *flint*, *opal*, and *quartz*. The conchoidal fracturability of obsidian and flint was readily recognized by prehistoric Stone Age peoples who found obsidian and flint ideal for making tools.

✦ *Earthy*—crumbly; examples are *chalk* (*limestone* variety) and *kaolinite*.

✦ *Even*—relatively flat surfaces, smoothly broken; for example, *jasper*.

✦ *Fibrous*—see "Splintery" below.

✦ *Hackly*—jagged, sharp-edged; common in native metals.

✦ *Irregular*—see "Uneven" below.

✦ *Rough*—not smooth.

✦ *Splintery* (also called "Fibrous")—a woodlike break; examples are *garnet* and *nephrite*.

✦ *Subconchoidal*—not quite clean shell-like breakage.

✦ *Uneven*—moderately rough surfaces; examples are *arsenopyrite* and *pyrite*. Also called "irregular" fracture.

Parting

Parting is mineral breakage along weak planes that are unrelated to the atomic/molecular structure of the mineral. Parting is caused by layered inclusions, crystal twinning, or external pressure. It is not evident, therefore, in all specimens of a given mineral species.

Parting should not be confused with cleavage or fracture. Parting has a gross (large) structural reason for occurring in a mineral. Cleavage and fracture are due to the mineral's ultimate atomic/molecular structure. By chance, parting may coincidentally occur along crystalline planes and cleavage planes, leaving the observer to wonder exactly what is happening, mineralogically.

SPECIFIC GRAVITY (DENSITY)

Specific gravity (abbreviated "G" or "sp. gr."—and also known as *density*) is the mathematical ratio of the weight of a sample of a given material compared to (divided by) the weight of an equivalent volume of distilled water at 4° C. In other words, specific gravity is the relative density of a substance compared with water.

Water is "as dense as itself"—meaning that it has a specific gravity (G) value of 1.00. A material with a sp. gr. greater than 1 is heavier than water, and it will sink in it. A material with a sp. gr. less than 1 is lighter in weight than water, and it will float upward to the water's surface.

The density of a material is due to its

SPECIFIC GRAVITY RANGES

Specific Gravity (G)	Weight Category	Mineral Examples
1–2	Lightweight	Borax (1.7) Kernite (1.95) Ulexite (1.9)
2–4	Average or Medium Weight	Bauxite (2.4–2.6) Calcite (2.7) Fluorite (3.0–3.2) Gypsum (2.3–2.4) Halite (2.16) Orthoclase (2.5–2.6) Quartz (2.65) Realgar (3.5–3.6) Sulfur (2.0–2.1)
4–6	Heavyweight	Barite (4.3–4.6) Bornite (4.9–5.1) Chalcopyrite (4.1–4.3) Hematite (4.9–5.3) Marcasite (4.8–4.9) Pyrite (4.9–5.2) Stibnite (4.6) Zircon (4.6–4.7)
Above 6	Very Heavy	Cassiterite (6.8–7.1) Cinnabar (8.0–8.2) Cobaltite (6.3) Native copper (8.9) Native gold (19.3) Vanadinite (6.7–7.2) Wulfenite (6.5–7.0)

chemical composition and interatomic/intermolecular structure (for example, crystals, if applicable). Metallic minerals tend to be about twice as heavy as non-metallic minerals. Most minerals have a sp. gr. of 2 to 4; that is, they are 2 to 4 times as heavy as water. Experienced mineral collectors can estimate the sp. gr. of a mineral specimen just by holding it in their hand. Minerals can be classified from "lightweight" to "very heavy" according to these sp. gr. ranges:

Of course, handheld estimates of specimen densities should be correlated with specimen volumes. Although pure *gold* is seven times as heavy as pure *quartz*, a tiny leaf of gold will obviously weigh less than a massive quartz crystal, but such differences are understood by the intelligent observer.

Density Ranges

Density ranges exist for certain mineral species, but density is independent of direction in a given homogeneous (pure) crystal. Density can vary in a single crystal due to impurities, inclusions, and crystal intergrowth (for instance, *barite* [G 4.5] and *gypsum* [G 2.3] may be intergrown, with a resulting composite average density).

Mineralogical reference books often give a range of commonly measured mineral densities, as well as a pure specimen density, for each mineral species.

Mineral Identification with Densities

A specific gravity test can help to identify minerals at home or in the field. Mineral look-alikes, such as *barite* (G 4.5) and *gypsum* (G 2.3), can be distinguished by their densities in pure specimens (also by hardness in this case: *barite* H. 3–3.5, *gypsum* H. 1½–2).

Barite and *calcite* both have perfect cleavage, are the same hardness, and are often both whitish-colored. But barite is heavier, and calcite dissolves in dilute hydrochloric acid.

Although *diamond* and *graphite* could never be mistaken for each other, they show the principle of how compact crystal structure affects density. Both diamond and graphite have the same chemical composition (pure carbon), but diamond has a sp. gr. of 3.5, while graphite has a sp. gr. of 1.9–2.3. Diamond's compact atomic arrangement accounts for its higher specific gravity.

Densities of Less Than "1"

Pumice, the very porous variety of the volcanic rock *rhyolite*, often floats in water due to its spongy air pockets. Crushed pumice, however, will sink in water—as will a water-logged specimen of pumice, as I learned not too long ago. When I was demonstrating its floatability in my second-period Earth Science class, my pumice sample sank, to my embarrassment, after becoming water-logged during the first-period class. After that, I used a dry specimen of pumice whenever I wanted to show my students its equivalent specific gravity of less than 1. Furthermore, some pumice samples will never float, because their pores aren't voluminous enough to hold an amount of air that compensates for their dry mineral weight.

Mineral dust and small slivers of *mica*, for instance, will float on water. This is due to surface tension of the water, whereby water molecules refuse to "climb up" around and on top of the tiny specimen—not because such minerals are lighter in weight than water.

The mineral *water* will float as solid ice in liquid water, because water slightly expands just before it freezes. This is a very unusual physical property that gives solid water an effective specific gravity of less than 1 (and that keeps our planet from being in a permanent Ice Age, because icebergs in the polar regions can float away and melt, rather than pile up and contribute to intense polar refrigeration).

Measuring Specific Gravity

Specific gravity values are precisely determined by professional mineralogists in the laboratory using a Jolly balance, a pycnometer, or heavy liquids. A *pycnometer* employs the principle of different densities of liquids in determining specific gravities of samples.

Mineral collectors use one of three basic methods in home testing for mineral specific gravities:

Sample weight in air versus sample weight in water The specific gravities of nonporous, non-water-soluble solids can be determined by weighing them in air and then weighing them in water (with the water's buoyancy affecting the submerged specimen's measured weight). A *Berman torsion balance* or *spring scale* (of the kind used in physics classes) are commonly employed in this method of specific gravity testing. Water-soluble specimens can be weighed in oil or alcohol of known density. The mathematical formula for calculating specific gravity from weight in air versus weight in water is as follows:

$$\text{specific gravity} = \frac{(\text{weight in air}) \times (\text{immersion liquid's density})}{(\text{weight in air} - \text{weight in liquid})}$$

If pure water is used as the immersion liquid, its density equals 1.

Sample weight in air versus weight of the volume of displaced water (when sample is submerged in water) This is the easiest method, requiring minimal special equipment, for measuring specific gravity, provided that you can accurately weigh the sample's size and water's volume. The formula for calculating specific gravity by this method is as follows:

$$\text{specific gravity} = \frac{\text{specimen weight in air}}{\text{weight of water displaced by specimen}}$$

For example, weigh a piece of pure *fluorite* in air. Submerge it in a container of pure water, ideally a long glass tube with volumetric increments marked on it (such as a chemical lab's *graduated cylinder*), and notice how high the water has risen after completely submerging the mineral specimen. Then carefully pour off only the amount of rise in the column of water, and weigh this water in a container with appropriate deduction for the container's dry (empty) weight. The amount of water that rises is the amount of water that the solid mineral displaces, and this numerical value goes in the denominator of the fraction above. In the case of *fluorite*, you should find that its specimen weight in air is about triple its weight of displaced water volume, because fluorite is three times as heavy as water (sp. gr. of 3.0–3.2).

A major source of error with this method of measuring specific gravity is in trying to get accurate weight measurements for small mineral samples and small volumes of water. Large volume samples work better with amateur equipment at home. Small samples can be used if you have access to a high school, college, or company chemistry lab.

Heavy liquids—comparing their densities with a mineral sample You can buy a set of heavy liquids for specific gravity sample determination at mineralogical equipment supply companies, including some of the better local lapidary shops. If a mineral sample sinks, it is heavier than the liquid. If the mineral floats, it is lighter than the liquid. If the mineral stays randomly suspended in the liquid, they are of the same density.

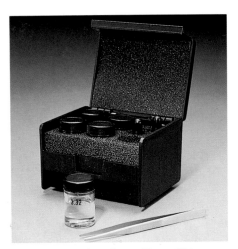

Specific gravity liquids test kit. © GIA.

For example, a certain set of heavy liquids for density tests on minerals includes the following liquids and their densities: bromoform, 2.88; tetrabrommetan, 2.95; Thoulet's Liquid, 3.19; methylene iodide, 3.3; Rohrbach's Solution, 3.58; and Clerici's Solution, 4.2

Sometimes a heavy liquids set is diluted with alcohols, benzol, or ether. So, be sure to use the densities listed with the set's instructions, and take care to avoid contamination of the liquids or getting them mixed up in unmarked containers.

TENACITY

The cohesive properties of minerals are divided into three basic categories: (1) *hardness* (tested by scratching, discussed earlier in this chapter), (2) *breakage* (cleavage, fracture, and parting, also discussed earlier in this chapter), and (3) *tenacity* (brittleness, ductility, elasticity, flexibility, malleability, sectility, and sometimes softness [not to be confused with "hardness" above] and toughness [explained in this section]).

Tenacity is a mineral's resistance to breakage, or how a mineral "holds itself together" in a specimen sample—especially when hammered. Do not confuse tenacity with hardness (resistance to scratching).

In mineralogy, there are six basic types of tenacity, and I also added softness and toughness:

✦ *Brittleness*—easily breaks when lightly struck; may shatter to pieces when hit with a steel-headed hammer. Examples: *diamond*, *obsidian*, *opal*, *quartz*, and *pyrite*. Brittle minerals are not malleable or ductile.

+ *Ductility*—can be drawn into a wire; native metals, such as *copper*, *gold*, *platinum*, and *silver*, are ductile.

+ *Elasticity*—resumes original position after bending; for example, *mica* cleavage plates are perfectly elastic.

+ *Flexibility*—stays deformed after bending; for example, *chlorite* cleavage plates (which resemble *mica* in outward appearance). Mica is both flexible and elastic, according to loose definitions of terms. Chlorite is flexible, but not elastic, according to any definitions of the terms.

+ *Malleability*—flattens when hammered (rather than breaks into pieces). Native metals can be hammered into thin sheets; thus, native metals are ductile and malleable. *Pyrite*, brassy yellow in color and often associated with *native copper* and *gold*, is not malleable—a basic test for pure *gold*. Malleable minerals are not brittle.

+ *Sectility*—can be sliced with a knife into thin sheets; the silver sulfide mineral *"acanthite"* (*argentite*) is perfectly sectile.

+ *Softness*—breaks easily into powder (instead of larger fragments) when hammered. *Graphite* and *talc* are soft minerals. Don't confuse with hardness. As used here in tenacity classifications, softness is in contradistinction to brittleness and malleability, not as a "low number" on the Mohs' Hardness Scale.

+ *Toughness*—resists breakage. There are varying degrees of toughness, of course. A mineral is tough if it is difficult to break with repeated moderately forceful hammer blows, but this also depends on the size of the specimen, the angle of hammer impact, and so forth. No mineral is "perfectly" tough, because every mineral can be broken.

MAGNETISM

Magnetism in minerals is of two types:

Naturally magnetized minerals These are minerals that are magnets themselves, and will attract iron filings (dust). "Lodestone" (a variety of the iron ore *magnetite*—not to be confused with magnesite) behaves as a natural magnet.

Magnetism can be used when prospecting for iron-rich minerals, and for distinguishing certain iron ore look-alikes—for example, *magnetite* and *chromite* are both blackish minerals with a specific gravity of about 5, but magnetite has a black streak and is more magnetic than chromite that has a dark brown streak and is weakly magnetic.

Magnetic minerals Those that are attracted to a magnet, specifically those with a high iron content. *Native iron* is strongly magnetic, and *native platinum* is weakly magnetic, but both of these are rare minerals in such a pure state. Pure *nickel* is magnetic, but it is never found as such in nature.

+ *Chromite*—weakly magnetic.
+ *Franklinite*—weakly magnetic.
+ *Hematite*—with very high iron content; may become slightly magnetic upon heating in a candle flame.
+ *Ilemite*—weakly magnetic.
+ *Limonite*—may become weakly magnetic upon heating.
+ *Magnetite*—highly magnetic, as well as often being a natural magnet itself.
+ *Pyrrhotite*—strongly magnetic.

+ *Siderite*—becomes weakly magnetic when heated in a candle flame.
+ *Wolframite*—weakly magnetic if of high iron content.

CHEMICAL PROPERTIES

Because minerals are made of *chemicals*, all mineralogical diagnostic tests are, in a sense, chemical, or at least based on chemical composition. But when we say "chemical tests," we customarily mean how a mineral responds when exposed to specific chemical reagents, such as water or acids (especially the mineral's solubility in such). We can also include the human observer's physiological chemical reactions, such as taste and smell, in mineral identification.

Chemical reagents for mineral testing can be purchased from rock and lapidary shops, chemical-supply firms, and school-supply firms—although many companies will not sell potentially dangerous chemicals to private individuals. You should be able to buy dilute hydrochloric acid at a rock shop, concentrated ethyl alcohol (with a small percentage of denaturing impurity of another alcohol) at your drugstore or grocery store, and distilled water from any grocery store. These are the most useful chemicals for routinely required mineral tests.

Mineral Solubility

Most minerals, such as *calcite* and *quartz*, are insoluble (not dissolvable) in pure water. Some minerals are very soluble (dissolvable) in water, such as *borax*, *chalcanthite*, *halite*, and *kernite*—and these minerals must be protected from moisture, which could melt them right on their display shelf!

Cold, dilute hydrochloric acid (HCl) will dissolve carbonates effervescently (with carbon dioxide bubbles generated). This is a convenient chemical test for *calcite*, *limestone*, *chalk*, and so forth. The chemical equation for the reaction of calcium carbonate (*calcite*) with hydrochloric acid is as follows:

$$CaCO_3 + HCl = CO_2 + CaCl_2 + H_2O$$
(calcium carbonate) +
(hydrochloric acid) =
(carbon dioxide gas) +
(calcium chloride salt) +
(liquid water)

Calcite and *quartz* both form clear hexagonal crystals with pyramidal caps, but calcite effervesces in hydrochloric acid, while quartz doesn't. *White calcite* and *white gypsum* look similar and have close specific gravities, but calcite fizzes in hydrochloric acid, which has no effect on gypsum (gypsum, however, will dissolve in hot hydrochloric acid). *Limestone* with high *calcite* or *aragonite* content will dissolve effervescently in cold, dilute hydrochloric acid, but similarly appearing *dolomite* will not. Use *dilute* acids only in field tests, and don't damage nice crystals with excess acid application.

Some noncarbonate minerals, like *howlite* (hydrated calcium silico-borate), will also dissolve in hydrochloric acid.

Hot acid tests should only be performed by experienced chemists. Be careful not to spill acids on your hands or eyes! The first-aid treatment for acid burns is flushing the wound with plenty of cold water; this must be done immediately. Always have a jar of cold water nearby, for first-aid use, when making acid tests on minerals.

Native (pure) *gold* and *platinum* are unaffected by either hydrochloric acid (HCl) or nitric acid (HNO$_3$) alone. These noble metals will dissolve in *aqua regia* ("kingly water," or "royal water"), which is a mixture of hydrochloric and nitric acids. This is a good test for gold in the field. Plain nitric acid will dissolve gold look-alikes such as *pyrite*, but it will not affect pure gold.

HEAT CONDUCTIVITY

Native metals (*gold*, *silver*, and so forth) feel colder to the touch than, say, the organic minerals of *amber* or *coal*, due to the greater *heat conductivity* of the metals. Sometimes jewelers can tell the difference between a genuine gemstone and a glass imitation by feeling them against their cheek; the stone feels colder than the glass, even though they are the same temperature.

Small pieces of certain minerals, such as *borax*, *calaverite*, *cerussite*, *galena*, *stibnite*, and *sylvanite*, will melt in a candle or Bunsen burner flame.

Be careful that you don't get burned when performing heating tests on minerals. Always wear protective eye goggles when making open-flame tests. The first-aid treatment for skin burns is immediately flooding the burn site with cold water; keep a jar or bucket of cold water nearby whenever you are working with open flames.

Some minerals will spatter or explode into hot flying fragments when heated. Expect this to happen every time that you heat a mineral, and wear your eye goggles.

ELECTRICAL CONDUCTIVITY

Certain minerals *conduct electricity* better than others. A mineral specimen on a zinc plate submerged in an aqueous solution of copper sulfate will gather a layer of pure copper where its mineral surface touches the zinc surface, *if* the mineral conducts electricity.

Pyroelectric substances gain an electric charge when heated or cooled, thereby exhibiting electrical *polarity* (one end becomes positively charged, the other end negatively charged). *Quartz* shows marked pyroelectrical effects: when a warmed quartz crystal is dusted with a powdered mixture of red lead and sulfur dust, the red lead accumulates on the negative end, and the sulfur on the positive end, of the crystal.

Piezoelectric substances gain an electric charge when pressure is applied. *Analcite*, *diamond*, *quartz*, *sulfur*, *topaz*, and *tourmaline* are some minerals that exhibit piezoelectricity: when their crystals are vigorously rubbed, they pick up little bits of paper by static electricity. Quartz and tourmaline both show prominent pyroelectric and piezoelectric effects. Like pyroelectric materials, piezoelectric substances show crystal electrical polarity when charged.

RADIOACTIVITY

Radioactive minerals give off invisible radiation from the spontaneous decay in

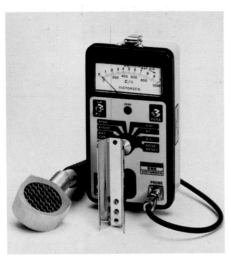

This Geiger counter with "pancake probe" is used for detecting radioactive minerals. Instrument is courtesy of Victoreen, Inc. Photo courtesy of Victoreen, Inc.

mild low-dosage radiation constantly—to which you are exposed whenever you go camping or cave exploring in granitic mountains, although this is not considered a health hazard. People who live in stone-faced houses or stone-walled basements also receive mild radiation doses from the stones over a long period of time, but it's probably nothing to worry about in most situations. Lying on the beach in the sun all day or taking a high-altitude airplane trip for a few hours will expose you to more radiation than you'll receive from handling a few average radioactive rock specimens. And a medical X ray is a massive radiation dose—compared to touch-

their atomic nuclei. This radiation takes the forms of (1) alpha particles (two protons and two neutrons stuck together—a "helium" atomic nucleus), (2) beta particles (electrons or positrons), and (3) gamma rays (high-energy electromagnetic radiation of shorter wavelength than X rays).

Most radioactive minerals are considered harmless as they are found in nature by prospecting with a portable *Geiger counter*, a device that converts radioactive radiation into visible or audible clicks on its metres.

Note: When radioactive elements are extracted from their minerals and concentrated, they become a serious health hazard. So, beginning collectors are advised to get help and advice before keeping collections of radioactive minerals.

Actually, even rocks like *granite* give off

This faceted "hot" (radioactive) green zircon specimen on a Geiger counter probe shows a radiation reading of more than 0.4 milliroentgens (mR) per hour. As normal environmental background level is about 0.02 mR/hour, this stone might be unsafe to wear in jewelry. © GIA.

ing the typical radioactive mineral sample.

Radioactive minerals will take their own photograph (an "autoradiograph") when left sitting on a sealed sheet of unexposed photographic film for 24 hours or

Natural zircon crystal from Australia. The mineral zircon is a simple zirconium silicate, which can be slightly radioactive when admixed with sufficient uranium and thorium. A popular gemstone whose refractive index approaches that of diamond. Courtesy of Max Faulkner, photo by Robert Weldon. © GIA.

MISCELLANEOUS MINERAL TESTS

Depending on the minerals involved, some of the following tests may be useful in species identification.

Touch

By *touching* minerals, you can help identify them. For example, both *graphite* and *talc* feel slippery and greasy when handled, and graphite will leave pencil lead marks on your skin and paper.

Chalk and *kaolinite* feel dry—but, while kaolinite feels smooth, chalk tends to feel a bit rough. *Sandstone* feels rough, like sandpaper, *milky quartz* feels hard and glassy and cold and *granite* feels as permanent as it does . . . when you're feeling your way around inside granite caves in the dark!

Sulfur will sometimes crumble in your hand. *Chrysocolla* will sometimes stick to your tongue.

Weight, or Mass

Weight, or *mass*, of mineral specimens can be measured with a weighing scale or metric balance, both for sale at good rock shops and lapidary stores. Get a scale that will work for the weight of the specimens that you intend to collect.

A common bathroom scale may be adequate for weighing 50-pound boulders of collected rock. But you may have to invest in an *electronic gemstone balance* if you intend to collect gemstones seriously.

longer. When the film is developed and printed by normal processing, the auto-radiograph is present. So, radioactive minerals can accidentally ruin film if they are placed near it, whether the film is inside or outside a camera.

Uranium minerals, such as *autunite*, *carnotite*, *torbernite*, and *uraninite-pitch-blende* are radioactive. Autunite is both radioactive and highly fluorescent.

Thorium minerals, such as *monazite* and *thorite*, are radioactive.

Radioactive minerals are frequently green, orange, or yellow.

Of course, all minerals give off some type of radiation in the sense that they emit heat waves and reflect visible light—but only minerals that release invisible radiation due to nuclear disintegration are called radioactive.

cient size so that the specimens don't get stuck inside the tube. You must use a liquid in which the tested mineral is insoluble. This means that you'll be using water for many minerals, but not for evaporites.

After partially filling the cylinder with liquid to a predetermined level, you cautiously slide the mineral specimen into the cylinder and submerge it in the liquid. Don't break the cylinder's glass or the mineral specimen itself by carelessly "throwing" the specimen into the cylinder.

The volume to which the liquid rises in the cylinder is a close indication of the mineral specimen's volume. Graduated cylinders are sold by chemical-supply companies and science-supply firms (especially those that sell to school science departments) and at well-stocked lapidary shops.

Analytical balance, used to weigh small mineral specimens. © GIA.

Linear Measurement

Linear measurements can be made accurately on mineral specimens by using a simple ruler, with either English or metric units, for gross (large) lengths. A hand caliper may be necessary for measuring the dimensions of tiny crystals, little fossils, or cut gemstones—but be careful that you don't squeeze and crush the specimen with the caliper! A protractor (like the one you used in geometry class) measures crystal angles, or at least estimates them.

Volume

The most convenient way to determine the *volume* of rock and mineral specimens is with a glass *graduated cylinder* of suffi-

Temperature

The temperature of a rock is measured with a thermometer inserted inside a crack in the rock. You may want to measure the rock temperatures in a cave, under ice, near a hot spring, or at a fresh volcanic eruption—but be sure that your thermometer won't burst in excessively high heat. Volcanologists use special thermometers to record temperatures above the boiling point of water; you can buy these thermometers from science-supply companies.

Taste

Water-soluble minerals can be tested by *taste*, but I don't recommend it for safety and sanitary reasons. For example, the mineral *witherite* is water-soluble and poisonous!

The brazen collector will discover, however, that *halite* tastes salty, *epsomite* tastes salty-bitter, and "rock candy" (crystallized *sucrose*) tastes sweet. Prehistoric people undoubtedly tasted many minerals—to their benefit or detriment.

Odor

When rubbed or struck with a piece of metal, some minerals, such as *arsenopyrite*, *fluorite*, or *sulfur*, give off characteristic *odors* that are recognizable by the experienced mineral collector. For example, *arsenopyrite* smells like garlic when it is hit with a hammer and *kaolinite* smells like clay when it is damp. A mineral-hunting dog, trained to smell and locate certain minerals, would be of great value to a mineral prospector—provided that the dog didn't get distracted by rabbits or frightened in a cave!

chapter eight

MINERAL OPTICAL PROPERTIES

"Ever drifting down the stream—
Lingering in the golden gleam—
Life, what is it but a dream?"
Lewis Carroll (1832–1898), *Through the Looking Glass*

Optical properties deal with how light affects, and is affected by, minerals that it contacts. Although optics is a physical property, it is discussed separately in this chapter for convenience.

In nature, the wide variation of the chemical and physical conditions under which minerals form has a correspondingly diverse influence on their resultant optical properties—even within a given mineral species from a single collecting site. So, expect a range of measured values for optical studies in a given species. For example, *calcite* appears in many natural colors from white to black, is transparent to varying degrees of translucency, sometimes fluoresces brilliantly, and sometimes not, but displays double refraction when a colorless variety (such as "Iceland spar").

Mineral crystal *morphology* (shape), *color, lustre,* and *diaphaneity* (degree of transparency) together can often serve as positive identification by sight for many minerals *in situ* (in their bedrock matrix in the field)—even without considering other physical properties, such as *density* or *hardness*. The determined collector uses as many tests as necessary to identify a specimen, and experience will permit this quickly for many species.

Although there is some overlap in certain optical properties, I have divided this chapter into the following sections: (1) asterism, (2) chatoyancy, (3) color, (4) diaphaneity, (5) luminescence, (6) lustre, (7) photosensitivity, (8) polarization, (9) refraction, and (10) streak—with their appropriate subcategories.

———————————— ◆ ————————————

ASTERISM

Asterism is the starlike effect produced when light is transmitted through, or reflected from, a mineral's surface. Some *phlogopite mica* shows asterism with transmitted light. The highly prized "star rubies," "star sapphires," and "star garnets" exhibit asterism, due to reflected light, when cut in the rounded cabochon style.

Polished cabochon of chrysoberyl, showing the optical property of chatoyancy ("cat's-eye effect"). © GIA.

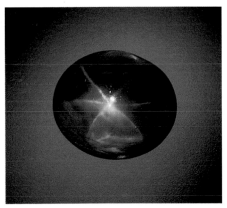

Natural star sapphire. Photo by S. McClure. © GIA.

An unusually large phosphophyllite crystal, 7.8 centimetres long and weighing 220 grams. Few minerals have the color shade of phosophyllite. Photo by Robert Kane. © GIA.

CHATOYANCY

Chatoyancy is a changeable silky sheen, often seen in minerals with a fine fibrous structure, such as *chrysoberyl* ("cat's-eye"), *crocidolite* ("tiger-eye"), and *satin-spar gypsum*. Chatoyancy is also called "Cat's-eye effect."

COLOR

Apparent color, observable in gross (large) specimens, should not be confused with a mineral's *true color*, the color of its pow-der, explained later in this chapter under "Streak." Apparent color (gross specimen color) is highly variable for many mineral species, especially nonmetallic ones, such as *calcite*, *fluorite*, *quartz*, and *tourmaline*, but true color (streak powder color) is constant for a given mineral species.

"Intraspecific" (within a given mineral species) color variation can be caused by changes in the mineral's chemical composition, impurities in the atomic structure, impurities as contaminants, visible inclusions, and crystal structural defects. Because of this variability, color alone cannot be relied upon for positive mineral identification. When I taught Earth Science classes, I used to place many whitish and greyish minerals on the "lab practical identification test" for my students, so that they couldn't identify a specimen by color alone.

Mineral color tends to change (darken or bleach) when exposed to weather, so a freshly fractured piece may be needed to evaluate a mineral's color. Although color is positively diagnostic in native metals, they, and their ores (compounds), tend to oxidize (tarnish) over time and their surface color is dulled; pure *gold*, of course, is an exception.

Alexandrite, *a color-change variety of* chrysoberyl, *photographed in incandescent light. From Sri Lanka. Courtesy* M. Allbritton, *photo by Robert Weldon,* © *GIA.*

Mineral Colors

The 10 basic colors for rocks and minerals are black, blue, brown, colorless (clear like window glass), grey, green, purple, red, white (not colorless, but white like a piece of paper), and yellow. Pink is considered a red tint, tan a brown tint, violet a purple tint, and so on.

Mineral colors are best observed in natural light, including direct sunlight. A mineral's color may change with different light sources—for example, *alexandrite* (a variety of *chrysoberyl*) is greenish in sunlight but rose-violet in artificial light.

Commercial gemstones often have had their colors changed completely or artificially enhanced by heat treatment or irradiation (both treatments render the stones safe to touch). *Amethyst* (purple *quartz*) changes into yellow *citrine* (also called "Madeira topaz") upon heating, and greenish-blue *aquamarine* becomes blue when heated. Most of the deep blue

The same alexandrite *as in previous photo, but under fluorescent light. Courtesy of M. Allbritton, photo by Robert Weldon.* © *GIA.*

topaz sold in jewelry stores has been produced by irradiating light blue or brown *topaz*. One would hope that if you paid good money for a richly colored gemstone, its deep color will be somewhat permanent, even if artificially created—some color-enhanced stones have slowly reverted towards their original pale shades over time!

Unusual colors of minerals, if genuine, may be worth a premium for their rarity, when offered for sale. Examples include red *topaz*, blue *quartz*, colorless *chrysoberyl*, and *achroite* (colorless *tourmaline*).

Greatly magnified stress fractures in a heat-treated sapphire from Sri Lanka. Gemstones are often heated or irradiated to improve their color for sale in the jewelry business. © GIA.

Achromatism

Achromatic minerals are colorless. Light rays are completely transmitted through the specimen without being absorbed in the visible spectral colors. Examples are the colorless varieties of *calcite*, *diamond*, *halite* (*rock salt*), *quartz* (*rock crystal*), and *topaz*.

"Rock crystal" specimen, the transparent colorless variety of quartz, *the most common mineral in the Earth's crust, and composed of simple silicon dioxide. Photo by Robert Weldon. © GIA.*

Allochromatism

Allochromatic minerals have highly variable colors for a given species, usually due to the presence of chemical impurities or inclusions. Color alone is therefore often unreliable in identifying such minerals, although you can narrow the possibilities when considered along with crystal form and habit.

When *quartz* is pure, it is colorless *rock crystal*; when violet, it is *amethyst*; when pink, it is *rose quartz*; and when grey or brown, it is called *smoky quartz*. Amethyst and rose quartz are due to traces of iron and titanium, respectively, whereas smoky quartz is colored by radioactivity, which is common deep underground. Within a quartz color variety, we may find many shades—for example, amethyst ranges from almost imperceptibly light violet to deep "Siberian" purple.

Pure *beryl* is colorless. But when less than 1-percent chromium impurity is substituted for the element aluminum in the mineral's beryllium aluminum silicate molecule, the color is green. Iron makes beryl blue or yellow. Manganese makes beryl pink.

Amethyst *terminations on* milky quartz *crystals, a common occurrence for amethyst.* © *GIA.*

Fluorite is most commonly seen at rock and mineral shows in blue, violet, and yellow shades, but it also comes in brown, green, pink, white, and colorless. *Smithsonite* has no single diagnostic color, being found in shades of blue, brown, colorless, grey, green, pink, purple, white, and yellow. *Tanzanite* is blue *zoisite*.

Color variations of a given mineral species often have their own variety, or subspecies, name, especially in the gemstones. For example, blue *tourmaline* is known as *indicolite*, pinkish-red tourmaline as *rubellite*, colorless as *achroite*, and *schorl* when it is opaque blackish-blue. A *suite* (pronounced "sweet") is a group of specimens that are color varieties of the same mineral; so, you'll see a jeweler or gem dealer offering a suite of *tourmalines* for sale, in a variety of pinks and greens, all lined up on a little display shelf. The word "suite" is most commonly used for cut gemstones, but it can refer to rough minerals as well.

Color "zoning" occurs when completely different colors are in one specimen of the same mineral. *Calcite, fluorite,* and *tourmaline* are well known for zoning. *Tourmaline* from San Diego County, California, is often bicolored (two colors) or tricolored (three colors), with combinations of vivid green, pink, and colorless bands. *Fluorite* crystals and cleavage bodies are often zoned with purple, yellow, and/or colorless regions. Don't confuse color zoning with *dichroism* and *trichroism*, which are *pleochroic* properties (differential coloration when viewed from different angles).

This 162.26-carat bicolored rough sapphire *from Australia is unusual both for its large size and the sharp demarcation between color zones. Photo by S. McClure.* © *GIA.*

Idiochromatism

Idiochromatic minerals occur in a single, relatively consistent color (although they may be shades thereof) due to an element that is always present. Examples are the following:

Mineral	Color	Element
Autunite	Yellow	Uranium
Azurite	Blue	Copper
Crocoite	Orange-red	Chromium
Malachite	Green	Copper
Sulfur	Yellow	Sulfur

Pleochroism

Pleochroic minerals change color when viewed by transmitted light in different directions through the specimen. Various colors come into view as the mineral is rotated in front of a light source. Pleochroism is called *dichroism* when two optical directions are present and *trichroism* when three optical directions are evident. Pleochroism is not seen in *isotropic* materials (materials having a homogeneous composition and single refractive index), because light travels at the same velocity in all directions in such materials.

Examples of strongly pleochroic minerals are *andalusite* (green one way, red another) and *cordierite* (blue one way, yellow another).

While not technically pleochroism, a mineral may exhibit different colors in *reflected* light versus *transmitted* light. *Fluorite* crystals may appear bluish-violet in reflected light, but green in transmitted light (viewed against a light source).

Pseudochromatism

Pseudochromatic minerals have an "apparent" color that is not an "intrinsic" color of the pure mineral (which, in turn, may or may not be the same as the "true" color of its powder streak). Pseudochromatism can have many causes, such as diffraction, dispersion, interference, reflection, or refraction of light.

Asterism (starlike effect), caused by crystal inclusions, is technically pseudochromatic, as is *iridescence*—the rainbow sheen from cleavage separations or surface oxidations, common on metallic lustred opaque minerals, such as *chalcopyrite* and *pyrite*.

Iridescent orthoamphibole *from Wyoming. Courtesy U.S. Museum of Natural History. Photo by Robert Weldon.* © *GIA.*

"Color play" (also called "schiller" or "fire") is the change in apparent reflected color when viewed at different angles. Color play is prominent in the *feldspar* varieties of *moonstone* and *labradorite*, and also in *opal*—where it is called "fire" in precious gem opals and "opalescence" in nongem opals. Opalescence in opal is due to light's refraction and diffraction on silicon dioxide beads and water inclusions.

This unusually large (14.0 × 10.2 × 4.10 centimetres) specimen of rough opal *displays pinfire "play of color" throughout. Color play in opals is called "fire" in precious gem opals and "opalescence" in nongem opals. Photo by Tino Hammid. © GIA & Tino Hammid.*

A *stereomicroscope* is useful for studying three-dimensional rocks and minerals— for identifying crystal inclusions, which can help to name the mineral species, and for observing tiny specimens for crystal shape, cleavage, and fracture types. With adjustable eyepieces, you can get an effective magnification of 10× to 60× (10 times to 60 times natural size), which is adequate for most mineralogical work.

DIAPHANEITY

Diaphaneity is the ability to transmit light, or the degree to which light penetrates a mineral. Diaphaneity is some-

A mounted gemstone being examined with a quality microscope. © GIA.

times called *transparency*, although the word "transparency" is also used for the clearest type of diaphaneity.

The optical test for diaphaneity is to examine specimens of varying thickness against a strong light source, such as a light bulb. In general, the more dense the mineral, the less transparent it is, but there are exceptions. Large samples of some minerals (such as *gypsum*, *mica*, and *obsidian*) may be opaque or translucent, but transparent in thin slices. Chemical purity and crystal perfection also affect the diaphaneity of a given mineral sample: transparent minerals can become translucent to opaque when contaminated with impurities or inclusions.

There are five categories of diaphaneity:

Transparency   Complete or nearly complete light transmission; a mineral sample is transparent if you can read this print easily through it. Mineral examples: clear *calcite*, clear *diamond*, rock crystal (*clear quartz*), *halite* (*rock salt*), and clear *topaz*.

Semitransparency (also called "subtransparency")   Indistinct images are transmitted, but they are not so hazy as translucent materials (below). *Emerald* (green *beryl*) and *rose quartz* are often semitransparent.

Translucency There is partial light transmission, but with no clear image. *Chalcedony*, *chert*, *flint*, *orpiment*, *milky quartz*, and *sulfur* display translucency. Certain granular aggregates—such as *calcite*, *gypsum*, *marble*, and *mica*—may be translucent in large pieces, but transparent in thin sections. Translucent semiprecious stones, like *chalcedony*, are popular for cabochon jewelry.

Nontransparency Light is transmitted in thin sections, but not in thick pieces. Nontransparency is sometimes eliminated as a diaphaneity category by collectors who go directly from translucency to opaqueness, and some collectors use the words "opaqueness" and "nontransparency" synonymously. *Amphibole*, *augite*, and *schorl* (black *tourmaline*) are nontransparent by my definition.

Opaqueness No light transmission, even through thin sections. Examples are *magnetite*, *pyrite*, most sulfides, and native metals (unless you hammer them ultra-thin!).

LUMINESCENCE

Luminescence is the conversion of some type of energy (chemical, electrical, light, mechanical, or thermal) into visible light, due to a material's ability to absorb energy in its atomic electrons, and later emit light from these energized electrons. A luminescent mineral displays colors generated by external stimulation from pressure,

heat, visible light, ultraviolet light, or X rays.

Luminescence is not constant for many mineral species; hence, it cannot alone be relied upon for positive identification of a mineral. Luminescence often varies in intensity between samples of the same species, often from different mines; for example, *rubies* and *sapphires* exhibit variable luminescence, according to their source site. Luminescence is not usually considered to include normal colors observable in visible light.

Photoluminescence is caused by exposure to light, visible or otherwise; but mineral collectors usually use it to refer to *fluorescence* and *phosphorescence* exhibited by minerals exposed to ultraviolet light (see below).

Fluorescence

Fluorescence is the production of a color other than a material's color in normal light, caused when ultraviolet light is falling on the specimen. The word "fluorescence" comes from the mineral name *fluorite*, which often fluoresces blue or green. But not all fluorite fluoresces. Fluorescence is more common than phosphorescence—some minerals do both, some just one, some neither. Both fluorescence and phosphorescence can be induced by exposure of certain minerals to ultraviolet light, X rays, or high electrical charges in a vacuum tube.

Many minerals will not respond to ultraviolet stimulation without having an impurity element as an activator—for example, manganese activates many minerals to fluoresce, whereas iron may stop it. From 1- to 5–percent manganese in

Fluorescence in a rough diamond *crystal.* © *GIA.*

resces blue or yellow. *Calcite, fluorite, halite,* and *willemite* often fluoresce brilliantly, but not all specimens will fluoresce—some localities will, while others are "cold."

Fluorescent minerals are notable from the mines near Franklin Furnace, New Jersey. Examples are the red-fluorescing *calcite* and green-fluorescing *willemite*.

Phosphorescence

Phosphorescence is similar to fluorescence (above), but it persists from several seconds to many minutes, unlike fluorescence, which observably stops when the ultraviolet source is blocked. *Calcite, colmanite, diamond,* and *strontianite* are often highly phosphorescent.

Thermoluminescence

Thermoluminescent minerals emit light when heated. They are best observed, like all luminescent properties, in total darkness. Thermoluminescence exists in *apatite, calcite, diamond, fluorite, lepidolite,* and *scapolite*—in commonly collected minerals. Note: When heat testing mineral samples, be careful that you don't burn yourself, and always wear protective eye goggles.

Triboluminescence

Triboluminescent minerals emit visible light when crushed or rubbed. Some emit a dramatic sparking flash of light when scratched by a metal point, which is best seen in total darkness. Triboluminescence is displayed by all *flint* samples and by many samples of *calcite, fluorite, hemi-*

calcite will make calcite fluoresce; less than 1-percent or greater than 5-percent manganese will not produce fluorescence in calcite. It is believed that *fluorite* fluoresces due to the presence of uranium, rare earths, or hydrocarbon inclusions. The scientific study of mineral fluorescence began with fluorite.

Fluorescence is best observed in a darkened room or special display case by using an ultraviolet (UV) lamp to test specimens.

Note: Be extremely cautious when using ultraviolet lamps—because the UV radiation can damage your eyes or burn your skin. Never look into an ultraviolet lamp when it is on, and keep such lamps hidden from small children and pets. Get advice on the proper use of UV lamps from a lapidary shop or a company that sells mineral-collecting supplies.

During World War II, amateur prospectors found quantities of *scheelite*, a valuable tungsten ore, by prospecting with portable UV lamps. Scheelite fluo-

morphite, magnesite, pectolite, quartz, and *sphalerite.*

Flame Tests and Spectroscopic Analysis

Mineral fusibility, volatility, and flame color can be determined from simple flame tests with a candle or Bunsen flame. The addition of a *spectroscope* allows the positive identification of many minerals, based on their elements. A spectroscope allows the observer to recognize which particular visible color wavelengths are being absorbed by a mineral as light passes through it. This is called an *absorption spectrum*, and it is useful in identifying gemstones:

light source → mineral
→ spectroscope → eye

For example, a spectroscope allows *almandine garnet* to be distinguished from *ruby* of a similar color red. A good-quality spectroscope is not cheap, and it is not needed by the average mineral collector. A compromise can be arranged whereby specimens are flame-tested for certain elements, and a cheap spectroscope purchased for emission-spectroscopy observations, whereby the mineral's flame color is analyzed for elements present.

Some minerals, like *flint*, will emit sparks when struck with rocks or steel implements in the dark.

Flame tests can be done by inserting small samples of dry minerals into the flames of candles or Bunsen burners. Blowpipe flame tests are sometimes used in element diagnosis. A clean *platinum* or

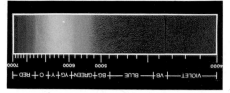

The color spectrum of a dyed-green jadeite *specimen. Dyed jadeite and dyed* emerald *are common in the gemstone and jewelry trade, and sometimes unethically sold as purported natural deep green color.* © *GIA.*

Examining a mineral specimen with a spectroscope. © *GIA.*

Nichrome wire that is dipped into a powdered-mineral sample, then inserted into a flame, will reveal characteristic colors of yellow-orange for sodium (*halite*), blue-green for *copper* ores (*malachite,* etc.), and crimson-red for strontium (*strontianite*)—and will melt other minerals, like *galena*, or fuse them, like *borax*.

LUSTRE

Lustre is the ability to reflect light off a mineral's surface. Lustre is not color: lustre refers to how light appears when reflected, whereas color is the precise wavelength of the visible light spectrum.

Lustre is caused by the surface condition of the atomic/molecular aggregation of a mineral sample, such that the light falling on the specimen's surface is differentially reflected, absorbed, or refracted. Lustre should be observed on the fresh, unweathered surface of a mineral that has just been fractured or naturally cleaved.

Lustre may vary in a single specimen. It increases with a smooth surface, decreases with a rough surface. Lustre is often greater on crystals than on granular aggregates of the same mineral (for example, *magnetite*). A crystal may have a dull base but a vitreous termination. Mineral cleavage planes often have a brighter lustre than crystal faces. The lustres of highly granular minerals can be observed under magnification. *Gypsum*, for example, can have a pearly, silky, or vitreous lustre.

Lustre can be subdivided into four main categories: (1) metallic, (2) submetallic, (3) nonmetallic, and (4) dull (or earthy)—although some mineral collectors just use two classifications: metallic and nonmetallic. These categories are discussed below.

Metallic lustre (also called full or splendent lustre) The highly reflective appearance that is typical of fresh metals and their ores. Metallic lustre is common in opaque ores, native metals, and sulfide ores. It is best observed on cleavage planes, crystal faces, and freshly fractured surfaces of ores, such as *chalcopyrite*, *galena*, *magnetite*, and *pyrite*—and, of course, on native metals, like *gold* leaf or *silver* wire.

Submetallic lustre Uneven, almost metallic reflection from a mineral's surface.

Common in dark, almost opaque crystals. Submetallically lustred minerals often have one or more metal atoms in their molecular structure, such as *chromite*, *covelite*, *cuprite*, *ilmenite*, *psilomelane*, *rutile*, *sphalerite*, and *wolframite*.

Nonmetallic lustres These can be of the following types:

+ *Adamantine*—brilliant, sparkling, gemlike; also called "diamond lustre," as it shines like a cut *diamond*'s light reflection. Found only on transparent or translucent minerals with refractive indices of 1.92 or greater. Mineral examples: *cerussite*, *corundum*, *diamond*, and *zircon*.

+ *Greasy*—oily appearance; common lustre in heavily microscopically included minerals, such as *apatite*, *diamond*, *quartz*, *serpentine*, and the organic mineral *amber*.

+ *Pearly*—lustre like mother-of-pearl; also called iridescent lustre. Common in transparent or semitransparent minerals with perfect cleavages. Examples: *gypsum*, *muscovite mica*, *stilbite*, and, of course, the organic mineral *pearl*.

+ *Resinous*—waxlike lustre; also called waxy lustre. Examples: *cryptocrystalline quartz*, *opal*, *realgar*, *sulfur*, and *vesuvianite* (*idocrase*).

+ *Silky*—lustre from a fine, parallel fibrous structure; examples are fibrous asbestos minerals, such as *chrysotile* (*serpentine* variety) and *crocidolite* (*riebeckite* variety), as well as *gypsum* (*alabaster* and *selenite*) and *fibrous limestone*.

+ *Vitreous*—glassy lustre. Found often on transparent and subtransparent

Faustite, *a zinc, copper, aluminum phosphate hydroxide, which crystallizes in apple-green masses with waxy lustre. Forms triclinic crystals, but this specimen is polished.* © GIA.

Carved jadeite *usually exhibits a vitreous lustre. The term "jade" refers to lapidary-quality specimens of the silicate mineral* jadeite *and the "nephrite" variety of the amphibole mineral* actinolite. © GIA and Tino Hammid.

minerals with refractive indices of 1.3 to 1.9. Common in gemstone minerals. Examples: *calcite, corundum, cryolite, fluorite, halite, obsidian, quartz* (and other crystal silicates), *topaz*, and *tourmaline*.

Dull (earthy) lustre Little or nonexistent lustre. Typical of low-refractive minerals. May display itself as the worst lustre in a mineral species that has a lustre range; for example, *kaolinite* has a dull lustre but is pearly on cleavages. *Borates* (such as *colemanite, howlite*, and *kernite*) tend to have dull lustres, as do other earthy or powdery minerals. *Lazulite* and *turquoise* can have dull lustres, but still be nicely colored blue. Other dull-lustred

minerals are *carnotite, pyrolusite, vivianite*—and *azurite* and *malachite* when they're not of brighter lustre.

PHOTOSENSITIVITY

Photosensitivity is usually mineralogically defined as "color change or fading of a mineral after light exposure over time." If the original color intensity can be restored, the mineral has reversible photosensitivity: for example, pinkish-violet *hackmanite* fades to white by exposure to natural light, but it can be temporarily restored to pinkish-violet by exposure to ultraviolet light, after which it begins to fade again.

Prolonged sunlight exposure is especially devastating to the colors of many minerals, and all mineral collections should be kept away from direct sunlight. *Amethyst* (purple quartz), *emerald* (green *beryl*), and *rose quartz* fade in sunlight over time. Golden *calcite* fades to pale lemon-yellow. *Topaz* can change from blue to green. Red *realgar* becomes yellow orpiment. The *silver* ores of *acanthite*, *proustite*, and *pyrargyrite* will blacken after light exposure, so they should be stored in total darkness.

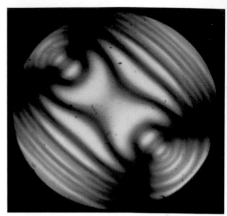

Biaxial optical effect of cerussite, *as viewed through a polariscope.* © *GIA.*

POLARIZATION

All minerals that aren't isotropic (isometric), or symetrically homogeneous in composition, are anisotropic and exhibit polarized light (light rays that vibrate in a single plane, rather than in all planes, as is the case with nonpolarized light in isometric crystal travels). Light travels at the same velocity in any direction in an isotropic material (for example, isometric crystals and amorphous glass), but it travels at different velocities in anisotropic materials.

A *polariscope* is used to detect polarized light in crystals, by using a Nicol prism made from optical calcite. *Polarizing microscopes* are also available for observing polarized light from tiny specimens. This light phenomenon is usually of more interest to the gemstone specialist than to the general mineral collector; beginning collectors will find other tools more useful than a polariscope. If two Nicol prisms are rotated at right angles to each other, no light will pass through to the observer, and this principle is used to test minerals for polarized light.

Examining a mineral specimen with a polariscope, an instrument used to detect polarized light in crystals. © *GIA.*

REFRACTION

Refraction is the bending of light. As applied to mineralogy, refraction is the bending of light as it passes between the two different media of mineral and air. The *refractive index* (index of refraction) is a mineral's property of bending the light that enters it at a constant angle. Refraction of light is a constant (unchangeable) optical property of a given pure mineral. Refractive indices are measured with a *refractometer*, a rather expensive instrument used mostly by jewelers for gemstone identification. A refractometer also measures *birefringence*, the splitting of light into two polarized components.

Examining a mineral specimen with a refractometer. A polariscope and a microscope are also on the table. © GIA.

Light is slowed down and refracted (bent) as it crosses an interface (boundary) between two media, such as air and a mineral crystal. The index of refraction is the ratio of the velocity of light in one medium to another, specifically air to mineral, according to the following formula:

$$n = \frac{1}{v}$$

In this formula, "n" is the refractive index, "1" is the velocity of light in air, and "v" is the velocity of light in the mineral (the denser medium). Because light moves slower in a mineral than in air, "v" is always less than "1" for minerals and the refractive index ("n") is always greater than 1 for minerals. Accurate refractive indices cannot be measured in opaque or

heavily translucent materials by using a refractometer. And refractive index can change substantially with the presence of chemical impurities incorporated into the mineral's molecular structure.

All *isotropic* (symetrically homogeneous) minerals have a single refractive index—for example, *diamond*, which also has the highest refractive index (2.417). The higher the refractive index, the greater the mineral's "fire" (precious gemstone's color play) and the more desirable it is as a gemstone. Diamond's high refractive index causes dispersion—the breaking up of white light into its component colors, because differently colored wavelengths of light have different refractive indices. This is what causes a diamond to show many colors beside its natural color.

Refractive indices often vary with color within a single mineral species; for example, *red spinel* has a RI of 1.715–1.735,

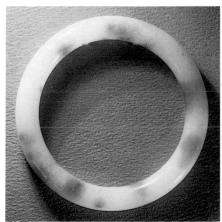

Dyed calcite may resemble jadcite, as in this piece of jewelry, and calcite's refractive index may be confused with jadeite's. However, jadeite is much harder and has monoclinic crystals. © GIA.

blue *spinel* 1.715–1.747, and all others 1.712–1.717—with an average of 1.72. Hence, refractive index tables in mineralogy texts may include RI ranges, averages, pure mineral value (colorless, unincluded, and so on), and/or most common value—and, if the table doesn't state which RI numbers are listed, you have to interpret what you are reading.

Here are some refractive index values for some gemstones (most are averages for relatively pure specimens as encountered in the jewelry trade): *diamond*, 2.42; *zircon*, 1.925–1.984; *garnet*, 1.7–1.9; *asteriated sapphire*, 1.76; *alexandrite* (*chrysoberyl*), 1.75; *spinel*, 1.72; *chrysolite*, *peridot* (*olivine*), 1.6–1.7; *pearl* (organic), 1.53–1.69; *kunzite* (*spodumene* variety), 1.67; *jadeite*, 1.65; *tourmaline*, 1.62–1.64; *turquoise*, 1.62; *topaz*, 1.61; *aquamarine*, *emerald*, *heliodor*, *morganite* (*beryl* varieties), 1.57; *black coral* (organic), 1.56; *lapis lazuli* (*lazurite*), 1.56; *amethyst*, *chalcedony*, *citrine*, *rose quartz*, *smoky quartz*, 1.553; *amber* (organic), 1.54; "glass" (including *obsidian*), 1.49–1.51—useful for distinguishing imitation gemstones made of glass; and precious *opal* 1.44–1.47.

Double Refraction

Double refraction occurs when rays of light split into two components when passing through certain anisotropic mineral crystals. Many minerals display mild double refraction, but the most pronounced is seen in transparent ("optical") calcite crystals. Normal window glass does not show double refraction, and glass imitation gemstones should not have double refraction either.

Calcite *crystal showing the optical property of double refraction.* © *GIA.*

STREAK

Streak is the color of a mineral's powder, a mineral's "true color"—as opposed to its "apparent color" (gross specimen color). Streak tests are useful for identifying richly colored opaque or semitransparent minerals. Streak color may vary, however, if foreign chemical impurities and inclusions are present.

Streak is a more reliable diagnostic optical property than a mineral's apparent color. For example, *fluorite* comes in many colors, but its streak is always white. Metallic lustred minerals tend to have dark streaks. Nonmetallic lustred minerals tend to have lighter-colored streaks. Most minerals that are transparent in pure form have a white or colorless streak.

Some minerals have been even named for their streak's color: *crocoite* (saffron-yellow), *hematite* (blood), and *xanthoconite* (yellow).

Metallic lustred minerals often have streaks of very different color than the whole specimen color: *black cassiterite* has an almost colorless streak, *black he-*

matite has a reddish-brown streak, *yellow pyrite* has a greenish-black streak, and *black wolframite* has a brown streak. Sometimes streak refers to the mineral's whole color: *grey galena* has a black streak. But a streak is often lighter in color than the deeply colored mineral that produces it.

The two darkly colored iron ores, *hematite* and *magnetite*, often look very similar in gross specimen form, but *hematite* always has a reddish-brown streak, whereas *magnetite* always has a black streak (if pure, of course). Colorless or nonmetallic lustred minerals have white or colorless streaks, and they cannot be identified by streak alone.

Streak Test

A *streak test* should be done with the surface of a freshly fractured mineral specimen. Rub the mineral piece across an unglazed white porcelain tile ("a streak plate"), whose finely abrasive surface will rub off some mineral powder. The color of this powder is the mineral's streak.

Because porcelain has a hardness of 6 to 6.5, minerals harder than that will scratch the streak plate and produce white porcelain powder instead of their own powder! Minerals harder than 6–6.5 must first be ground to powder in a mortar and pestle or with a steel hammer. Then this powder is rubbed on the streak plate to observe its streak. Remember, streak color is constant for pure minerals (that is, those minerals that aren't heavily contaminated with impurities and inclusions).

A MINERALOGICAL IDENTIFICATION EXAMPLE

Here is an example of how our knowledge of the physical properties (including optical properties) of minerals can help us identify them in our geological detective work. *Graphite* and *molybdenite* are very similar minerals in many respects. Both graphite and molybdenite:

♦ have a metallic to opaque lustre,
♦ can be cut with a steel knife,
♦ leave a mark when rubbed on paper and feel greasy,
♦ cleave perfectly in one direction into plates that are flexible but not elastic,
♦ can be found associated with *granite* or *quartz* deposits,
♦ have similar hardnesses (1–2 for *graphite*, 1–1½ for *molybdenite*),
♦ are primarily grey to greyish-black in gross specimen color, and
♦ have similarly appearing hexagonal crystals that are rare in nature.

But, there are some differences between graphite's and molybdenite's physical properties:

♦ Molybdenite has a *bluish tint*; graphite doesn't.
♦ Graphite is a good electrical conductor; molybdenite isn't.
♦ Molybdenite's streak shows a bluish or greenish tint along with black; graphite's streak is just grey to black.
♦ Molybdenite is twice as heavy as graphite (specific gravities of 4.6–5.1 and 1.9–2.3, respectively); therefore, graphite is lighter in weight for a given volume.
♦ Molybdenite has a more metallic lustre than graphite.

MINERAL CLASSES

*"Material objects are of two kinds, atoms
and compounds of atoms."*
Titus Lucretius Carus (circa 99–55 B.C.), Roman philosopher and
poet

Only some of the more than 3,000 known mineral species are described in this chapter, having been chosen as representative popular minerals that you are most likely to hear about, read about, see in museums, find during field collecting, or buy from mineral dealers.

Scientists classify minerals by their chemical composition and related crystal structure, such as in James D. Dana's *System of Mineralogy*. This chapter follows Dana's classification system of 15 mineral classes: (1) native elements, (2) sulfides, arsenides, and tellurides, (3) sulfosalts, (4) simple oxides, (5) hydroxides, (6) multiple oxides, (7) halides, (8) carbonates, (9) borates, (10) sulfates, (11) chromates, (12) phosphates, arsenates, and vanadates, (13) vanadium oxysalts, (14) molybdates and tungstates, and (15) silicates—in that order, the sequence in which they are traditionally arranged, from simple to complex in crystal chemistry. Mineral classes can be formally divided into families, then into groups, species, and varieties.

In this chapter, I have selected the more typical and common mineral species of each class, and I give their chemical formulae, synonyms, prominent crystal characteristics, some physical/chemical properties, geological collecting locations, and tips on choosing quality specimens.

The so-called "mineraloids" (the rocks of organic origin, such as *amber*, *coal*, and *pearl*) are discussed with sedimentary rocks in Chapter 2, as such substances are not usually considered true minerals because they are amorphous (lack crystal form) and of inconsistent composition.

———————————— ◆ ————————————

1. Native Elements

Native elements are found in free elemental form in nature, uncombined with other elements as compounds. Native elements include metallic elements (such as *copper*, *gold*, and *silver*), semimetallic elements (*antimony* and *arsenic*), and nonmetallic elements (*carbon* and *sulfur*). Some native elements, such as iron and nickel, are so rare in pure elemental form in nature that they aren't discussed here.

ANTIMONY Sb. Color: tin-white. Streak: steel-grey. Hardness: 3–3½. Cleavage: perfect, unidirectional. Specific gravity: 6.6–6.7. Crystals: rhombohedral hexagonal. Occurrence: rare in North America, but some in Kern County, California; Wolfe County, Quebec; and Chihuahua, Mexico. Often found mixed with arsenic, iron, and silver.

ARSENIC As. Color: tin-white. Streak: tin-white. Hardness: 3–4. Cleavage: perfect, unidirectional. Specific gravity: 5.6–5.7. Crystals: hexagonal, pseudocubic. Occurrence: rare in North America, more common in Europe. Often mixed with antimony, iron, nickel, silver, and sulfur. Poisonous.

BISMUTH Bi. Color: Silver-white, turns to red. Streak: lead-grey. Hardness: 2–2½. Cleavage: good, unidirectional. Specific gravity: 9.7–9.8. Crystals: hexagonal (trigonal) and rare. Occurrence: rare in North America, more common in Europe (especially Germany).

COPPER Cu. A native metal. Color: copper-red, tarnishing to brown, blue, green, and black. Streak: copper-red. Hardness: 2½–3. Cleavage: none. Specific gravity: 8.93. Crystals: cubic and dodecahedral, rarely octahedral. Occurrence: superb specimens from Michigan and Arizona. Often mixed with antimony, arsenic, bismuth, iron, and silver. Beware of acid-cleaned specimens offered for sale as pristine native copper.

DIAMOND C—pure carbon with compact arrangement of atoms. The most valuable precious stone. Colors: colorless, grey, yellow, brown, green, blue, black, and sometimes "fancy colors" of red or orange; the most prized diamonds in the gemstone trade are colorless. Hardness: 10, the hardest natural substance. Cleavage: perfect in four directions. Specific gravity: 3.52. Crystals: mostly isometric octahedrons, and often rounded and irregularly shaped. Lustre: adamantine. Occurrence: concentrated in South Africa and the former U.S.S.R., scattered many other places (collectible specimens in Arkansas). Rough diamonds often look like *quartz* pebbles, so check their hardness in the field. Often found in stream deposits. The only known rock in which diamond has been discovered as an ingrown mineral is the *kimberlite* variety of *peridotite*. Warning: Many diamonds are overpriced, either rough or cut, especially if they are colored and/or heavily included.

GOLD Au. The most famous metal in the world, and one of the most sought after. Because it doesn't oxidize, gold is usually found in native form, although often alloyed with silver, copper, or platinum. Color: gold-yellow. Streak: gold-yellow, shining. Hardness: 2½–3. Cleavage: none. Specific gravity: 19.28 when pure, 15.5 to 19.3 with admixtures. Crystals: isometric—usually cubic, dodeca-

Natural placer gold nugget. When such nuggets have character in an interesting shape, they sell for a collector-based premium price over the current bullion value of the gold metal alone. © GIA.

hedral, or octahedral, often distorted. Often forms nuggets, leaves, and wire. Occurrence: South Africa and the former U.S.S.R.; many other places, including collectible and commercial desposits in the American West and Mexico. Recovered by panning placer gravels and hardrock mining, often in *milky quartz* veins. Choice collector specimens are worth more than bullion value.

GRAPHITE C—pure carbon, but of less compact atomic arrangement than *diamond*. Color: dark steel-grey. Lustre: metallic. Streak: grey to black, glossy. Hardness: 1–2. Cleavage: perfect, unidirectional. Specific gravity: 1.9–2.3 (depending on impurities). Feel: greasy, and rubs off on your skin or paper. Crystals: hexagonal and rare. Synonyms: *black lead* and *plumbago*. Occurrence: mostly in metamorphic rocks. Found in Bavaria, the Bohemian Forest of Czechoslovakia, Sri Lanka (Ceylon), Quebec, and Alabama.

PLATINUM Pt. A native metal, almost always found with admixtures of iridium,

iron, copper, gold, nickel, osmium, palladium, and/or rhodium. Color: silvery-white, steel-grey. Streak: steel-grey. Hardness: 4–4½. Cleavage: none. Specific gravity: 14–19 with admixtures (pure platinum is 21.45, but it is not found pure in nature). Crystals: isometric, usually distorted cubes. Occurrence: rare in nice cubes or large nuggets, hence uncommon in private mineral collections; found in various mining districts in North America and Africa.

SILVER Ag. A native metal, often found with admixtures of antimony, arsenic, bismuth, copper, gold, mercury, and/or platinum. Color: silver-white, gradually tarnishing to black. Streak: silver-white. Hardness: 2½–3. Cleavage: none. Specific gravity: 10–12, depending on admixtures (pure silver is 10.5, but it is rarely found pure). Crystals: isometric; in cubic, dodecahedral, or octahedral forms. Rare as crystals. Occurrence: in native form, in wire, grains, plates, and dendrites; found in many mining districts in Nevada, Michigan, and Arizona, as well as Ontario and Mexico.

SULFUR S. A nonmetallic native element, sometimes found with admixtures of selenium (especially), as well as arsenic, tellurium, and thallium. Color: yellow, but with brownish or greenish tones due to admixtures. Streak: white, but sometimes light yellow. Hardness: 1½–2½ with admixtures, brittle. Cleavage: poor in two directions. Specific gravity: 2–2.1 (pure sulfur is 2.07). Crystals: orthorhombic, usually bipyramidal, best when large and transparent deep yellow. Occurrences: as sublimates in volcanoes, hot springs, and coal piles, as well as in certain sedimentary deposits in Louisiana and Texas; superb crystals come from Sicily, known since ancient Roman times.

2. Sulfides, Arsenides, and Tellurides

Because of space considerations, I left out some of the rarer minerals in this class because they are less likely to be encountered by the average collector—specifically, *calaverite* (the ditelluride of gold: $AuTe_2$), *cobaltite* (the sulfarsenide of cobalt, often mixed with iron: $CoAsS$), *millerite* (nickel sulfide: NiS), *molybdenite* (molybdenum sulfide: MoS_2), *nickeline* (also called *niccolite*, nickel arsenide: $NiAs$), *pentlandite* (iron and nickel sulfide: $[Fe, Ni]_9S_8$), *skutterudite* (also called *smaltite*, cobalt and nickel arsenide: $[CoNi]As_3$), and *sylvanite* (the telluride of gold and silver: $AuAgTe_4$).

ACANTHITE (ALSO CALLED "ARGENTITE")

Ag_2S. The sulfide of silver, often mixed with copper. Color: lead-grey to black, darkens on exposure to light. Streak: black, shining. Hardness: 2–2½. Cleavage: indistinct, but perfectly sectile (may be cut by a steel knife). Specific gravity: 7.3. Crystals: dimorphic—isometric (in cubes, dodecahedra, and octahedra) in *acanthite* below 173°C, and twinned as *argentite* above 173°C. So, at room temperature, call it *acanthite*, although you'll often hear it termed *argentite*, and maybe its vernacular name, "silver glance." Occurrence: Kongsberg, Norway; Butte, Montana; Aspen and Leadville, Colorado; and Virginia City, Nevada (the famous "Comstock Lode").

ARSENOPYRITE (ALSO CALLED "ARSENICAL PYRITE" AND "MISPICKEL")

$FeAsS$—iron arsenide sulfide, usually with cobalt mixed in. Color: silver-white, steel-grey. Streak: black. Hardness: 5½–6, brittle. Cleavage: good in one direction. Specific gravity: 6.0–6.2. Crystals: monoclinic, but pseudoorthorhombic. Occurrences: many mining districts, famous from Freiberg, Germany; also in western U.S., Canada, and Mexico.

BORNITE (ALSO CALLED "PEACOCK COPPER ORE")

Cu_5FeS_4—copper iron sulfide. Color: copper-red to bronze-brown, often tarnished with iridescent blue/violet. Streak: greyish black. Hardness: 3, brittle. Cleavage: imperfect. Specific gravity: 4.9–5.1. Crystals: isometric, with cubic and dodecahedra more common than octahedra, but any crystals are rare. Occurrence: various mining districts in western U.S. Get this in crystals if you're lucky, otherwise in large colorful lumps.

CHALCOCITE (ALSO CALLED "COPPER GLANCE")

Cu_2S—copper sulfide. Color: lead-grey, tarnishing to black with bluish/greenish tint. Streak: dark grey, metallic. Hardness: 2½–3, brittle. Cleavage: poor in one direction. Specific gravity: 5.5–5.8. Crystals: orthorhombic, often prismatic or tabular. Occurrences: mining districts of western U.S., especially Butte, Montana, and Bisbee, Arizona.

CHALCOPYRITE (ALSO CALLED "COPPER PYRITES" OR "YELLOW COPPER ORE")

$CuFeS_2$—copper iron sulfide. Color: brass-yellow or honey-yellow, often tarnished with iridescent blue, purple, or black, easily recognized by early miners. Streak: greenish-black. Hardness: 3½–4, brittle. Cleavage: poor in one direction. Specific gravity: 4.1–4.3. Crystals: tetragonal, often pseudotetrahedral. Occurrence: widespread in copper-mining districts the world over.

CINNABAR (SOMETIMES CALLED "NATURAL VERMILLION") HgS— mercury sulfide. Color: red to brownish-red. Streak: red to brownish-red. Lustre: adamantine to dull. Hardness: 2–2.5, brittle. Cleavage: perfect in three directions. Specific gravity: 8.1 if pure. Crystals: hexagonal. Occurrence: famous from Almadén, Spain, where Romans mined it in pre-Christian times; also from California, Nevada, Oregon, and Texas.

COVELLITE (ALSO CALLED "COVELLINE" AND "INDIGO COPPER") CuS—copper sulfide. Discovered at Mount Vesuvius by Italian mineralogist Niccolo Covelli (1790–1829), and named in his honor. Color: dark blue, often iridescent with yellow and red tones. Streak: grey to black. Hardness: 1½–2, brittle. Cleavage: perfect in one direction. Specific gravity: 4.6–4.8. Crystals: hexagonal. Occurrence: superb crystals from Butte, Montana; also from Alaska, Colorado, and Utah.

GALENA (ALSO CALLED "LEAD GLANCE" AND "BLUE LEAD" IN MINING LORE) PbS—lead sulfide. Color: lead-grey. Streak: greyish-black. Hardness: 2½, and very brittle. Cleavage: perfect in three directions. Specific gravity: 7.3–7.6. Crystals: isometric, with cubic and octahedral most common. Occurrence: fine crystals from the Joplin district of Kansas, Missouri, and Oklahoma; also from Colorado and Idaho.

MARCASITE (HAS BEEN CALLED "WHITE IRON PYRITE") FeS_2— disulfide of iron, the same chemical formula as *pyrite*, but different crystal structure. Color: light yellow, tarnishes to brown. Streak: greenish-grey to brownish. Hardness: 6–6½, brittle. Cleavage: distinct in two directions. Specific gravity: 4.8–4.9. Crystals: orthorhombic (whereas pyrite is isometric). Occurrence: nice crystals from the Joplin district of Kansas, Missouri, and Oklahoma; also from Guanajuato, Mexico.

ORPIMENT As_2S_3—arsenic trisulfide. Color: lemon-yellow to orangish-brown. Streak: lemon-yellow. Hardness: 1½–2. Cleavage: good in one direction. Specific gravity: 3.48 if pure. Crystals: monoclinic. Occurrence: Nevada and Utah in the U.S. Used as one ore of arsenic.

PYRITE (ALSO CALLED "IRON PYRITE" OR "FOOL'S GOLD") FeS_2—iron disulfide, the same formula as *marcasite*, but different crystal structure. Color: pale yellow to brass-yellow, often with variegated tarnish colors. Streak: greenish-black. Hardness: 6–6½, brittle. Cleavage: none. Specific gravity: 4.9–5.2. Crystals: isometric, mostly cubes and pyritohedra with parallel facial striations. Occurrence: many locations, many specimens from Peru in rock shows.

PYRRHOTITE (ALSO CALLED "MAGNETIC PYRITE") FeS—iron sulfide. Color: yellowish-brown to bronze, tarnishes dark brown. Streak: grey-black.

Natural specimen of the common iron sulfide mineral pyrite *from Tuscany, Italy. Courtesy of Natural History Museum of Los Angeles County.*

Hardness: 3½–4½, brittle. Cleavage: none. Specific gravity: 4.5–4.6. Crystals: orthorhombic, but pseudohexagonal. Occurrence: Germany and Sweden; also in Connecticut and Maine on the East Coast, and Tennessee and California. *Pyrrhotite* is magnetic; *chalcopyrite* and *pyrite* are not.

REALGAR AsS—arsenic sulfide. Becomes yellowish orpiment on exposure to light, so store in total darkness. Color: orangish-red. Streak: orangish-yellow. Hardness: 1½–2. Cleavage: good in one direction. Specific gravity: 3.5–3.6. Crystals: monoclinic, usually prismatic. Large crystals are rare and in demand by collectors. Occurrence: Utah, Nevada, and California.

SPHALERITE (HAS BEEN CALLED "BLACK JACK," "BLENDE," "MOCK ORE," AND "ZINC BLENDE") ZnS—zinc sulfide. Color: yellow, brown, red, green, black, sometimes grey or white. Streak: light brown. Hardness: 3.5–4, brittle. Cleavage: perfect in six directions. Specific gravity: 3.9–4.1. Crystals: iso-metric, with tetrahedra and dodecahedra common. Occurrence: in zinc mines in many places; nice specimens of crystals from the tristate region near Joplin, Missouri; also New Jersey and Mexico. Named from the Greek *sphaleros* ("misleading"), referring to the ease in confusing it with other minerals.

STIBNITE (ALSO CALLED "ANTIMONITE," "ANTIMONY GLANCE," AND "GREY ANTIMONY") Sb_2S_3—antimony trisulfide. Color: lead-grey, tarnishes to black, sometimes iridescent. Streak: lead-grey. Hardness: 2. Cleavage: perfect in one direction. Specific gravity: 4.63 if pure. Crystals: orthorhombic, often slender in radiated groups or in columnar masses. Occurrence: the largest and best crystals are from Shikoku Island, Japan, where they have been collected since ancient times; also found in Idaho and Nevada, as well as Rumania and Quebec. According to Pliny, it was used in cosmetics in the first century A.D. Roman world. Don't confuse *stibnite* with the silicate mineral *stilbite*.

3. Sulfosalts

Sulfosalts are mostly rare minerals composed of metallic and nonmetallic elements, along with sulfur. I discuss the common sulfosalts, *tennantite* and *tetrahedrite*, in detail here, but I will only list some others:

BOULANGERITE $Pb_5Sb_4S_{11}$—lead antimony sulfide.

BOURNONITE (ALSO CALLED "ENDELLIONITE" AND "WHEEL ORE") $PbCuSbS_3$—lead copper antimony sulfide.

ENARGITE Cu_3AsS_4—copper arsenic sulfide.

JAMESONITE $Pb_4FeSb_6S_{14}$—lead iron antimony sulfide.

PROUSTITE (ALSO CALLED "LIGHT RED SILVER ORE") Ag_3AsS_3—silver arsenic sulfide.

PYRARGYRITE (ALSO CALLED "DARK RED SILVER ORE") Ag_3SbS_3—silver antimony sulfide.

STEPHANITE (ALSO CALLED "BRITTLE SILVER ORE") Ag_5SbS_4—silver antimony sulfide.

TENNANTITE $Cu_{12}As_4S_{13}$—copper arsenic sulfide. Forms a series with *tetrahedrite* (below). Color: steel-grey to black. Streak: steel-grey with red tint. Hardness: 3–4, brittle. Cleavage: none. Specific gravity: 4.6–4.7. Crystals: isometric, usually tetrahedra. Occurrence: Colorado, British Columbia, Ontario, Germany, Sweden, and Namibia. Important copper ore.

TETRAHEDRITE (ALSO CALLED "FAHLERZ" AND "GREY COPPER") $Cu_{12}Sb_4S_{13}$—copper antimony sulfide. Forms a series with *tennantite* (above), called the "tetrahedrite series." Color: steel-grey to black. Streak: black. Hardness: 3–4, brittle. Cleavage: none. Specific gravity: 4.6–5.2, depending on admixtures. Crystals: isometric, mostly tetrahedra. Occurrence: more common than tennantite; famous from the Sunshine Mine in Idaho; also found in Mexico, British Columbia, Austria, Czechoslovakia, and Germany.

4. Simple Oxides

Simple oxides are compounds of single metallic elements combined with oxygen. The mineral *water* (H_2O)—hydrogen oxide—is an oxide, and it is the only mineral commonly found in both solid (ice) and liquid state on the Earth's surface.

BIXBYITE $(Mn,Fe)_2O_3$—iron manganese oxide. Rare.

CASSITERITE (ALSO CALLED TIN-STONE) SnO_2—tin oxide. Color: brown, black, rarely yellow to grey. Streak: white or light brown. Hardness: 6–7, brittle. Cleavage: indistinct. Specific gravity: 6.8–7.1. Crystals: tetragonal, generally prismatic and twinned. Occurrence: Bolivia, England, Indonesia, and Malaysia. The richest tin ore.

CORUNDUM (ALSO CALLED "RUBY" AND "SAPPHIRE," FOR THE GEM VARIETIES) Al_2O_3—aluminum oxide, often found with impurities as coloring agents. Colors: *ruby* red is due to chromium; *sapphire* blue is caused by iron and titanium; colorless, transparent corundum is called *leucosapphire*; *corundum* also comes in yellow, green, and violet; *common corundum* is grey; in the jewelry business, deep *red corundum* is *ruby*, and all other colors are called *sapphire*. Streak: white. Hardness: 9. Cleavage: none, but may easily part. Specific gravity: 3.9–4.1. Crystals; hexagonal, with various forms. Occurrence: Burma, Thailand, and Sri Lanka (Ceylon) have the best rubies and sapphires; Montana and North Carolina have gem-quality corundum in the U.S. Warning: Don't be impressed by the names "ruby" and "sapphire"—a lot of junk stones are for sale at exorbitant prices; quality is all-important when seeking corundum, rough or cut.

CUPRITE (ALSO CALLED "RED OXIDE OF COPPER") Cu_2O—copper oxide. Color: brownish-red to black. Streak: brownish-red. Hardness: $3\frac{1}{2}$–4, brittle. Cleavage: poor. Specific gravity: 6.15. Crystals: isometric, usually octahedral. Occurrence: superb crystals from Arizona, New Mexico, and Utah. Named after the Latin *cuprum* ("copper").

HEMATITE (ALSO CALLED "IRON GLANCE" AND "FERRIC OXIDE") Fe_2O_3—iron oxide. Color: reddish-brown to black. Streak: cherry-red or reddish-brown. Hardness: 5–6, brittle. Cleavage: none. Specific gravity: 5.25 if pure. Crystals: hexagonal. Occurrence: many places the world over. Common iron ore. Forms reniform (kidney-shaped) aggregates. Causes the reddish color of soil and many rocks.

MAGNETITE (ALSO CALLED "LODESTONE" AND "MAGNETIC IRON ORE") Fe_3O_4—iron oxide. Natural magnet, and important iron ore. Color: iron-black. Streak: black. Hardness: $5\frac{1}{2}$–$6\frac{1}{2}$. Cleavage: none. Specific gravity: 4.9–5.2. Crystals: isometric, usually octahedra. Occurrence: many places the world over; fine crystals from California, New Mexico, New York state, and Vermont, as well as Nova Scotia and Ontario.

PYROLUSITE MnO_2—manganese dioxide. Important manganese ore. Color: greyish-black. Streak: black. Lustre: metallic to dull. Hardness: 6–$6\frac{1}{2}$. Cleavage: perfect in one direction. Specific gravity: 4.4–5. Crystals: tetragonal, rare when

large and well-formed. Occurrence: Georgia and Minnesota, as well as Germany and many other places.

RUTILE TiO_2—titanium dioxide. From the Latin word *rutilus* ("reddish"). Color: yellow, red, brown, to black. Streak: yellowish-brown or brownish-red. Lustre: adamantine, submetallic. Hardness: 6–$6\frac{1}{2}$. Cleavage: distinct in two directions, poor in a third. Specific gravity: 4.2–4.3. Crystals: tetragonal, often long needles, often as inclusions in quartz. Occurrence: Arkansas, California, and Georgia in U.S.

URANINITE (ALSO CALLED "PITCHBLENDE" AND "PITCH ORE") UO_2—uranium oxide, often found with *thorium*. Radioactive. Color: greenish to brownish-black. Streak: brown, grey, or green. Lustre: submetallic, dull. Hardness: 5–6, brittle. Cleavage: none. Specific gravity: 9–9.5 for pure specimens, often higher or lower for admixtures. Crystals: isometric, usually cubes and octahedra. Occurrence: Europe, Africa, and only a few sources in North America (including Colorado and Ontario). Commonly found in *pegmatites* with alteration products colored yellow, orangish-red, or green.

ZINCITE (ALSO CALLED "RED OXIDE OF ZINC") ZnO—zinc oxide. A rare mineral. Color: red to orangish-brown.

5. Hydroxides

Hydroxides are metallic elements compounded with water or hydroxyl (OH^{-1}) groups.

BAUXITE a group of hydrated aluminum oxides; for example, "gibbsite"—

$Al(OH)_3$—aluminum hydroxide. Physical properties vary, depending on the bauxite variety. Hardness: 1–3. Specific gravity: 2.4–2.6. Color: generally whitish, but often stained red or brown by iron oxides. Sometimes called the "pea-soup rock" for its appearance. Occurrence: Arkansas and France.

BRUCITE $Mg(OH)_2$—magnesium hydroxide. Scarce in U.S.

GOETHITE (ALSO CALLED "ACICULAR IRON ORE" OR "NEEDLE IRONSTONE") $HFeO_2$—hydrogen iron oxide. Found in Michigan and Colorado.

LIMONITE (ALSO CALLED "BROWN HEMATITE" OR "YELLOW IRON ORE") A mixture of iron ores with water, variable composition, for example: $Fe_2O_3 \cdot 3H_2O$—hydrous iron oxide. Usually a decomposition product of iron minerals. Color and streak: yellowish-brown. Hardness range: 4–5½. Cleavage: none. Specific gravity: 2.7–4.3. Amorphous. Occurrence: widespread, including New England in the U.S.; Finland; and Sweden, where it is called "bog iron ore" or "lake ore."

MANGANITE (ALSO CALLED "BROWN MANGANESE ORE") $MnO(OH)$—basic manganese oxide. Color: steel-grey to brownish-black. Streak: dark brown to black. Hardness: 4, brittle. Specific gravity: 4.2–4.4. Crystals: monoclinic. Occurrence: the best crystals come from China, England, and Germany.

PSILOMELANE $(Ba, H_2O)Mn_5O_{10}$—basic oxide of barium and manganese. Color: black. Streak: black, brown. Hardness: 5–6, brittle. Specific gravity:

4.5–4.7. Crystals: monoclinic, massive. Occurrence: widespread, Arizona and Virginia in U.S.

6. Multiple Oxides

Multiple oxides are compounds of two or more metallic elements with oxygen. I've left out species such as *franklinite* and the *columbite-tantalite* series, but here are some popularly collected species:

CHROMITE (ALSO CALLED "CHROMIC IRON" OR "CHROME IRON ORE") $FeCr_2O_4$—iron chromium oxide. Color: iron-black, brownish-black. Streak: dark brown. Hardness: 5½. Cleavage: none. Specific gravity: 4.3–5. Crystals: isometric octahedra, but rare. Occurrence: widespread, in U.S.A., Africa, Turkey, and Philippines. Chromium ore.

CHRYSOBERYL $BeAl_2O_4$—beryllium aluminum oxide. Gemstone when transparent. Colors: shades of yellow, green, and brownish-green. Streak: white. Hardness: 8½. Cleavage: good in one direction. Specific gravity: 3.5–3.8. Crystals: orthorhombic. Occurrence: various gem mines in former U.S.S.R. in central Urals and Asia Minor, Colorado, and New England. *Alexandrite* is chrysoberyl that is green in natural light, but red in artificial light. Chrysoberyl is harder and heavier than *beryl*, with which it often associates.

ILMENITE (ALSO CALLED "TITANOFERRITE") $FeTiO_3$—iron titanium oxide. Titanium ore. Color: black. Streak: brownish-black. Cleavage: none. Hardness: 5–6. Specific gravity: 4.5–4.7. Crystals: hexagonal. Occurrence: in North America, in Massachusetts, Virginia, Wyoming, and Quebec; named after the Ilman Mountains in the former U.S.S.R., where it was first found.

SPINEL $MgAl_2O_4$—magnesium aluminum oxide. An important gemstone when transparent. The "Black Prince's Ruby" and the "Timur Ruby" in the Crown Jewels of England are actually red spinels. Colors: red, blue, and green are the most prized; also found brown to black. Streak: white. Hardness: 7½–8. Cleavage: none. Specific gravity: 3.6–4. Crystals: isometric, usually octahedra. Occurrence: best gem quality from Burma, Thailand, and Sri Lanka (Ceylon); also found in

Faceted red spinel of 1.54-carat weight, a popular gemstone mineral composed of magnesium, aluminum multiple oxide. The "rubies" in the Crown Jewels of England are actually red spinels. © GIA.

California and New Jersey. Occurs in metamorphic rocks and alluvial sand, sometimes with *corundum*.

7. Halides

Halides are minerals in which a halogen element (that is bromine, chlorine, fluorine, or iodine) is the only anion (negatively charged ion). Halides tend to be soft, brittle, and very soluble in water; hence, their cubic crystals are rarely found in the field—many crystal halides for sale to mineral collectors are actually laboratory preparations.

CHLORARGYRITE (ALSO CALLED "CERARGYRITE" AND "HORN SILVER") AgCl—silver chloride. Color: colorless to grey, darkens upon exposure to light. Streak: white. Hardness: 2½. Cleavage: none. Specific gravity: 5.5–5.6. Crystals: isometric, usually cubic. Occurrence: rather scarce, but at *silver* mines in western U.S. and Mexico; a mass of chlorargyrite weighing over 6 tons was found at Treasure Hill, Nevada.

CRYOLITE Na_3AlF_6—sodium aluminum fluoride. Color: colorless, white, reddish, and brown. Streak: white. Hardness: 2½–3. Cleavage: none. Specific gravity: 2.9–3. Crystals: monoclinic. Occurrence: Greenland, and Colorado at the base of Pike's Peak. Named from the Greek words *kryos* ("ice") and *lithos* ("stone").

FLUORITE (ALSO CALLED "FLUOR SPAR," AND "ORE BLOOM" BY THE OLD BOHEMIAN MINERS) CaF_2—calcium fluoride. Color: colorless, pink, yellow, green, blue, violet, brown, and black. Streak: white. Hardness: 4, brittle. Cleavage: perfect in four directions, forming octahedra. Specific gravity: 3–3.25 with impurities, 3.18 if pure. Crystals: isometric, usually cubic or penetration twins. Occurrence: many localities, especially Hardin County, Illinois; also Colorado, Kentucky, and Ohio, as well as Ontario. Named from the Latin word *fluere* ("to flow") because it melts easily and is used as smelting flux. Be choosy when buying fluorite, the only halide gemstone (collectible, but not wearable)—seek quality specimens. Often fluoresces in ultraviolet light.

HALITE (ALSO CALLED "ROCK SALT") NaCl—sodium chloride. Color: colorless, white, yellow, orange, red, blue, and violet. Streak: white. Hardness: 2–2½. Cleavage: perfect in three directions at 90°. Specific gravity: 2.16 if pure, but usually found with other salts of calcium and magnesium. Crystals: isometric, usually cubic. Other properties: salty taste, slippery feel, brittle, may fluoresce in ultraviolet light, and readily dissolves in water. Store away from high humidity. Occurrence: widespread evaporite, found on dry lake beds and ancient sea deposits. Rock shows often have pink halite crystal clusters for sale, from Searles Lake, California.

8. Carbonates

Carbonates are minerals compounded with the carbonate radical (CO_3^{-2}). Carbonate minerals are often white and brittle, sometimes richly colored and in demand by collectors. Carbonates are generally common species, but even some of the scarcer ones are affordable. They often dissolve in hydrochloric acid.

ARAGONITE $CaCO_3$—calcium carbonate, the same chemical formula for calcite, but different crystal system and less common than calcite. Color: colorless, white, yellow, grey, green, violet, and brown. Streak: white. Hardness: 3½–4, brittle. Cleavage: good in one direction. Specific gravity: 2.9–3. Crystals: orthorhombic, often needles and stalactitic ag-

gregates. Occurrence: Arizona and New Mexico. Named after Aragon, Spain, where it was first found.

AURICHALCITE $(Zn,Cu)_5(CO_3)_2(OH)_6$ —zinc and copper basic carbonate. Scarce. From Arizona, California, New Mexico, and Mexico.

AZURITE (ALSO CALLED "CHESSYLITE" AND "BLUE CARBONATE OF COPPER") $Cu_3(CO_3)_2(OH)_2$— basic copper carbonate. Color: azure-blue, dark blue. Streak: blue. Hardness: 3½–4, brittle. Cleavage: good in two directions. Specific gravity: 3.7–3.8. Crystals: monoclinic. Occurrence: Arizona and Utah, as well as Mexico and Namibia. Named from the Persian word *lazhward* ("blue"). Often associated with *malachite* or other copper ores.

CALCITE (ALSO CALLED "CALC-SPAR," "ICELAND SPAR," AND "CARBONATE OF LIME") $CaCO_3$—calcium carbonate. The most common mineral, after *quartz*. Occurs in many forms, including the prime mineral of *limestone*. Color: colorless, white, grey, yellow, red, green, blue, brown, to black, depending on impurities. Streak: white. Hardness: 3, brittle. Cleavage: perfect rhombohedra. Specific gravity: 2.7. Crystals: hexagonal, common—with rhombohedra, scalenohedra, prisms, and twinning. Occurrence: all over the world. Forms stalactites and stalagmites in caverns. "Iceland spar" is transparent calcite exhibiting double refraction. "Dogtooth spar" is long, pointed crystals. Also forms alabaster, *chalk*, *satin-spar*, *travertine*, *tufa*, and so forth. An excellent mineral for beginning collectors and specialists.

CERUSSITE (ALSO CALLED "WHITE LEAD ORE") $PbCO_3$—lead carbonate. Color: colorless, white, yellow, brown, grey, black. Streak: white. Hardness: 3–3½, brittle. Cleavage: good in one direction. Specific gravity: 6.4–6.6. Crystals: orthorhombic. Lustre: often adamantine or silky. Occurrence: Leadville, Colorado; also in Czechoslovakia and Africa.

DOLOMITE $CaMg(CO_3)_2$—calcium magnesium carbonate. Similar to *calcite* in *limestone*, but with magnesium present. Whole mountain ranges are sometimes made of dolomite—for example, the Dolomite Alps of the Austrian Tyrol. Color: colorless, white, pink, grey, and brown are common. Streak: white. Hardness: 3½–4, brittle. Cleavage: perfect in three directions, forming rhombohedra. Specific gravity: 2.8–2.9. Crystals: hexagonal. Distinguishable from calcite: dolomite is harder, reacts slowly with hydrochloric acid, and rarely fluoresces. Occurrence: widespread, but nice crystals may be hard to find; pink crystals in Ontario and the Mississippi Valley.

MAGNESITE (ALSO CALLED "BITTER SPAR" $MgCO_3$—magnesium carbonate. Similar to *calcite* and *dolomite*, but magnesite is harder and denser. Color: usually dull white; may also be grey, yellow, or brown; often greyish with *dolomite* admixture or yellowish with *siderite*. Streak: white. Hardness: 3½–4½, Cleavage: perfect in three directions, forming rhombohedra. Specific gravity: 2.96–3.12. Crystals: hexagonal and rare. Occurrence: widespread, the coast ranges of California, Chewelah in Washington, Gabbs in Nevada, and the Yukon River.

MALACHITE (ALSO CALLED "GREEN CARBONATE OF COPPER") $Cu_2CO_3(OH)_2$—basic copper carbonate. Color: emerald-green, dark green. Streak: light green. Hardness: 3½–4, brittle. Cleavage: good in one direction. Specific gravity: 3.9–4. Crystals: monoclinic, but rare. Occurrence: copper mines in Arizona at Bisbee, and Namibia—for most commercial specimens. Used as a cabochon gemstone and lapidary sculpture. Get it with dramatic concentric patterns of alternating light and dark bands.

RHODOCHROSITE (ALSO CALLED "MANGANESE SPAR") $MnCO_3$—manganese carbonate. Color: pink to reddish-brown; best color is as red as possible. Streak: white. Hardness: 3½–4. Cleavage: perfect in three directions, forming rhombohedra. Specific gravity: 3.3–3.6. Crystals: hexagonal, usually rhombohedra. Occurrence: Rumania and Colorado have produced the best specimens, rare in large crystals. A popular cabochon gemstone.

Rhodochrosite *crystals are usually rhombohedrons—brittle, transparent to opaque but commonly translucent, and often having surface growth.* © GIA.

SIDERITE (ALSO CALLED "CHALYBITE" AND "SPATHIC IRON") $FeCO_3$—iron carbonate. A minor iron ore, named after the Greek work for iron: *sideros*. Interesting crystals from Colorado and Connecticut, as well as Greenland. Common ore in Europe.

SMITHSONITE (ALSO CALLED "CALAMINE," "GALMEI," AND "ZINC SPAR") $ZnCO_3$—zinc carbonate. A zinc ore, sometimes used as a gemstone, named after James Smithson (1765–1829), the Smithsonian Institution founder. Color: many colors, including white, yellow, pink, green, blue, and purple. Streak: white. Hardness: 4–4.5. Cleavage: perfect in three directions, forming rhomobohedra. Specific gravity: 4.3–4.5. Crystals: hexagonal, but rare. Occurrence: many localities, including Austria, Germany, Greece, and Namibia, as well as various western states in the U.S. Smithsonite forms from the weathering of zinc ores. Excellent for a specialized collection.

STRONTIANITE $SrCO_3$—strontium carbonate. Scarce mineral. Used for red color in fireworks.

WITHERITE $BaCO_3$—barium carbonate. Rare. Source of barium used in medical X rays for opaque gastrointestinal photos.

9. Borates

Borates are metallic elements compounded with boron. There are two types of borates: *anhydrous* (without water), which form in igneous and metamorphic deposits, and *hydrous* (with water), which form in sedimentary deposits, usually evaporites. Hydrous borates are white, brittle, and soft, and they tend to dissolve easily in water.

BORAX (HAS BEEN CALLED "TINCAL") $Na_2B_4O_7 \cdot 10H_2O$—sodium borate with 10 parts water. Forms when alkali lakes evaporate. Once carried by "20-mule" teams from Death Valley, California. Color: colorless, white, and grey. Streak: white. Hardness: 2–2½, brittle. Cleavage: perfect in one direction. Specific gravity: 1.7–1.8. Crystals: monoclinic, prismatic. Occurrence: Borax Lake and Clear Lake in California; also Nevada and New Mexico. Soluble in water; melts in a candle flame.

COLEMANITE $Ca_2B_6O_{11} \cdot 5H_2O$—calcium borate with five parts water. Color: white, grey. Streak: white. Hardness: 4–4½ (harder than borax). Cleavage: perfect in one direction. Specific gravity: 2.4. Crystals: monoclinic, prismatic. Occurrence: Death Valley, Boron, and Yermo localities in California. Named after San Francisco businessman and mine owner, William T. Coleman (1824–1893).

HOWLITE $Ca_2B_5SiO_9(OH)_5$—hydrated calcium silico-borate. Color: white. Streak: white. Hardness: 3½. Cleavage:; none. Crystals: monoclinic, but rare. Usually occurs as compact nodular masses, which are often dyed blue and sold as fake turquoise to tourists. Occurrence: as an evaporite, usually associated with *ulexite* and *colemanite* in California and Nova Scotia. Named after Nova Scotia mineralogist, Henry How (died 1879), who first described it.

Polished howlite, *a basic silicoborate of calcium. Specimens of natural white color, and blue-dyed. Howlite is often dyed blue to imitate* turquoise *for the cheap jewelry trade.* © *GIA.*

KERNITE $Na_2B_4O_7 \cdot 4H_2O$—sodium borate with four parts water. Similar to *borax*, but kernite has less water, is harder, and is slightly denser. Color: colorless, white, and grey. Streak: white. Hardness: 2½–3. Cleavage: perfect in two directions, good in third. Specific gravity: 1.95. Crystals: monoclinic, twinning and elongated. Occurrence: as an evaporite in old lake beds and clays of the Mojave Desert in Kern County, California. Named for this county. Mined for boron and borax. Soluble in water.

ULEXITE (ALSO CALLED "TV ROCK" FOR ITS ABILITY TO TRANSMIT LIGHT IMAGES IN ITS FIBRES) $NaCaB_5O_9 \cdot 8H_2O$—sodium calcium borate with eight parts water. Easily confused with *fibrous asbestos*, but ulexite is an evaporite and usually associated with other evaporites, while asbestos (serpentine) is metamorphic. Color: colorless, white; get it very transparent for best optical effect. Streak: white. Hardness: 2½,

brittle. Cleavage: perfect in one direction. Specific gravity: 1.9. Crystals: triclinic, but rarely well-formed. Occurrence: borax lakes in Kern and Inyo counties of California. An excellent gift mineral. Named after German chemist, Georg Ludwig Ulex (1811–1883).

10. Sulfates

Sulfates are minerals with metallic elements compounded with the sulfate (SO_4^{-2}) radical. A large class of minerals with diverse properties, but generally lightly colored, soft, and fragile. I've decided not to describe scarce sulfates that you are unlikely to encounter, such as: *anglesite* ($PbSO_4$—lead sulfate); *brochantite* ($Cu_4[SO_4][OH]_6$—basic copper sulfate); *chalcanthite* ($CuSO_4 \cdot 5H_2O$—hydrous copper sulfate); *cyanotrichite* ($Cu_4Al_2SO_4[OH]_{12} \cdot 2H_2O$); *glauberite* ($Na_2Ca[SO_4]_2$—sodium calcium sulfate); *jarosite* ($KFe_3[SO_4][OH]_6$—basic hydrous potassium iron sulfate); and *linarite* ($PbCu[SO_4][OH]_2$—basic sulfate of lead and copper).

ANHYDRITE $CaSO_4$—calcium sulfate, the same formula as *gypsum*, but without the water. Color: usually white or grey, sometimes bluish, reddish, or violet. Streak: white. Hardness: 3–3½. Cleavage: good in three directions at 90°. Specific gravity: 2.9–3. Crystals: orthorhombic, but rare. Occurrence: Arizona, New Mexico, Ontario, and Austria. Often found with gypsum, and may alter to gypsum by water absorption. *Anhydrite* means "without water" in Greek.

BARITE (ALSO SPELLED "BARYTE"; ALSO CALLED "HEAVY SPAR") $BaSO_4$—barium sulfate. A common mineral, soft and heavy, known since earliest times by miners of sulfide ores. Color: colorless, white, grey, red, yellow, blue, and brown. Streak: white. Hardness: 3–3½, brittle. Cleavage: perfect in one direction, good in two others. Specific gravity: 4.3–4.6. Crystals: orthorhombic, usually plates, rarely prisms. Occurrence: widespread, including Colorado, Oklahoma, and South Dakota, as well as British Columbia, England, and Germany. Named for the greek word *barys* ("heavy").

CELESTITE $SrSO_4$—strontium sulfate. Forms as an evaporite in sedimentary rocks or hydrothermal veins. Color: colorless, white, yellow, and red, but the light blue crystal masses are most popular at rock shows. Streak: white. Hardness: 3–3½. Cleavage: perfect in one direction, good to distinct in two others. Specific gravity: 3.9–4. Crystals: orthorhombic, usually plates. Occurrence: many localities, with excellent crystals from California, New York state, Ohio, and San Luis Potosí in Mexico. Named from the Latin word *coelestis* ("of the sky"), referring to this mineral's common handsome pale blue color.

EPSOMITE (ALSO CALLED "BITTER SALT" OR "EPSOM SALTS") $MgSO_4 \cdot 7H_2O$—magnesium sulfate with seven parts water. Often associated with *aragonite* and *gypsum*. Loses water and dulls when exposed to air. Color: colorless, white, grey, sometimes yellowish or reddish. Streak: white. Hardness: 2–2½, brittle. Cleavage: good in one direction. Specific gravity: 1.68 if pure. Crystals: orthorhombic, often needles. Occurrence: widespread, including Death Valley, California; in the salt lakes of Kruger Hills, Washington; and at Epsom, England, from which it derives its name. Used as a medicinal cathartic since ancient times.

GYPSUM $CaSO_4 \cdot 2H_2O$—calcium sulfate with two parts water. The same formula as *anhydrite*, but with water added. *Alabaster* (compact and translucent), *satin spar* (fibrous and silky), and *selenite* (colorless and glassy) are common varieties of gypsum. Color: colorless when pure, admixtures make it white, yellow, grey, red, brown, and bluish. Streak: white. Hardness: 1½–2. Cleavage: perfect in one direction, distinct in another. Specific gravity: 2.3–2.4. Crystals: monoclinic, with many forms. Occurrence: mostly as an evaporite in sedimentary deposits in many countries; in the U.S., nice crystals have been found in Oklahoma, New York state, and Utah; gypsum crystals more than 3 feet long have been found in Chihauhua, Mexico, and Braden, Chile. Named from the Green word *gypsos* ("gypsum" or "plaster"), gypsum has been used to make plaster for centuries: when gypsum is heated to drive out the water, then crushed into powder and reconstituted with water, it hardens into plaster of Paris.

MELANTERITE (ALSO CALLED "COPPERAS" AND "GREEN VITRIOL") $FeSO_4 \cdot 7H_2O$—iron sulfate with seven parts water. Color: green or yellowish-green. Streak: white. Hardness: 2. Cleavage: perfect in one direction, distinct in another. Specific gravity: 1.9. Crystals: monoclinic, often prisms and plates. Occurrence: many localities in the American West, including California, Montana, Nevada, and Utah.

THENARDITE Na_2SO_4—sodium sulfate. Forms as an evaporite in salt lakes and fumaroles. Often associated with *halite* and *borax*. Color: mostly white and grey. Streak: white. Hardness: 2½–3. Cleavage: perfect in one direction. Specific gravity: 2.67 if pure. Crystals: orthorhombic, often intergrown. Originally derived from a salt lake in Spain, thenardite was named after the French chemist Louis J. Thénard (1777–1857). Occurrence: found in fumaroles at Mount Vesuvius, Italy; also in Arizona, California, Nevada, and Canada.

11. Chromates

Chromates are a small class of usually brightly colored minerals with metallic elements compounded with the chromate ($CrO_4{}^2$) radical. *Crocoite* is the only chromate found in most private mineral collections.

CROCOITE (ALSO CALLED "RED LEAD ORE") $PbCrO_4$—lead chromate. Color: bright orange-red. Streak: orange-yellow. Hardness: 2½–3. Cleavage: distinct in one direction, poor in two directions. Specific gravity: 5.9–6.1. Crystals: monoclinic, usually prismatic or long needles. Occurrence: famous crystals from Tasmania, Australia, measuring 7 inches long; also from a few mines in Arizona and California. Crocoite is a rare mineral, but its color makes it popular with collectors.

Natural crystal of crocoite, *a rare mineral of lead chromate that is popular with collectors.* © *GIA.*

12. Phosphates, Arsenates, and Vanadates

Phosphates, arsenates, and vanadates are a large class of minerals whose metallic elements are compounded with the phosphate ($PO_4{}^{-3}$), arsenate ($AsO_4{}^{-3}$), or vanadate ($VO_4{}^{-3}$) radicals. For this mineral class, I list more species than I discuss in detail, as many are scarce and unlikely to be encountered by the average collector.

ADAMITE $Zn_2(AsO_4)(OH)$—basic arsenate of zinc. Brownish-yellow crystals from Durango, Mexico, are common at mineral shows.

AMBLYGONITE $(Li,Na)Al(PO_4)(F,OH)$ —basic fluorophosphate of aluminum, sodium, and lithium. At hardness 5½–6, it is used as a minor gemstone.

APATITE $Ca_5(F,Cl,OH)(PO_4)_3$—calcium fluorine-chlorine-hydroxyl phosphate. Named from the Greek word *apatao* ("I am misleading" or "to deceive"), because early mineralogists easily confused apatite with other minerals. As a collector gemstone, it is found in *pegmatite* dikes and sedimentary deposits.

Color: colorless, white, yellow, red, green, violet, and brown. Streak: white. Hardness: 5, brittle. Cleavage: poor in one direction. Specific gravity: 3.1–3.2. Crystals: hexagonal, short or long prisms and plates. Occurrence: choice specimens from Germany and Spain; Ontario and Quebec in Canada; and Durango, Mexico.

AUSTINITE $CaZnAsO_4OH$—basic arsenate of calcium and zinc. Scarce mineral. Found in Utah and Mexico.

AUTUNITE (ALSO CALLED "LIME URANITE") $Ca(UO_2)_2(PO_4)_2 \cdot 10–12H_2O$—calcium and uranium phosphate with 10 to 12 parts water. A radioactive ore of uranium. Highly fluorescent under ultraviolet light. Yellowish-green. Emitted radiation can be detected with a Geiger counter or scintillometer. Named after its early locality in Autun, France.

CONICHALCITE $CaCu(AsO_4)(OH)$—basic arsenate of calcium and copper. Grass-green copper mineral from Arizona, Nevada, and Utah.

DESCLOIZITE SERIES Two scarce vanadate minerals from western U.S. and Mexico. *Descloizite*'s formula is $Pb(Zn,Cu)VO_4OH$, and it is zinc-rich. The other member is copper-rich *mottramite*: $Pb(Cu,Zn)VO_4OH$. Brown to green.

ERYTHRITE (ALSO CALLED "COBALT BLOOM") $Co_3(AsO_4)_2 \cdot 8H_2O$—cobalt arsenate with eight parts water. Scarce purple-red mineral. Famous from the mines at Bou Azzer, Morocco; also from Schneeberg, Germany.

LAZULITE (ALSO CALLED "BLUE SPAR") $(Mg,Fe)Al_2(PO_4)_2(OH)_2$—basic phosphate of magnesium, iron, and aluminum. Scarce blue mineral. Not to be confused with the tectosilicate *lazurite*—both are used as gemstones. *Lazulite* comes from California and Georgia in the U.S.

LEGRANDITE $Zn_2(AsO_4)(OH) \cdot H_2O$—hydrous basic zinc arsenate. Rare yellow mineral from Lampazos and Mapimí, Mexico.

MIMETITE (ALSO CALLED MIMETESITE) $Pb_5(AsO_4)_3Cl$—lead chloroarsenate. Scarce yellow, orange, or brown mineral, with choice specimens from Australia and Namibia. Named from the Greek word *mimos* or *mimetes* ("imitator"), because it resembles *polymorphite*.

MONAZITE $CePO_4$—cerium phosphate, but usually contains admixtures of lanthanum, yttrium, and thorium (*cheralite* variety has up to 33-percent thorium). A scarce brownish-yellow radioactive mineral, used as a source of rare earth elements and thorium. From Colorado and North Carolina in U.S.

OLIVENITE Cu_2AsO_4OH—basic arsenate of copper. A scarce olive-green to yellowish-brown mineral, found in Idaho, Nevada, and Utah in the U.S. Do not confuse with the common neosilicate *olivine*.

PYROMORPHITE (ALSO CALLED "GREEN LEAD ORE") $Pb_5(PO_4)_3Cl$—lead chlorophosphate. A scarce lead ore found in British Columbia, Idaho, and Durango (Mexico) in North America; also found in Europe.

TORBERNITE (ALSO CALLED "COPPER URANITE") $Cu(UO_2)_2(PO_4)_2 \cdot 8\text{-}12H_2O$ —copper and uranium phosphate with eight to 12 parts water. A radioactive uranium ore, greener than autunite. An alteration product of *uraninite* (*pitchblende*). Choice crystals from Sonora, Mexico.

TRIPHYLITE SERIES A two-member phosphate series, with iron-rich *triphylite* at one end and manganese-rich *lithiophilite* at the other end: $Li(Fe^{+2},Mn^{+2})PO_4$. From New England and San Diego County, California.

TURQUOISE (HAS BEEN CALLED "CALLAITE") $CuAl_6(PO_4)_4(OH)_8 \cdot 4\text{-}5H_2O$—hydrous basic phosphate of copper and aluminum, sometimes containing iron. Occurs in hydrothermal replacement deposits. Color: sky-blue, bluish-green, and apple-green. Streak: white. Hardness: 5–6, brittle. Cleavage: none. Specific gravity: 2.6–2.9. Crystals: triclinic, but cryptocrystalline (crystals cannot be seen). Uses: as an opaque gem and lapidary stone. Prized by Native Americans in Arizona and New Mexico, who fashion turquoise in silver jewelry. Cheap turquoise may be dyed blue. The finest turquoise comes from Iran (Persia), where it has been mined for centuries. Named from the French word *turquoise* ("Turkish"), due to a misconception of where Persian turquoise was mined. Sometimes spelled without the "e."

VANADINITE $Pb_5(VO_4)_3Cl$—lead chlorovanadate. Handsome orangish-red mineral, displaying hexagonal crystal prisms. Found in southwestern U.S. and Mexico.

VARISCITE $Al(PO_4) \cdot 2H_2O$—hydrated aluminum phosphate, sometimes with admixtures of iron or arsenic. Green to bluish-green. Translucent and waxy. From Nevada and Utah.

VIVIANITE (ALSO CALLED "BLUE IRON EARTH") $Fe_3(PO_4)_2 \cdot 8H_2O$—iron phosphate with eight parts water. Color: colorless when freshly fractured, changing to dark blue on exposure to light. Streak: white, immediately changing to indigo blue. Occurrence: Maryland, New Jersey, Colorado, Idaho, and Utah.

WAVELLITE $Al_3(PO_4)_2(OH)_3 \cdot 5H_2O$—hydrous basic aluminum phosphate, often with fluorine and iron. Mostly whitish in color, with orthorhombic crystals usually radially fibrous or globular. The best wavellite in America comes from Garland, Hot Springs, and Montgomery counties in Arkansas; also well known from Cerhovice, Czechoslovakia.

13. Vanadium Oxysalts

Vanadium oxysalts are a small class of minerals of metallic elements compounded with the vanadate (VO_4^{-3}) radical. These minerals are soft, brittle, and brightly colored.

CARNOTITE The most likely collected species of the vanadium oxysalts, and a hydrous potassium uranium vanadate: $K_2(UO_2)_2(VO_4)_2 \cdot 3H_2O$. A yellowish radioactive ore of uranium found in weathered sandstones and sometimes on petrified wood—in the Colorado Plateau region of Arizona, Colorado, New Mexico, and Utah. Specific gravity: 4–5. Crystals are monoclinic, usually powdery aggregates on another rock.

14. Molybdates and Tungstates

Molybdates and tungstates are minerals with metallic elements compounded with the molybdate (MoO_4^{-2}) or tungstate (WO_4^{-2}) radicals. These minerals tend to be soft, brittle, and heavy in bright or dark colors. Three members of this mineral class are commonly collected: *scheelite*, *wolframite*, and *wulfenite*:

SCHEELITE (ALSO CALLED "CALCIUM TUNGSTATE") $CaWO_4$—calcium tungstate. Color: usually lighter colors, including white, yellow, orange, greenish, reddish, and sometimes brownish. Streak: white. Hardness: 4½–5. Cleavage: distinct in one direction. Specific gravity: 5.9–6.1. Crystals: tetragonal, usually dipyramidal pseudooctahedral. Luminescence: fluoresces bluish-white like *fluorite*, but is harder and heavier than fluorite. Occurrence: many localities in western U.S. and British Columbia, often in *quartz* veins or at metamorphic contact zones.

WOLFRAMITE SERIES A three-member tungstate mineral series, consisting of manganese-rich *hübnerite* ($MnWO_4$), intermediate *wolframite* (Fe,Mn)WO_4, and iron-rich *ferberite* ($FeWO_4$). Color and streak: ranges from reddish-brown in *hübnerite* to black in *ferberite*. Hardness: 4–5½. Cleavage: perfect in one direction. Specific gravity: 6.4–7.5. Crystals: monoclinic, often plates and prisms. Occurrence: nice crystals of series species from Colorado and Germany.

WULFENITE (ALSO CALLED "YELLOW LEAD ORE") $PbMoO_4$—lead molybdate. Color: mostly shades of yellow, orange, and light brown—often resembles butterscotch candy. Streak: white or yellowish-white. Hardness: 3, brittle. Cleavage: distinct in one direction. Specific gravity: 6½–7. Crystals: triclinic, but pseudotetragonal due to twinning. Crystals often thin square plates in large groups. Occurrence: Arizona and New Mexico; also the famous specimens from Sierra de Los Lamentos in Chihuahua, Mexico.

15. Silicates

Silicates are the largest class of minerals and the most widely distributed. They comprise about 25 percent of all known mineral species (40 percent of the common ones) and 95 percent by volume of all minerals in the Earth's crust. The Earth's mantle is thought to be almost entirely silicates, also.

Most rock-forming minerals are silicate families—that is, aluminosilicates (feldspars, feldspathoids, and clay minerals), amphiboles, micas, olivines, pyroxenes, quartz, and zeolites. For example, continental *granite* is made entirely of silicates (*feldspar*, *mica*, *quartz*, and so forth), except for stray impurities. Pyroxenes (especially *augite*) are common in *basalt* and *gabbro*. *Olivine* is found in dark igneous rocks, and it is believed to be common in the Earth's mantle. Clay minerals are aluminum silicates derived from *feldspar* weathering.

Silicate minerals are usually hard, acid-resistant, extremely insoluble, with glassy lustre, relatively lightweight, often vividly colored, and often transparent or translucent; hence, they make excellent gemstones. Many thousands of people in America earn all or most of their yearly income from commercial uses of silicate minerals—from stone masons and ceramic workers to jewelers and mineral dealers.

All silicate minerals are molecularly based on the geometrical tetrahedral arrangement of the silicate group. In this arrangement, one silicon atom is in the middle of an imaginary tetrahedron (a solid figure with four triangular faces), with four equally spaced oxygen atoms at the four corners:

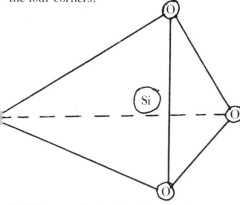

Building on the basic silicate molecular group, increasing molecular complexity and added elemental impurities produce the hundreds of species and varieties of silicate minerals.

Silicates can be divided into three general categories:

Ferromagnesian silicate minerals (*also called the "mafic" minerals*) Those with iron and magnesium:
+ *Amphibole* group (for example, *actinolite*, *hornblend*, and *tremolite*)
+ *Biotite* mica
+ *Olivine* group

+ *Pyroxene* group (for example, *augite*, *diopside*, and *enstatite*)

Nonferromagnesian silicate minerals (*also called the "felsic" minerals*) Those without iron and magnesium:
+ *Feldspar* group:
 • *Orthoclase* group (for example, if we include *microcline*)—high in potassium and aluminum
 • *Plagioclase* group (for example, *albite*, *anorthite*, and *labradorite*)—high in calcium, aluminum, and sodium
+ *Muscovite* mica—high in potassium and aluminum
+ *Quartz*—silicon and oxygen

All other silicate minerals For example, *beryl, garnet, topaz, tourmaline, zircon*, and so forth—a grouping that includes some of the most sought gemstones.

Here are some selected species from the hundreds of known silicate minerals:

ACTINOLITE AND TREMOLITE (AMPHIBOLE GROUP) $Ca_2(Mg,Fe)_5Si_8O_{22}(OH)_2$ —a basic calcium, magnesium, and iron silicate. When iron content predominates, it is called *actinolite*. High magnesium content makes it *tremolite*. Color: green in *actinolite*—white, grey, or colorless in *tremolite*. Streak: colorless. Hardness: 5–6. Cleavage: perfect in two directions. Specific gravity: 3.0–3.5 for *actinolite*, 2.9–3.1 for *tremolite*. Crystals: monoclinic, prisms or fibrous. Occurrence: New England, California, and Ontario. *Nephrite* "jade" is usually a combination of actinolite and tremolite, colored translucent green, and found in Alaska, Wyoming, British Columbia, China, and Siberia.

Cut slab of nephrite, a type of "jade," which is usually a combination of the basic silicate minerals of actinolite and tremolite and colored translucent green. © GIA.

ANDALUSITE Al_2SiO_5—aluminum silicate. Color: grey, reddish-grey, and brownish. Streak: white. Hardness: 7½, brittle. Cleavage: good in two directions. Specific gravity: 3.1–3.2. Crystals: orthorhombic, often thick columnar. Occurrence: mostly in metamorphic rocks—nice crystals from California, and *chiastolite* variety from Massachusetts. Named after its locality in Andalusia, Spain. Andalusite is trimorphic with *kyanite* and *sillimanite*—meaning that these three minerals have the same empirical chemical formula, but different crystal structures.

APOPHYLLITE $KCa_4Si_8O_{20}(F,OH)$ • $8H_2O$—hydrous calcium potassium fluorsilicate, sometimes with iron and nickel impurities. Color: usually colorless, white, or greenish (the green tint is from iron). Streak: white. Hardness: 4½–5, brittle. Cleavage: perfect in one direction. Specific gravity: 2.3–2.4. Crystals: tetra-

gonal, usually short-columnar or tabular. Occurrence: Poonah, India; also Michigan, New Jersey, and Mexico.

AUGITE (PYROXENE GROUP) $Ca(Mg,Fe,Al)Si_2O_6$—calcium, magnesium, iron, aluminum silicate, sometimes with sodium and titanium admixtures. Found in dark igneous rocks. Color: dark green to black. Streak: greyish-green. Hardness: 5–6, brittle. Cleavage: good in two directions. Specific gravity: 3.2–3.6. Crystals: monoclinic, often short prisms. Occurrence: rock-forming mineral in basic igneous rocks—basalts, tuffs. Many localities. Nice crystals in Colorado, New York state, Oregon, and Ontario. Famous from Luková, Czechoslovakia.

BENITOITE $BaTiSi_3O_9$—barium titanium silicate. Discovered in 1906, this rare blue mineral was first believed to be sapphire. Color: colorless, blue, and bluegrey. Streak: white. Hardness: 6–6½, brittle. Cleavage: none. Specific gravity: 3.6. Crystals: hexagonal, characteristically triangular and flattened. Occurrence: California, Texas, and Belgium—but the only gemstone-quality benitoite is from the Gem Mine in San Benito County, California, from which it derives its name. Not to be confused with the weathered volcanic ash "bentonite" from Rock River, Wyoming.

BERYL $Be_3Al_2Si_6O_{18}$—beryllium aluminum silicate. A famous genstone, with the following color varieties:
- ✦ *Aquamarine*—blue or bluish-green, color caused by ferrous iron (Fe^{+2}) impurity; the deeper the blue, the better the aquamarine as a gemstone.
- ✦ *Bixbite*—rose-red, due to manganese.

- *Common beryl*—opaque, not gem quality, any color.
- *Emerald*—intense green, due to chromium; according to Pliny, the Roman Emperor Nero had eyeglasses made of emerald crystals.
- *Golden beryl*—golden yellow, due to ferric iron (Fe^{+3}).
- *Goshenite*—pure, colorless beryl.
- *Green beryl*—green color not due to chromium, possibly colored by vanadium; not technically an emerald.
- *Heliodor*—yellow or orangish-yellow, due to ferric iron.
- *Morganite*—pink or peach colored, due to manganese (and possible heat treatment!).

Beryl's streak: white. Hardness: 7½–8, brittle. Cleavage: indistinct in one direction. Specific gravity: 2.66–2.92. Crystals: hexagonal columnar prisms, striated lengthwise, often cracked and heavily included. Occurrence: Colorado, New England, North Carolina, and San Diego County in California for U.S. beryl localities; quality *emeralds* from Columbia; *aquamarines* from Brazil (in 1910, a 243-pound transparent aquamarine crystal was found in Brazil). Inferior-quality emeralds and aquamarines are common and often overpriced.

BIOTITE (ALSO CALLED "IRON MICA") $K(Mg,Fe)_3(Al,Fe)Si_3O_{10}(OH,F)_2$ —basic potassium, magnesium, iron, and aluminum silicate. Dark-colored mica, common in *granite* (the dark flecks) and the metamorphic rocks of *gneiss* and *schist*. Color: dark green, greenish-brown, to black. Streak: white or grey. Diaphaneity: opaque to transparent, depending on how many plates are stacked up.

Hardness: 2½–3. Cleavage: perfect in one direction, cleaves into thin plates. Tenacity: elastic. Specific gravity: 2.8–3.2. Crystals: monoclinic, tabular. Occurrence: widespread the world over, especially in *pegmatites* with reddish *feldspar*; biotite crystals are found on Mount Vesuvius, Italy.

CHORITE A group of minerals of which a green mica is commonly collected: $(Mg,Fe)_6(AlSi_3)O_{10}(OH)_8$—basic iron, magnesium, and aluminum silicate. Color: usually green, but can be white to black. Similar to *biotite* (above), but chlorite is green, flexible (not elastic), and softer (hardness 2–2½). Occurrence: widespread, with nice crystals from California and New York state.

CHRYSOCOLLA $Cu_2H_2Si_2O_5(OH)_4$— basic copper silicate. Used as a gemstone when mixed with *chalcedony*. Color: green, bluish-green, and blue. Streak: light green to light blue. Diaphaneity: translucent to opaque. Hardness: 2–4. Cleavage: none. Specific gravity: 2–2.2. Crystals: monoclinic, microscopic in aggregates. Occurrence: Arizona, Idaho, Nevada, New Mexico, Utah, and Mexico for North America. Chrysocolla high in *quartz* has a hardness near 7. Chrysocolla mixed with *malachite* is called "Eilat Stone."

CORDIERITE (ALSO CALLED "DICHROITE" OR "IOLITE") $(Mg,Fe)_2Al_4Si_5 O_{18}$—magnesium aluminum silicate, often with iron as admixture. Color: blue, grey, to violet. Streak: white. Hardness: 7–7½, brittle. Cleavage: distinct in one direction. Specific gravity: 2.6–2.7. Crystals: orthorhombic, but rare. Occurrence: transparent blue cordierite is called *iolite* and used as a gemstone—found in Connecticut and Canada's Northwest Territories, as well as Burma, India, Sri Lanka, and Africa.

DANBURITE $CaB_2Si_2O_8$—calcium borosilicate. Colors: colorless, white, to yellow and brown. Hardness: 7–7½. Specific gravity: 2.9–3. Crystals: orthorhombic, usually prisms. Occurrence: named for Danbury, Connecticut, where it was first found (this city presently covers the collecting site); also from Russell, New York, and Charcas, Mexico. Used as a gemstone.

DIOPSIDE (PYROXENE GROUP) $CaMgSi_2O_6$—calcium magnesium silicate. Color: usually white to greyish-green shades, often pale. Streak: white. Hardness: 5–6, brittle. Cleavage: good in two directions. Specific gravity: 3.3–3.6, with higher range for iron admixture. Crystals: monoclinic, often short prisms. Occurrence: choice crystals from Piedmont, Italy; also from Ontario, Quebec, and New York state. Not to be confused with "dioptase" below.

A polished lapidary specimen of diopside, *variety* violane *(for violet color). Diopside is a calcium, magnesium silicate mineral.* © *GIA.*

DIOPTASE $CuSiO_2(OH)_2$—basic copper silicate. An emerald-green collectible gemstone (not wearable due to softness). Streak: pale bluish-green. Hardness: 5, brittle. Cleavage: perfect in one direction. Specific gravity: 3.3–3.4. Crystals: hexagonal, usually short prisms. Occurrence: Namibia and Zaire in Africa produce the finest dioptase; tiny crystals from Arizona.

Dioptase, *a basic copper silicate mineral that is cut into emerald-green collectible gemstones, but not wearable in jewelry due to moderate softness.* © *GIA.*

EPIDOTE GROUP $Ca_2(Al,Fe)_3Si_3O_{12}(OH)$—basic calcium, aluminum, and iron silicate. A group of minerals often found in contact metamorphic rocks, especially igneous/*limestone* zones. With admixtures, the epidote group includes *allanite*, *clinozoisite*, *epidote* (proper), *hancockite*, *piedmontite*, and *zoisite*.

Tanzanite (blue *zoisite*) is a soft (Hardness 6–6½), but popular gemstone from Tanzania, East Africa. Specific gravity: 3.2–3.4. Orthorhombic, long prismatic crystals. Named "tanzanite" by Tiffany & Company, famous American jewelers.

GARNET GROUP A number of silicate minerals with similar structure but variable chemical composition and physical properties; commonly used as gemstones. Most garnets have a vitreous lustre, hardness 6½–7½, no cleavage, and a specific gravity range of 3.4–4.6, depending on the type. All garnets have isometric crystals, typically dodecahedra and trapezohedra. All garnets are brittle and fracture conchoidally. Garnets come from many places in the U.S. and elsewhere, often found in crystalline schists and alluvial deposits. Garnets range from opaque to transparent, from cheap mineral specimens to choice gemstones. The following are the popular garnet species.

✦ *Almandine*—$Fe_3Al_2Si_3O_{12}$—iron aluminum silicate. Deep red to brownish. Also called "common garnet."

✦ *Andradite*—$Ca_3Fe_2Si_3O_{12}$—calcium iron silicate.
  • *Demantoid* variety—deep green, colored by chromium.
  • *Melanite* variety—brown or black, colored by titanium.
  • *Schorlomite* variety—contains titanium, like *melanite*.
  • *Topazolite* variety—yellowish-green.

✦ *Grossular*—$Ca_3Al_2Si_3O_{12}$—calcium aluminum silicate. Many colors, white to black, including the following:
  • *Hessonite* variety—brownish-orange.
  • *Rosolite* variety—pink, from Mexico.
  • *Tsavorite* variety—emerald-green, from East Africa; popular emerald substitute in jewelry, but not cheap.

Rough tsavorite garnet, *the emerald-green variety of* grossular garnet, *from Kenya, East Africa. Photo by Tino Hammid.* © GIA and Tino Hammid.

✦ *Pyrope* (also called "Bohemian garnet")—$Mg_3Al_2Si_3O_{12}$—magnesium aluminum silicate. Deep red to purplish-red, due to iron and chromium. Pure pyropes are believed to be unknown in nature; they always have some *almandine* and *spessartine* ingredients.

So-called "rhodolite" garnet is intermediate between *almandine* and *pyrope*, with a magnesium-iron ratio of 2:1, and doesn't warrant a separate mineral species. Rhodolite is always purplish-red.

✦ *Spessartine* — $Mn_3Al_2Si_3O_{12}$ — manganese aluminum silicate. Red, reddish-orange, to reddish-brown. A rare garnet, typically found in *pegmatites* and *rhyolite*. Choice specimens from Ramona, California, and Amelia, Virginia.

✦ *Uvarovite*—$Ca_3Cr_2Si_3O_{12}$—calcium chromium silicate. A rare dark green garnet, found in *serpentine* and *chromite*-invaded *limestone*. In the U.S., found in California, Oregon, and Texas; also found in Finland, Norway, South Africa, and Quebec.

Rhodolite garnet *from East Africa, a 2.34-carat "rose octagon" cut by, and courtesy of, Don Clary. Photo by Robert Weldon.* © GIA.

HEMIMORPHITE (ALSO CALLED "CALAMINE," "GALMEI," AND "SILICATE OF ZINC")

$Zn_4Si_2O_7 \cdot H_2O$—hydrous zinc silicate. A scarce mineral, often pale blue, but seen at mineral shows—from the mines at Mapimí (Durango) and Santa Eulalia (Chihuahua), Mexico.

HORNBLENDE (AMPHIBOLE GROUP)

$(Ca,Na,K)_{2-3}(Mg,Fe^{+2},Fe^{+3},Al)_5$ $(SiAl)_8O_{22}(OH)_2$—a complex basic silicate of calcium, sodium, potassium, magnesium, iron, and aluminum. A common rock-forming mineral of plutonic and metamorphic rocks. Color: green to black. Streak: colorless. Hardness: 5–6, up to 6½ in magnesium-rich specimens. Cleavage: perfect in two directions. Specific gravity: 3.0–3.4. Crystals: monoclinic, but scarce in nice specimens. Occurrence: widespread.

HYPERSTHENE (PYROXENE GROUP)

$(Mg,Fe)SiO_3$—magnesium iron silicate. Common rock-forming mineral of plutonic and metamorphic rocks. Color: grey, green, to brownish-black. Streak: greyish-white. Hardness: 5–6, brittle. Cleavage: perfect in one direction. Specific gravity: 3.4–3.9. Crystals: orthorhombic, nice specimens rare. Occurrence: widespread.

JADEITE (PYROXENE GROUP)

$NaAlSi_2O_6$—sodium aluminum silicate. The word "jade" includes the lapidary-quality specimens of two minerals: *jadeite* (described here) and "nephrite" (the fibrous variety of the amphibole mineral *actinolite*—see page 157). The following are jadeite's properties. Color: white and green shades common, also grey and yellow. Streak: white. Hardness: 6½–7. Cleavage: distinct in two directions. Specific gravity: 3.2–3.3. Crystals: monoclinic, but rare. Occurrence: best jadeite comes from Burma, but specimens can be found in San Benito County, California.

KAOLINITE (ALSO CALLED "KAOLIN" OR "CHINA CLAY")

$Al_2Si_2O_5(OH)_4$—hydrous aluminum silicate. Used to make porcelain in China since the 6th century A.D., and named after Kao-Ling, a mountain there where this mineral was mined. Color: white, yellowish, and grey. Streak:

At approximately 33 metric tons, this is reportedly the largest jadeite boulder ever mined in Myanmar (Burma). Photo by Robert Kane. © GIA.

white. Hardness: 1–2. Cleavage: perfect in one direction. Specific gravity: 2.6. Crystals: monoclinic, usually tiny plates in masses. Occurrence: widespread, but nice crystals are rare.

KYANITE (ALSO CALLED "DISTHENE"; ORIGINALLY SPELLED "CYANITE") Al_2SiO_5—aluminum silicate. Trimorphic with *andalusite* and *sillimanite*. Usually found in *gneiss* and *schist*. Color: colorless, white, blue, grey, green, and yellow. Named from the Greek word *kyanos* ("dark blue"). Streak: white. Hardness: 4–5 lengthwise, 6–7 crosswise. Cleavage: perfect in one direction, good in another.

Specific gravity: 3.6–3.7. Crystals: triclinic, usually bladed aggregates. Occurrence: nice specimens from California, Georgia, and North Carolina.

LAZURITE (ALSO CALLED "LAPIS LA-ZULI" BY JEWELERS AND LAPIDARIES) $(Na,Ca)_8(Al,Si)_{12}O_{24}(S,SO_4)$—silicate of sodium, calcium, aluminum, with sulfur. The opaque blue gemstone known as "lapis lazuli" is actually a rock composed mostly of lazurite, often with *calcite* and *pyrite*. The following are lazurite's properties. Color: azure-blue, dark blue, and greenish-blue. Streak: light blue. Hardness: 5–5½, brittle. Cleavage: poor. Specific gravity: 2.38–2.45 if pure. Crystals: isometric, but rare; dodecahedra. Occurrence: the finest lapis lazuli comes from a mine in Badakshan, Afghanistan, which has been operating for 7,000 years; some in California and Colorado. The word *lazurite* comes from the Persian word *lazhward* ("blue"). Lazurite is in the sodalite subgroup of tectosilicates. Do not confuse *lazurite* with the phosphate mineral *lazulite*.

Polished cabochons of naturally mottled "lapis lazuli" from Afghanistan, where it has been mined for 7,000 years. The old masters used crushed grains of lapis lazuli for the ultramarine color in their oil paintings. © GIA.

LEPIDOLITE (ALSO CALLED "LITHIUM MICA") $K(Li,Al)_3(Si,Al)_4O_{10}(F,OH)_2$ —basic potassium, lithium, aluminum fluorsilicate mica group. A pinkish or lavender *mica* known especially from Maine and San Diego County, California. Hardness: 2½–3. Specific gravity: 2.8–2.9.

MUSCOVITE (ALSO CALLED "COMMON MICA," "ISINGLASS," AND "MUSCOVY GLASS"—FROM ITS USE AS GLASS IN RUSSIA) $KAl_3Si_3O_{10}(OH,F)_2$—basic potassium aluminum silicate. A common rock-forming mineral, especially in granitic pegmatites. Color: white to yellowish to greenish, and brown. Streak: white. Hardness: 2–2½. Cleavage: perfect in one direction. Specific gravity: 2.7–2.8. Crystals: monoclinic, tabular. Occurrence: widespread.

NEPHELINE $(Na,K)AlSiO_4$—sodium, potassium aluminum silicate. Mostly white or grey, to greenish or brown. Common in *nepheline syenite pegmatites*. Found in Maine and Ontario; also on Mount Vesuvius, Italy.

OLIVINE GROUP A solid solution series of three neosilicate minerals: *forsterite* (Mg_2SiO_4) at one end, *fayalite* (Fe_2SiO_4) at the other end, and *olivine* $([Mg,Fe]_2SiO_4)$ in the middle. Color: yellowish-green to reddish-brown. Transparent yellow-green olivine is the gemstone *peridot* or *chrysolite* (not to be confused with "chrysotile" serpentine). *Olivine* streak: white. Hardness: 6½ (*fayalite*) to 7 (*forsterite*), brittle. Cleavage: indistinct in two directions. Specific gravity: 3.27 (*forsterite*) to 4.20 (*fayalite*). Crystals: orthorhombic; rare as crystals, usually short prisms or rounded grains.

Occurrence: opaque *olivine* (called "dunite") is a common rock-forming mineral in *basalt*, *gabbro*, and *peridotite*.

The best *peridot* comes from Zebirget Island (Isle of St. John) off the coast of Egypt in the Red Sea. Small peridot stones come from Arizona and New Mexico. Peridot has been called "evening emerald," because it seems to lose its yellowish tint at night and therefore looks green like *emeralds*. Most cut peridot gemstones are heavily included or cracked—check them with a 10-power magnifier, and don't buy inferior quality.

Rough (9.17 carats) and cut (1.63 and 1.65 carats) peridot *from Zebirget Island (Isle of St. John) in the Red Sea. Gemstone-quality peridot (sometimes called "chrysolite") is actually transparent yellow-green olivine mineral. Photo by Tino Hammid. © GIA & Tino Hammid.*

ORTHOCLASE $KAlSi_3O_8$—potassium aluminum silicate. A "potash feldspar," sometimes containing sodium or barium admixtures. Color: mostly white, yellow, or pink. When transparent and glassy, it is called *sanidine*. When colorless and transparent or translucent, often with a bluish opalescence, it is called *adularia* and termed "moonstone" in the jewelry business (see "Plagioclase" for other moonstones). Streak: white. Hardness: 6–6.5. Cleavage: good in two directions. Specific gravity: 2.5–2.6. Crystals: monoclinic for *orthoclase*, in prisms, plates, and twins. *Microcline* feldspar has the same chemical formula and similar physical properties as orthoclase, but microcline has triclinic crystals. A light bluish-green microcline variety called "amazonite" (or "amazonstone") is polished as a cabochon gemstone. Occurrence: widespread in North America for common orthoclase and microcline; fine amazonite comes from Colorado, Pennsylvania, and (especially) Amelia, Virginia; also from the former U.S.S.R.

PHLOGOPITE $KMg_3AlSi_3O_{10}(OH,F)_2$ —basic potassium, magnesium, aluminum silicate mica, often with fluorine and iron admixtures. Phlogopite mica is similar to *biotite* mica, and it may be found with it, but phlogopite is usually found in *marbles* (biotite and muscovite rarely are). Color: usually brown. Streak: white. Hardness: 2–3. Cleavage: perfect in one direction. Specific gravity: 2.7–2.9. Crystals: monoclinic, in prisms, plates, and scales. Occurrence: widespread; a phlogopite crystal 33 feet long, 14 feet wide, and weighing 90 tons was found at the Lacy Mine in Ontario.

PLAGIOCLASE GROUP A mixture of sodium and calcium aluminum silicate *feldspars*, from sodium-rich *albite* ($NaAlSi_3O_8$) at one end—through *oli-* *goclase* (not to be confused with *orthoclase*), *andesine*, *labradorite*, *bytownite*— to calcium-rich *anorthite* ($CaAl_2Si_2O_8$) at the other end. The plagioclase feldspars are common rock-forming minerals in igneous and metamorphic rocks. Color: mostly white, grey, and bluish. Streak: white. Hardness: 6–6½, brittle. Cleavage: good in two directions. Specific gravity: 2.62–2.76. Crystals: triclinic, often granular aggregates. Occurrence: widespread; opalescent oligoclase, one type of the jewelry trade's "moonstone," is found in Norway and Canada, and is polished into cabochons; the best labradorite ("sunstone") gems, with blue, green, and red color changes (known as "labradorescence"), come from East Labrador in Canada, Finland, and the Ukraine. Some albite is polished as "moonstone" also.

QUARTZ SiO_2—silicon dioxide. The most common mineral in the Earth's crust, in many rocks (igneous, sedimentary, and metamorphic), resistant to chemical weathering and metamorphism. So, sand from weathered *granite* will have a high quartz content, as will *sandstone* made from such sand.

Quartz is of three main types: *crystalline* with large, well-formed crystals (opaque, translucent, or transparent), *cryptocrystalline* (microscopic crystals), and hydrous *noncrystalline* (*opal*). Quartz specimens, rough or fashioned into gems and lapidary art, range from "junk" to "jewels" and are priced accordingly. Quartz is an obvious mineral for a specialist collection, as there are specimens for every budget and taste—from boulders of *milky quartz*, so heavy that you can't move them, to precious *fire opal* pebbles, so expensive that you dare not wear them in jewelry (and risk scratching or shattering them, due to opal's softness).

Crystalline quartz—with large visible crystals—has varieties named for their colors (due to impurities):
+ *Amethyst*—purple.
+ *Blue quartz*—blue.
+ *Citrine* (pronounced "sih'treen")— yellow; sometimes called "false topaz."
+ *Milky quartz*—white; opaque to translucent.
+ Rock crystal—colorless and transparent.
+ *Rose quartz*—pink to rose-red.
+ *Smoky quartz*—yellowish-grey to brownish-black; also known as "cairngorm." If there's any grey at all in its color, call it *smoky quartz* instead of *citrine*.

Aventurine is quartz embedded with flecks of *hematite* or *mica*. "Cat's eye" is a pseudomorph of quartz from *amianthus* or *asbestos* minerals. "Rutilated quartz" is called *sagenite* (for the quartz portion itself). "Tiger's eye" is a pseudomorph of quartz from weathered *crocidolite*.

Cryptocrystalline quartz is also called *chalcedony*, and subtypes are classified by their colors and patterns:
+ *Agate* has varicolored bands. "Moss agate" has mosslike inclusions of mineral oxides. Petrified wood is usually agate.
+ *Carnelian* is orangish-red, due to *hematite*.
+ *Chrysoprase*, sometimes mistaken for *jadeite*, is green, due to nickel.
+ *Flint* is grey, brown, or black; *chert* (also called "hornstone") is impure flint.

Rough and cabochon-cut specimens of chrysoprase, a chalcedony quartz variety, from Brazil. The cut stone weighs 11.18 carats. Chrysoprase is colored apple-green, due to the presence of nickel, and it is sometimes mistaken for the slightly heavier silicate mineral of jadeite. Photo by Robert Weldon. © GIA.

+ *Heliotrope* (also called "bloodstone") is dark green with red *jasper* spots.
+ *Jasper* is mottled red, yellow, and brown.
+ *Onyx* is banded black and white *chalcedony*.
+ *Sard* is like *carnelian*, but more reddish-brown; "carnelian" and "sard" are sometimes used synonymously.
+ *Sardonyx* is banded (mixed) *sard* and *onyx*.

Opal is hydrous noncrystalline quartz. Opal varieties include the following:
+ *Black opal*—dark body color, with gemstone "fire."
+ *Common opal*—without "fire," white to black.
+ *Diatomite* (also called *tripolite* or "diatomaceous earth")—chalklike stone

Natural black opal. *"Black" in opal refers to a dark body color, with accompanying prominent gemstone "fire," and not to an actual black color as such.* © GIA.

The following are the properties of quartz. Color for crystalline, cryptocrystalline, and opaline quartz is described above. Streak: white. Hardness: 7 for crystal *quartz* and *chalcedony*, 5½–6½ for *opal*. Cleavage: none. Specific gravity: 2.65 for crystalline *quartz* (very constant), 2.57–2.64 for *chalcedony*, and usually 2.0–2.2 for *opal*. Notice that opal is a little less heavy than regular quartz. Crystals: hexagonal prisms for crystalline *quartz*, none or microscopic in *chalcedony*, and none (amorphous) for *opal*. Occurrence: common *quartz*, *chalcedony*, and *opal* are widespread: choice gemstone-quality specimens are more localized; Australia, Mexico, and Nevada—in that order—are good sources of *precious opal*.

composed of microscopic shells of diatoms (fossil algae).

✦ *Fire opal*—orange to red; "fire" refers to the stone's body color, not to "play of color."

✦ *Geyserite*—porous residue found at geysers and hot springs; white to light brown. (All opal is not precious.)

✦ *Hyalite*— clear and glassy, colorless opal; found as lumps in volcanic cavities.

✦ *Hydrophane*—dull, opaque, porous, and light-colored: becomes transparent and opalescent in water, which is why you often see cheaper opal in vials of water at rock shows.

✦ *Precious opal*—opal of any color with "fire" (play of color).

✦ *White opal*—white body color, with or without "fire." Usually used for "white opal with fire" to distinguish it from "common opal," but sometimes "white opal" and "common opal" are used synonymously by jewelers.

✦ *Wood opal*—opalized petrified wood.

RHODONITE (ALSO CALLED "FOWLERITE" OR "MANGANESE SPAR") $MnSiO_3$—manganese silicate, often with calcium. Do not confuse with *rhodolite*, a *pyrope garnet* variety. Color:

Polished specimen of rhodonite, *a manganese silicate mineral with triclinic crystals, not to be confused with the manganese carbonate mineral* rhodochrosite *or with* rhodolite garnet. © GIA.

pink to reddish-brown. Streak: white. Hardness: 5½–6½, brittle. Cleavage: good in two directions. Specific gravity: 3.5–3.7. Crystals: triclinic, prisms or plates. Occurrence: in the U.S., best known from Franklin, New Jersey. As a cabochon gemstone, it is often spotted or streaked.

SERPENTINE GROUP $Mg_3Si_2O_5(OH)_4$ —magnesium silicate. The three common serpentine group varieties sought by mineral collectors are *antigorite* (common *serpentine*, translucent to opaque), *chrysotile* (containing iron, and fibrous, a source of asbestos), and "serpentine marble" (mottled dark green, used as a building stone). Do not confuse the "chrysotile" variety of *serpentine* with the "chrysolite" variety of *olivine*. Serpentine properties include the following. Color: green to black, often mixed. Streak: white. Hardness: 3–4. Cleavage: good in one direction in *antigorite*, nonexistent (or along fibres) in *chrysotile*. Specific gravity: 2.5–2.6. Crystals: monoclinic, plates and scales in *antigorite*, fibres in *chrysotile*. Occurrence: widespread; serpentine is the official California "state rock," and you can see roadside cliffs of it along Highway 49 in the Gold Rush country. Massive serpentine tends to have a greasy or waxy lustre and feel, as well as a mottled green-and-black color pattern with translucency. Serpentine comes from the Latin word *serpens* ("snake"), because the mineral resembles snakeskin and was used as a remedy for snakebite.

SILLIMANITE (ALSO CALLED "FIBROLITE") Al_2SiO_5—aluminum silicate. Trimorphic with *andalusite* and

Williamsite, *a translucent light green variety of the basic magnesium silicate mineral serpentine.* © *GIA.*

kyanite. Color: greyish-white to greenish-brown. Streak: white. Hardness: 6–7, brittle. Cleavage: perfect in one direction. Specific gravity: 3.2. Crystals: orthorhombic, fibrous, and radial aggregates. Occurrence: somewhat scarce, but in Connecticut, Massachusetts, and South Carolina in the U.S.

SODALITE $Na_4Al_3(SiO_4)_3Cl$—sodium aluminum silicate with chlorine. Found in *nepheline syenite pegmatites.* Nice specimens from British Columbia and Ontario. *Lazurite* is in the sodalite group of minerals. A variety of sodalite called *hackmanite* (from Ontario) is normally white, but it may temporarily turn red after exposure to short-wave ultraviolet light, then fade back to white in sunlight, a cycle which can be repeated. Sodalite is typically white, blue, grey, or green. Hardness: 5½–6. Specific gravity: 2.3. Crystals are isometric, but rare (and in dodecahedra).

SPODUMENE (OLDER NAME: "TRIPHANE") $LiAlSi_2O_6$—lithium aluminum silicate. A pyroxene group

A 187.9-gram specimen of natural sodalite, a sodium, aluminum silicate with chlorine added. From the GIA stone collection. Photo by Maha DeMaggio. © GIA.

mineral found only in *granitic pegmatites*—often associated with *beryl*, *lepidolite*, *quartz*, and *tourmaline*. Color: grey, yellowish-white; two color varieties are used as transparent faceted gemstones—green (*hiddenite*) and pink to purple (*kunzite*). Streak: white. Hardness: 6½–7, brittle. Cleavage: good in two directions. Specific gravity: 3.1–3.2, gems usually 3.18. Crystals: monoclinic, long flattened crystals with longitudinal grooves. Occurrence: *hiddenite* from Alexander County, North Carolina; *kunzite* from San Diego County, California, as well as Maine, Brazil, and Madagascar; a *spodumene* crystal 42 feet long, 5 feet wide, and weighing 90 tons was found at the Etta Mine in the Black Hills of South Dakota. *Spodumene* comes from the Greek word *spodumenos* ("burnt to ashes"), referring to its common grey color.

TALC (ALSO CALLED "STEATITE," "SAPONITE," AND "SOAPSTONE")

$Mg_3Si_4O_{10}(OH)_2$—basic magnesium silicate. Occurs in metamorphic rocks hy-

A 327.8-gram natural rough crystal of kunzite, *the pink to violet shade of* spodumene—*a lithium, aluminum silicate mineral found only in* granitic pegmatites. © GIA & Tino Hammid.

drothermally altered from *peridotite* and thermally altered from *dolomite*. Often found with *chlorite*, *dolomite*, *schists*, and *serpentine*. Has a greasy, soapy feel. Steatite is massive talc that has been carved into useful and ornamental objects since ancient times by the Chinese, Babylonians, Eskimos, Egyptians, and Native Americans. The following are its properties. Color: talc is usually light green to white, sometimes brownish. Streak: white. Hardness: 1–1½. Cleavage: perfect in one direction, frequently foliated (sheetlike). Specific gravity: 2.6–2.8. Crystals: monoclinic, but rare crystals (usually foliated). Occurrence: widespread; quarried in Connecticut, New York state, and Vermont in the U.S. Talc is named from the Arabic word *talq* (the mineral's name). *Steatite* is derived from the Latin *steatis* ("stone"), from the Greek *steatos* ("fat"). The term *saponite* comes from the Latin *sapo* ("soap"), and mineralogically is talc with aluminum, and sometimes iron, admixtures.

THORITE $ThSiO_4$—thorium silicate. Color: brownish-yellow, reddish-brown, orange, and black. Streak: brown, orange-yellow. Hardness: 4½–5, brittle. Cleavage: indistinct. Specific gravity: 4.4–4.8. Crystals: tetragonal—dipyramidal, prisms. Other properties: highly radioactive, sometimes admixed with uranium; soluble in hydrochloric acid. Occurrence: San Bernardino County, California, in the U.S.

TITANITE   (ALSO   CALLED "SPHENE") $CaTiSiO_5$—calcium titanium silicate, often with thorium or iron. Used as a gemstone, although soft (hardness: 5–5½)—therefore, easy to scratch; brittle. Nice brown to green crystals from Baja state of Mexico—the dark green chromium-bearing specimens are called "chrome sphene," which mimics *emerald* color.

TOPAZ $Al_2SiO_4(F,OH)_2$—aluminum fluorsilicate. Used as a faceted transparent-colored gemstone. Color: colorless, yellow, pink, blue, green, orange, and brown; dark orange topaz is called *hyacinth*; orange crystals with chromium turn pink when heated; most deep blue topaz gemstones sold today have been irradiated and heat-treated from pale blue or brown shades—thus, blue topaz gems are not rare, and often overpriced as *aquamarine* substitutes. Streak: white. Hardness: 8. Cleavage: perfect in one direction.

Light blue natural topaz crystal, a facetable *specimen of transparent rough topaz, an aluminum fluorsilicate gemstone of Hardness 8.* © *GIA.*

Specific gravity: 3.5–3.6, roughly correlated with color: pink is 3.50–3.53; yellow is 3.51–3.54; and blue or colorless is 3.56–3.57. Crystals: orthorhombic, usually in short, vertically striated prisms. Occurrence: known from California, Colorado, New Hampshire, Texas, and Utah—but the best gem topaz comes from Brazil, Sri Lanka (Ceylon), and the former U.S.S.R. Topaz occurs in igneous rock cavities and in stream gravel.

TOURMALINE GROUP   A family of six principal mineral species with similar crystal structure, but widely varying chemical composition due to element substitutions in a complex boron aluminum silicate. The empirical formula for *elbaite*, the gemstone variety of *tourmaline*, is

$Na(Li,Al)_3Al_6(BO_3)_3Si_6O_{18}(OH,F)_4$. The six principal members of the tourmaline group are as follows:

✦ *Buergerite*—dark brown to black, with iridescence.

✦ *Dravite*—brown to black, sometimes colorless.

✦ *Elbaite*—many colors; the popular gemstone colors are given individual names in the jewelry business:

• *Achroite*—colorless, sometimes with green or black natural crystal terminations.

• *Indicolite*—blue, often dark.

• *Rubellite*—pink to red.

• *Verdelite* (sometimes called "Brazilian emerald")—green; natural tourmaline crystals are often color-zoned into bicolored, tricolored, etc., specimens—the so-called "watermelon tourmaline" is zoned green/red.

✦ *Liddicoatite*—a calcium analog of *elbaite*; many colors.

✦ *Schorl*—black or dark blue.

✦ *Uvite*—black, dark brown, dark green.

Color: described above; also pleochroic—crystals exhibit deeper colors in one direction than in another. Streak: white. Lustre: vitreous. Hardness: 7–7½. Cleavage: none. Specific gravity: 3.0–3.2. Crystals: hexagonal, long prisms with vertical striations. Occurrence: gem-quality tourmaline comes from Mount Mica, Maine, and Pala, California, in the U.S. also from Burma, Brazil, Madagascar, Mexico, and the former U.S.S.R. Gem tourmaline usually comes from granitic *pegmatites*, and it is often associated with *lepidolite*, *microcline*, and *spodumene*.

VERMICULITE $(Mg,Fe,Al)_3(Al,Si)_4$ $O_{10}(OH)_2 \cdot 4H_2O$—basic hydrous aluminum silicate with variable magnesium and iron admixtures: that is, a clay mineral with water, similar to *micas*. Soft (hardness: 1½) and lightweight (specific gravity: 2.3–2.7), this yellowish or

A 12-centimetre-long elbaite tourmaline natural crystal cluster from Minas Gerais, Brazil. Tourmalines are a complex silicate family of gemstone minerals that are popular for jewelry and as mineral collectibles. Photo © by Mike Ridding. Photo courtesy of Silverhorn, Santa Barbara.

Idocrase is a complex silicate mineral, also termed vesuvianite *from its locality on the slopes of Italy's Mount Vesuvius, where specimens have been found in volcanically expelled* limestone *blocks. Natural rough, tumble-polished, and faceted specimens are pictured here. © GIA.*

greenish-bronze mineral is often used for growing seedlings and plant cuttings.

VESUVIANITE (ALSO CALLED "IDOCRASE") $Ca_{10}Mg_2Al_4(SiO_4)_5(Si_2O_7)_2(OH)_4$—basic calcium, magnesium, aluminum silicate, often with beryllium and fluorine. A widespread mineral, usually dark brown or green, mostly in metamorphic rocks. Streak: white. Hardness: 6½. Specific gravity: 3.3–3.5. Crystals: tetragonal, usually short prisms. Occurrence: nice specimens from California, Montana, Quebec, and Mexico. *Californite* (so-called "California jade") is greenish-grey translucent *vesuvianite* used as a cabochon gem. Named after its original locality: Mount Vesuvius, Italy.

WILLEMITE $ZnSiO_4$—zinc silicate, often containing iron and manganese. Very fluorescent under ultraviolet light. Color: white, yellow, green, brown in natural light. Occurs in *crystalline limestone*, often associated with *calcite*, *hemimorphite*, or *zincite*. Named for the Dutch King Willem I (1772–1843). Best specimens from Sussex County, New Jersey.

WOLLASTONITE (ALSO CALLED "TABLE SPAR") $CaSiO_3$—calcium silicate. Color: white or grey, sometimes yellowish. Nice crystals from Diana, New York, and the Crestmore Quarry at Riverside, California. Nice fluorescent specimens from Franklin, New Jersey.

ZEOLITE GROUP Several dozen minerals similar to feldspars with water added, often occurring in basaltic cavities. Zeolites are widespread, but not major rock-forming minerals. Chemically, the zeolites are hydrous tectosilicates, and collectors seek such species as *an-*

alcite (*analcime*), *chabazite*, *heulandite*, *mesolite*, *natrolite*, *pectolite*, *prehnite*, and *stilbite*. Because stilbite is popular at mineral shows, I'm going to give its properties as a sample zeolite mineral.

✦ *Stilbite* (also called *desmine* or "bundle zeolite")—$CaAl_2Si_7O_{18}$ • $7H_2O$—calcium, aluminum silicate with seven parts water, and often sodium. Color: white, grey, yellow, red, and brown. Streak: colorless. Hardness: 3½–4, brittle. Cleavage: perfect in one direction. Specific gravity: 2.1–2.2. Crystals: monoclinic, bundle-shaped bunches and radial aggregates. Occurrence: choice crystals from Berufjord, Iceland, and Poonah, India. Stilbite is often associated with other zeolites, *calcite*, *quartz*, or *apophyllite*. Don't confuse the zeolite silicate *stilbite* with the common antimony ore *stibnite*.

ZIRCON $ZrSiO_4$—zirconium silicate, often with small admixtures of uranium, thorium, or rare earths. A popular gemstone whose high refractive index approaches that of diamond. Color: colorless, grey, yellow, green, red, and brown are natural colors, but zircon is often heat-treated to get artificial colors for the gemstone trade. Zircon is also called *hyacinth*, when transparent orange-red, and *jargon*, when transparent colorless or grey. Streak: white. Hardness: 7½, brittle. Cleavage: indistinct. Specific gravity: 4.0–4.7. Crystals: tetragonal, short prisms. Adamantine or vitreous lustre. Slightly radioactive when admixed with sufficient uranium and thorium. Occurrence: many localities; collectible crystals in the U.S. and Ontario, but the best gem zircon comes from Burma, Sri Lanka (Ceylon), and France.

c h a p t e r   t e n

ORES

"But gold shines like fire blazing in the night, supreme of lordly wealth."
Pindar (circa 518–438 B.C.), *Olympian Odes*

Ores can be defined as chemical compounds of metals and nonmetallic elements or chemical radicals, such as carbonates, oxides, silicates, sulfates, and sulfides. By that definition, *cassiterite* (tin oxide) and *pyrite* (iron sulfide) are ores, even in samples as small as a piece of dust. Ores are also defined as economically important metal-bearing rocks or minerals, in compound or elemental form, whether or not currently profitable to mine. In this book, however, the term "ore" refers to any metal-bearing rock or mineral that could be of commercial value if it was found in concentrated quantities.

◆

ORE DEPOSITS AND BODIES

An *ore deposit* is an ore concentration in the Earth's crust. An *ore body* (also called an "ore site" or "ore reserve") is an ore deposit that can be currently extracted profitably. A "bonanza" is an unusually rich ore body. *Ore resources* are known ore deposits as well as estimates of undiscovered ore deposits in a given country, state, county, and so forth.

Once located, an ore deposit's *size* ("tonnage") and *grade* ("tenor") are determined by techniques such as drill core ore sampling, exploratory mine shafts, and ore assays in order to decide if the deposit can be profitably mined. A *high grade* ore is "rich," whereas a *low grade* ore is "lean," in a given metallic content.

Ores are not evenly distributed on the Earth's surface. For example, in 100 tons of average igneous rock, there are 8 tons of *aluminum* metal, but only 1½ ounces of *uranium*.

Copper was perhaps the first metal used by humans in the Neolithic age. Until the 18th century, the only metals regularly used by man were *copper*, *gold*, *iron*, *lead*, *silver*, *tin*, and *zinc*. Increasing knowledge of scientific mining and metallurgy, especially in 18th-century Germany, allowed the extraction of other metals from their ores and subsequent use as industrial alloys of economic value.

The common rock-forming silicate minerals are rarely profitable to mine for ores because their valuable metal concentrations tend to be low, and metals are harder to separate from the strong silicate molecular bonds, compared to the typical ore compounds of chlorides, oxides, sulfates, and sulfides.

Ore Formation

Most metals have an igneous origin. Ore deposits tend to be in three forms:

Veins Veins fill bedrock cracks or fissures. They can be from about a centimetre to hundreds of metres thick or long. *Lodes* are ore deposits of veins that are close to each other. The "Mother Lode" on the western slopes of the Sierra Nevada Mountains in California is where the 1848–1849 Gold Rush originated.

Beds Layers in bedrock, beds are more often found for nonprecious than precious metals.

Disseminated ore Sparsely distributed in rock, disseminated ore contains a lot of what miners call "gangue," unprofitable waste minerals mixed in with the saleable metals.

Hydrothermal Ore Deposits

The most common ore deposits are *hydrothermal*—that is, precipitated from hot aqueous liquids and gases of igneous origin, as they rise towards the Earth's surface. Hydrothermal ore deposits can be classified according to the underground depth where they solidified:

Epithermal deposits Ores that crystallize near the Earth's surface; examples are the ores of *antimony*, *gold*, *mercury*, and *silver*.

Mesothermal deposits Ores that form at intermediate depths in the Earth's crust; examples are *copper*, *gold*-quartz, and *silver-lead*.

Hypothermal deposits Ores that form at the great pressures and temperatures characteristic of great depths below the Earth's surface; examples are *gold*-quartz, *tin*, *tungsten*.

Time of Ore Formation

Hydrothermal ores can be grouped into two general categories based on when they solidified relative to their surrounding rock ("country rock");

Syngenetic ores Formed at the same time as the country rock, often in sheets. Common in *placer* deposits.

Diagenetic ores Formed after the country rocks were deposited, but before they lithified. *Copper*, *lead*, *uranium*, and *zinc* deposits in sedimentary rocks are often syngenetic or diagenetic.

Epigenetic ores Formed after the country rock lithified. Often in the form of veins or lodes.

Primary and Secondary Ores

Primary ores (also called "hypogenetic deposits") are below-surface deposits that formed when the mineral deposits originated. In contrast, secondary ores (also called "supergenetic deposits") are formed by weathering of outcrops or groundwater deposition after the original rocks were formed.

Placer Deposits

The word *placer* (pronounced "plas′er"—rhyming with the word "as") is derived intact from the American Spanish *placer* ("sandbank"), from the Catalonian *plassa*, from the Latin *platea* ("a place"). A placer (also commonly and redundantly called "placer deposit") is a heavy ore-bearing deposit of sand or gravel that was transported by water or glacier from the erosion site at the original bedrock outcrop. Alluvial placers and beach placers are often rich in ores such as *gold*.

Placer gold panning is a popular and cheap, although labor-intensive, method of extracting gold. The ore particles can be concentrated at the bottom of a gold pan by washing out a swirling mixture of gold and gravel in the placer mix. Gold tends to remain behind because it is so heavy. Successful gold panning requires strong arms, much patience, a reasonable knowledge of placer geology, and permission to work private lands if you're not panning on public property.

The copper ores of blue azurite *and green* malachite *are usually found together, as in this specimen from Arizona. Photo by Robert Weldon.* © *GIA.*

USEFUL AND COLLECTIBLE ORES

The following list of economically important metals gives their typical ores as found in nature, as well as ore minerals popular with collectors. Many of these minerals are described in Chapter 9.

ALUMINUM *Bauxite.*

ANTIMONY *Stibnite* is the only common antimony ore. Native antimony is rare.

COPPER Over 150 copper ores are known, but most mineral collectors concentrate on *native copper*, *azurite*, *bornite*, *cuprite*, *chalcocite*, *chalcopyrite*, *chrysocolla*, *covellite*, *malachite*, and *tetrahedrite*.

CHROMIUM *Chromite* is the only economically important chromium ore, but the rare lead-chromium ore *crocoite* is popular with mineral collectors.

GOLD Generally occurs in native form, but also known as the ore *calaverite* ($AuTe_2$), compounded with tellurium, and as *sylvanite* $(Au,Ag)Te_2$, compounded with silver and tellurium.

IRON The only ores that are profitably mined for iron are *magnetite* (72-percent iron), *hematite* (70-percent iron), *limonite* (60-percent iron), and *siderite* (48-percent iron). *Marcasite*, *pyrite*, and *pyrrhotite* are lean iron ores appreciated by collectors. *Meteorites* can be almost entirely a mixture of iron and nickel.

LEAD Generally occurs with zinc in nature, so many lead mines are also zinc

Native gold *on* quartz, *a common mineralogical association for gold in nature.* © *GIA and Tino Hammid.*

mines. *Galena* is the main lead ore, with *anglesite* and *cerussite* being secondary lead ores. The largest lead-zinc mine in the world is at Kimberly, British Columbia. A lead-zinc mine in Mexico has been operating since the mid-1500s.

MAGNESIUM *Magnesite* is the main magnesium ore, with commercial extraction possible also from *dolomite*. Today, much industrial magnesium is produced from the electrolysis of sea water. *Spinel* is a scarce gemstone of magnesium-aluminum oxide.

MANGANESE The three most important manganese ores, each having over 60-percent manganese, are *manganite*, *psilomelane*, and *pyrolusite*, and they are often found in the same ore deposits. "Absolite" is cobaltous *psilomelane*, found in clay. *Rhodochrosite* and *rhodonite* are minor manganese ores used in lapidary work.

An octahedrite *iron* meteorite *from Odessa, Texas, where it fell about 50,000 years ago, and whose site was discovered in 1923. Octahedrites are iron meteorites with approximately 7- to 10-percent nickel content by weight, on the average. Photo courtesy of, and* ©, *New England Meteoritical Services.*

Rough rhodochrosite, *a manganese carbonate mineral, from South Africa. Courtesy of Natural History Museum of Los Angeles County.*

MERCURY   *Cinnabar*, with 86-percent mercury, is the only practical ore of this metal. Occasionally mercury is found in pure native form.

MOLYBDENUM   *Molybdenite* is the main ore.

NICKEL   *Pentlandite* is the main ore. The hydrosilicate of nickel called *garnierite* is a secondary ore.

PALLADIUM   A native precious metal, found typically with platinum in placer sites.

PLATINUM   A native precious metal.

SILVER   Occurs as native metal, also in ores of *argentite* and *sylvanite*. The silver antimony sulfide called *stephanite* is a rare ore from Nevada's Comstock Lode.

TIN   *Cassiterite*, at 78.6-percent tin in its tin dioxide formula, is the main tin ore.

TITANIUM   Found in *rutile* and *ilmenite* ores. *Titanite* ("sphene") is a calcium titanium silicate gemstone. Titanium is found in meteorites and in Moon rocks.

TUNGSTEN   *Scheelite* and *wolframite* are important ores. The tungstate minerals *ferberite* and *huebnerite* are actually end-series members of *wolframite*.

VANADIUM   *Carnotite* and *vanadinite* are best-known ores.

ZINC   Used in the ancient world as the alloy with copper to make brass, before it was known to be a separate metal. The main zinc ores are *sphalerite*, *smithsonite*, *franklinite*, and *hemimorphite/willemite*.

A 110.4-gram specimen of natural rough sphalerite, *a simple zinc sulfide mineral, which is a main ore of zinc.* © GIA.

APPENDICES

"Mathematics, rightly viewed, possesses not only truth, but supreme beauty—a beauty cold and austere, like that of sculpture . . ."
Bertrand Russell (1872–1970), *British philosopher and mathematician*

Appendix A is a "Table of the Elements," listed in alphabetical order, with their chemical symbols, atomic numbers, and atomic weights. Appendix B lists some "Common Ions" that are likely to be found in rocks and minerals in nature, as well as in laboratory chemical preparations. Appendix C lists some "Common Acids" that are either found in nature or used in the laboratory for mineralogical analytical tests. Appendix D lists some "Common Gases"—many found in nature or in the analytical laboratory. And Appendix E contains tables of metric-English equivalents.

APPENDIX A: TABLE OF THE ELEMENTS

Element Name	Symbol	Atomic Number	Atomic Weight	Element Name	Symbol	Atomic Number	Atomic Weight
Actinium	Ac	89	(227)	Copper	Cu	29	63.55
Aluminum	Al	13	26.98	Dysprosium	Dy	66	162.50
Antimony	Sb	51	121.76	Erbium	Er	68	167.26
Argon	Ar	18	39.95	Europium	Eu	63	151.97
Arsenic	As	33	74.92	Fluorine	F	9	19.00
Astatine	At	85	(210)	Francium	Fr	87	(223)
Barium	Ba	56	137.33	Gadolinium	Gd	64	157.25
Beryllium	Be	4	9.01	Gallium	Ga	31	69.72
Bismuth	Bi	83	208.98	Germanium	Ge	32	72.61
Boron	B	5	10.81	Gold	Au	79	196.97
Bromine	Br	35	79.90	Hafnium	Hf	72	178.49
Cadmium	Cd	48	112.41	Helium	He	2	4.00
Calcium	Ca	20	40.08	Holmium	Ho	67	164.93
Carbon	C	6	12.01	Hydrogen	H	1	1.01
Cerium	Ce	58	140.12	Indium	In	49	114.82
Cesium	Cs	55	132.91	Iodine	I	53	126.90
Chlorine	Cl	17	35.45	Iridium	Ir	77	192.22
Chromium	Cr	24	52.00	Iron	Fe	26	55.85
Cobalt	Co	27	58.93	Krypton	Kr	36	83.80

Element Name	Symbol	Atomic Number	Atomic Weight
Lanthanum	La	57	138.91
Lead	Pb	82	207.21
Lithium	Li	3	6.94
Lutetium	Lu	71	174.97
Magnesium	Mg	12	24.31
Manganese	Mn	25	54.94
Mercury	Hg	80	200.59
Molybdenum	Mo	42	95.94
Neodymium	Nd	60	144.24
Neon	Ne	10	20.18
Nickel	Ni	28	58.69
Niobium	Nb	41	92.91
Nitrogen	N	7	14.01
Osmium	Os	76	190.21
Oxygen	O	8	16.00
Palladium	Pd	46	106.42
Phosphorus	P	15	30.97
Platinum	Pt	78	195.08
Polonium	Po	84	(209)
Potassium	K	19	39.10
Praseodymium	Pr	59	140.91
Promethium	Pm	61	(145)
Protactinium	Pa	91	231.04
Radium	Ra	88	(226)
Radon	Rn	86	(222)
Rhenium	Re	75	186.21
Rhodium	Rh	45	102.91
Rubidium	Rb	37	85.47
Ruthenium	Ru	44	101.07
Samarium	Sm	62	150.36
Scandium	Sc	21	44.96
Selenium	Se	34	78.96
Silicon	Si	14	28.09
Silver	Ag	47	107.87
Sodium	Na	11	22.99
Strontium	Sr	38	87.62
Sulfur	S	16	32.07
Tantalum	Ta	73	180.95
Technetium	Tc	43	(98)
Tellurium	Te	52	127.60
Terbium	Tb	65	158.93
Thallium	Tl	81	204.38

Element Name	Symbol	Atomic Number	Atomic Weight
Thorium	Th	90	232.04
Thulium	Tm	69	168.93
Tin	Sn	50	118.71
Titanium	Ti	22	47.88
Tungsten	W	74	183.85
Uranium	U	92	238.03
Vanadium	V	23	50.94
Xenon	Xe	54	131.29
Ytterbium	Yb	70	173.04
Yttrium	Y	39	88.91
Zinc	Zn	30	65.39
Zirconium	Zr	40	91.22

APPENDIX B: COMMON IONS

An *ion* is an atom or group of compounded atoms with an electrical charge. Here are some common ions that are found in rocks and minerals—as well as in reagents in the chemistry laboratory. *Oxidation numbers* ("charged valences") are given for the most common forms that appear in nature. Each ion is named, then shown in its chemical symbol.

Positive Ions ("Cations")

Aluminum—Al^{+3}

Ammonium—NH_4^{+1}

Antimony—Sb^{+3}

Arsenic (III)—As^{+3}

Barium—Ba^{+2}

Cadmium—Cd^{+2}

Calcium—Ca^{+2}

Carbon—C^{+4}

Cerium—Ce^{+3}

Chromium (II)—Cr^{+2}

Chromium (III)—Cr^{+3}

Cobalt—Co^{+2}

Copper (I)—"cuprous"—Cu^{+1}
Copper (II)—"cupric"—Cu^{+2}
Gold (I)—Au^{+1}
Gold (III)—Au^{+3}
Hydrogen (actually "hydronium": $\{[H_3O]^{+1}\}$—but by custom: H^{+1})
Iron (II)—"ferrous"—Fe^{+2}
Iron (III)—"ferric"—Fe^{+3}
Lead (II)—"plumbous"—Pb^{+2}
Lead (IV)—"plumbic"—Pb^{+4}
Lithium—Li^{+1}
Magnesium—Mg^{+2}
Manganese—Mn^{+2}
Mercury (I)—"mercurous"—Hg_2^{+2} (an effective valence of $+1$ per mercury atom)
Mercury (II)—"mercuric"—Hg^{+2}
Nickel—Ni^{+2}
Nitrogen (III)—N^{+3}
Nitrogen (V)—N^{+5}
Potassium—K^{+1}
Silicon—Si^{+4}
Silver—Ag^{+1}
Sodium—Na^{+1}
Strontium—Sr^{+2}
Sulfur—S^{+4}
Tellurium (IV)—Te^{+4}
Thorium—Th^{+4}
Tin (II)—"stannous"—Sn^{+2}
Tin (IV)—"stannic"—Sn^{+4}
Titanium (II, III, IV)—Ti^{+2}, Ti^{+3}, Ti^{+4}
Uranyl—$(UO_2)^{+2}$
Zinc—Zn^{+2}
Zirconium (II, III, IV)—Zr^{+2}, Zr^{+3}, Zr^{+4}

Negative Ions ("Anions")

I give the empirical formulae, rather than the structural formulae, for complex anions here. You may see some of them written differently elsewhere.

Acetate—$(C_2H_3O_2)^{-1}$
Amide—$(NH_2)^{-1}$
Antimonide—Sb^{-3}
Arsenate—$(AsO_4)^{-3}$
Arsenide—As^{-3}
Arsenite—$(AsO_3)^{-3}$
Bicarbonate—$(HCO_3)^{-1}$
Biphosphate (also called "hydrogen phosphate")—$(HPO_4)^{-2}$
Bisulfate ("hydrogen sulfate")—$(HSO_4)^{-1}$
Bisulfite ("hydrogen sulfite")—$(HSO_3)^{-1}$
Borate—$(B_2O_4)^{-2}$ for "metaborate"
$(B_4O_7)^{-2}$ for "tetraborate"
$(B_5O_8)^{-1}$ for "pentaborate" . . . etc.
Boride—B^{-3}
Bromate—$(BrO_3)^{-1}$
Bromide—Br^{-1}
Carbide—C^{-4}
Carbonate—$(CO_3)^{-2}$
Chlorate—$(ClO_3)^{-1}$
Chloride—Cl^{-1}
Chlorite—$(ClO_2)^{-1}$
Chromate—$(CrO_4)^{-2}$
Cyanate—$(OCN)^{-1}$
Cyanide—$(CN)^{-1}$
Dichromate—$(Cr_2O_7)^{-2}$
Diphosphate—$(P_2O_7)^{-2}$
Diphosphite ("pyrophosphite")—$(H_2P_2O_5)^{-2}$
Disulfate ("pyrosulfate")—$(S_2O_7)^{-2}$
Disulfide—S_2^{-2}
Disulfite ("pyrosulfite")—$(S_2O_5)^{-2}$
Dithionite—$(S_2O_4)^{-2}$
Fluoride—F^{-1}
Hydrazide—$(N_2H_3)^{-1}$
Hydride—H^{-1}
Hydroxide—$(OH)^{-1}$
Hypochlorite—$(ClO)^{-1}$
Hyponitrite—$(N_2O_2)^{-2}$
Hypophosphite—$(H_2PO_2)^{-1}$
Imide—$(NH)^{-2}$
Iodate—$(IO_3)^{-1}$
Iodide—I^{-1}

Molybdate—$(MoO_4)^{-2}$
Nitrate—$(NO_3)^{-1}$
Nitride—N^{-3}
Nitrite—$(NO_2)^{-1}$
Oxalate—$(C_2O_4)^{-2}$
Oxide—O^{-2}
Perchlorate—$(ClO_4)^{-1}$
Permanganate—$(MnO_4)^{-1}$
Peroxide—O_2^{-2}
Phosphate—$(PO_4)^{-3}$
Phosphide—P^{-3}
Phosphite—$(PO_3)^{-3}$
Selenate—$(SeO_4)^{-2}$
Selenide—Se^{-2}
Selenite—$(SeO_3)^{-2}$
Silicate—$(SiO_3)^{-2}$ for "metasilicate"
  $(Si_2O_5)^{-2}$ for "disilicate"
  $(Si_4O_9)^{-2}$ for "tetrasilicate" . . .
    etc.
Silicide—Si^{-4}
Sulfate—$(SO_4)^{-2}$
Sulfide—S^{-2}
Sulfite—$(SO_3)^{-2}$
Tellurate ("metatellurate")—$(TeO_4)^{-2}$
Telluride—Te^{-2}
Tellurite—$(TeO_3)^{-2}$
Thiosulfite—$(S_2O_2)^{-2}$
Thiosulfate—$(S_2O_3)^{-2}$
Tungstate—$(WO_4)^{-2}$
Vanadate—$(VO_4)^{-3}$

APPENDIX C: COMMON ACIDS

These are some common acids in nature and/or the chemistry laboratory:

Acetic acid—$HC_2H_3O_2$

"Aqua regia" (literally: "kingly water" in Latin)—a mixture of *nitric* (HNO_3) and *hydrochloric* (HCl) *acids* in a 1:3 ratio; so-called because this acid will dissolve gold—an element impervious to most acids

Boric acid—H_3BO_3
Carbonic acid—H_2CO_3
Chloric acid—$HClO_3$
Chlorous acid—$HClO_2$
Chromic acid—H_2CrO_4
Cyanic acid—$HOCN$
Dichromic acid—$H_2Cr_2O_7$
Hydrobromic acid—HBr
Hydrochloric acid—HCl
Hydrocyanic acid—HCN
Hydrofluoric acid—HF
Hydroiodic acid—HI
Hydrosulfuric acid—H_2S
Hypochlorous acid—$HClO$
Hypophosphorous acid—H_3PO_2
Hyposulfurous acid (also called "dithionous acid")—$H_2S_2O_4$
Nitric acid—HNO_3
Nitrous acid—HNO_2
Perchloric acid—$HClO_4$
Permanganic acid—$HMnO_4$
Phosphoric acid—H_3PO_4
Phosphorous acid—H_3PO_3
Sulfuric acid—H_2SO_4
Sulfurous acid—H_2SO_3

APPENDIX D: COMMON GASES

These are some common gases at "room temperature" in nature and/or the chemistry laboratory.

Ammonia—NH_3
Argon—Ar
Bromine—Br_2—liquid, but forms a red vapor at room temperature
Carbon dioxide—CO_2
Carbon monoxide—CO
Chlorine—Cl_2
Fluorine—F_2
Helium—He

Hydrogen—H_2
Hyrdrogen chloride—HCl
Hydrogen sulfide—H_2S
Iodine—I_2—solid, but vaporizes at room temperature
Krypton—Kr
Methane—CH_4
Neon—Ne
Nitrogen—N_2
Nitrogen dioxide—NO_2
Nitrogen oxide—NO
Nitrous Oxide—N_2O
Oxygen—O_2
Ozone—O_3
Radon—Rn
Sulfur dioxide—SO_2
Sulfur trioxide—SO_3
Water vapor—H_2O
Xenon—Xe

APPENDIX E:
METRIC–ENGLISH
EQUIVALENTS

In the United States, rocks and minerals, as well as physical geological data, are measured in both metric and English units. Therefore, a working knowledge of some common equivalents is necessary for making conversions and comparisons when reading geological and geographical information, and when studying specimens in the field, at museums, or in the marketplace.

Although all scientists use the metric system, much popularized nature literature uses metric and English units interchangeably, as I do in this book, for reasons that often involve the simple desire to be understood by the intended audience.

Mineral collectors and dealers use both metric and English units. The United States is converting more and more to the metric system in everyday affairs, but you will always need to know something about the English system in order to understand older literature on rocks and minerals.

The *troy* system is used mostly for weighing precious metals and gemstones, and *English pounds* should not be confused with *troy pounds*.

The metric system has the *metric ton*, the (American) English system has the *short ton*, and the (British) English system has the *long ton*, which is used in shipping. One *long ton* = 1.12 *short tons* = 2,240 *pounds avoirdupois* (American English system) = 1.016047 *metric tons* = 1,016.047 *kilograms*.

Time is the same in all systems.

The formulae for *temperature* conversions for the *Celsius* (metric), *Fahrenheit* (English), and *Kelvin* (used especially by astronomers and chemists) temperature systems are as follows:

$$C = \left(\frac{5}{9}\right)(F - 32) = K - 273.15$$

$$\text{and } F = \left(\frac{9}{5}\right)C + 32$$

where C = degrees Celsius, F = degrees Fahrenheit, and K = degrees Kelvin.

In the following conversion tables, most decimal values are rounded off. When no decimal points are included in the whole numbers, they are usually exact amounts.

All numerical values within a given box on the charts are equivalent. For each chart, I first list the metric system in whole numbers, next the English system, and then common abbreviations for unit names. I left out uncommonly used units, such as deciliters (metric) and drams (English).

Commonly Used Mass ("Weight") Units and Their Equivalents

Metric System	English System	Troy System
1 gram = 0.001 kilogram (exactly)	= 0.03274 ounce (avoirdupois)	= 0.03215 ounce (troy)
1 kilogram = 1,000 grams	− 2.20462 pounds (avoirdupois)	= 2.67923 pounds (troy)
	= 35.27396 ounces (avoirdupois)	= 32.15075 ounces (troy
1 metric ton = 1,000 kilograms	= 2,204.6226 pounds (avoirdupois)	
	= 1.10231 short tons (U.S.)	
	= 0.98421 long ton (British)	
28.34952 grams	= 1 ounce (avoirdupois)	= 0.91146 ounce (troy)
453.59237 grams	= 1 pound (avoirdupois)	= 1.21528 pounds (troy)
	= 16 ounces (avoirdupois)	= 14.58333 ounces (troy)
907.18474 kilograms	= 1 short ton (U.S.)	
0.90718 metric ton	= 2,000 pounds (avoirdupois) (exactly)	
	= 0.089286 long ton (British)	
1,016.04691 kilograms	= 1 long ton (British)	
1.01605 metric tons	= 2,240 pounds (avoirdupois) (exactly)	
	= 1.12 short tons (U.S.) (exactly)	
31.10348 grams	= 1.09714 ounce (avoirdupois)	= 1 ounce (troy)
373.24172 grams	= 0.82286 pound (avoirdupois)	= 1 pound (troy)
	= 13.16568 ounces (avoirdupois)	= 12 ounces (troy)

Abbreviations:

gram	=	gm	ounce	=	oz avdp		
kilogram	=	kg	pound	=	lb avdp	ounce =	oz t
metric ton	=	ton (m)	short ton	=	ton (s)	pound =	lb t
			long ton	=	ton (l)		
			avoirdupois	=	avoir *or* avdp		

Commonly Used Linear ("Length") Units and Their Equivalents

Metric System		English System	
1 millimetre	= 0.001 metre (exactly)	= 0.03937 inch	= 0.00328 foot
1 centimetre	= 10 millimetres	= 0.39370 inch	= 0.03281 foot
1 metre	= 100 centimetres = 1,000 millimetres	= 39.37008 inches	= 3.28084 feet = 1.09361 yards
1 kilometre	= 1,000 metres	= 0.62137 statute mile	= 0.53996 nautical mile = 3,280.840 feet = 1,093.613 yards
25.4 millimetres (exactly)	= 2.54 centimetres (exactly)	= 1 inch = $\frac{1}{12}$ foot	= $\frac{1}{36}$ yard (all exactly)
304.8 millimetres (exactly)	= 30.48 centimetres (exactly) = 0.3048 metre (exactly)	= 1 foot = 12 inches	= $\frac{1}{3}$ yard (all exactly)
914.4 millimetres (exactly)	= 91.44 centimetres (exactly) = 0.9144 metre (exactly)	= 1 yard = 3 feet	= 36 inches (all exactly)
1,609.344 metres	= 1.609344 kilometres	= 1 statute mile	= 0.86898 nautical mile = 5,280 feet (exactly) = 1,760 yards (exactly)
1,852 metres (exactly)	= 1.852 kilometres (exactly)	= 1 nautical mile	= 1.15078 statute miles = 6,076.11549 feet = 2,025.372 yards = the length of a minute of longitude at the Earth's equator

Abbreviations:	millimetre = mm	inch = in	mile = mi
	centimetre = cm	foot = ft	statute = stat (sometimes)
	metre = m	yard = yd	nautical = naut (sometimes)
	kilometre = km		

Commonly Used Square ("Area") Units and Their Equivalents

Metric System		English System	
1 square millimetre		= 0.00155 square inch	
1 square centimetre	= 100 square millimetres	= 0.15499 square inch	
1 square metre	= 10,000 square centimetres	= 1.196 square yards	= 1,549.9 sq inches
	= 1,000,000 square millimetres	= 10.764 square feet	
1 hectare	= 10,000 square metres	= 2.47105 acres	= 107,639.1 sq feet
1 square kilometre	= 1,000,000 square metres	= 0.38610 square mile	= 247.1054 acres
6.4516 sq centimetres	= 645.16 sq mm	= 1 square inch	
929.0304 sq centimetres	= 92,903.04 sq mm	= 1 square foot	= 144 sq inches
0.83613 square metre	= 83,613 sq centimetres	= 1 square yard	= 9 sq feet
			= 1,296 sq inches
0.40469 hectare	= 0.0040469 square kilometre	= 1 acre	= 4,840 sq yards
			= 43,560 sq feet
258.99881 hectares	= 2.5899881 square kilometres	= 1 square mile	= 640 acres
			= 27,878,400 sq feet
			= 3,097,600 sq yards

Abbreviations:

square millimetre = sq mm = mm^2
square centimetre = sq cm = cm^2
square kilometre = sq km = km^2

Abbreviations:

square inch = sq in = in^2
square foot = sq ft = ft^2
square yard = sq yd = yd^2
square mile = sq mi = mi^2

Commonly Used Cubic ("Linear Volume") Units and Their Equivalents

Metric System		English System	
1 cubic millimetre	= 0.001 cubic centimetre (exactly)	= 0.000061024 cubic inch	
1 cubic centimetre	= 1,000 cubic millimetres	= 0.061024 cubic inch	
1 cubic metre	= 1,000,000 cubic centimetres = 1,000,000,000 cubic millimetres	= 61,023.74 cubic inches	= 35.31467 cu ft = 1.30795 cu yd

1 cubic kilometre	= 1,000,000,000 cubic metres	= 0.2399128 cubic mile
		= about 35,312,789,000
		   cubic feet
		= about 1,307,881,100
		   cubic yards	

16.38706 cubic centimetres	= 16,387.064 cu millimetres	= 1 cubic inch	
0.28317 cubic metre	= 28,316.847 cu centimetres	= 1 cubic foot	= 1,728 cubic inches
0.76455 cubic metre	= 764,554.86 cu centimetres	= 1 cubic yard	= 27 cubic feet = 46,656 cubic inches

4.168182 cubic kilometres	= 4,168,182,000 cubic metres	= 1 cubic mile
		
		= 147,197,952,000
		   cubic feet (exactly)
		= 5,451,776,000
		   cubic yards (exactly)	

Abbreviations:

    cubic millimetre = cu mm = mm^3
    cubic centimetre = cu cm = cm^3 = cc (medical)
    cubic metre = cu m = m^3
    cubic kilometre = cu km = km^3

Abbreviations:

    cubic inch = cu in = in^3
    cubic foot = cu ft = ft^3
    cubic yard = cu yd = yd^3
    cubic mile = cu mi = mi^3

Commonly Used Capacity ("Dry and Fluid/Liquid Volume") Units and Their Equivalents

Metric System		English System ("U.S. Units")	
1 millilitre	= 0.001 litre (exactly) = 1 cubic centimetre	= 0.033814 ounce (fluid)	= 0.0010567 quart (liquid)
1 litre	= 1,000 millilitres = 1,000 cubic centimetres	= 1.056688 quarts	= 33.81402 ounces (fluid) = 0.90808 quart (dry) = 61.02374 cubic inches
473.1765 millilitres	= 0.4731765 litre = 473.1765 cu cm	= 1 pint (liquid)	= 16 ounces (fluid) = ½ quart (liquid) = ⅛ gallon (liquid) = 0.8594 pint (dry) = 28.875 cubic inches
0.5506105 litre	= 550.6105 millilitres = 550.6105 cu cm	= 1 pint (dry)	= ½ quart (dry) = ⅛ gallon (dry) = 1.1636 pints (liquid) = 33.6003 cubic inches
0.9463529 litre	= 946.3529 millilitres = 946.3529 cu cm	= 1 quart (liquid)	= 32 ounces (fluid) = 2 pints (liquid) = ¼ gallon (liquid) = 0.8594 quart (dry) = 57.75 cubic inches

Commonly Used Capacity ("Dry and Fluid/Liquid Volume") Units and Their Equivalents

Metric System				English System		
1.101221 litres	=	1,101.221 millilitres	= 1 quart (dry)	=	2 pints (dry)	
	=	1,101.221 cu cm		=	¼ gallon (dry)	
				=	1.1636 quarts (liquid)	
				=	67.2006 cubic inches	
3.785412 litres	=	3,785.412 millilitres	= 1 gallon (liquid)	=	128 ounces (fluid)	
	=	3,785.412 cu cm		=	8 pints (liquid)	
				=	4 quarts (liquid)	
				=	231 cubic inches	
4.404884 litres	=	4,404.884 millilitres	= 1 gallon (dry)	=	8 pints (dry)	
	=	4,404.884 cu cm		=	4 quarts (dry)	
				=	1.1636 gallons (liquid)	
				=	268.8025 cubic inches	

Abbreviations:

millilitre = ml
litre = l
cubic centimeters = cu cm
= cm³
= cc (medical)

Abbreviations:

ounce	=	oz
pint	=	pt
quart	=	qt
gallon	=	gal
fluid	=	f or fl
liquid	=	l or lq or liq
dry	=	d or dr

sometimes { fluid, liquid, dry }

INDEX

A

Acanthite (argentite), 141
Achromatism, 125
Acids, common, 181
Actinolite, *46*
Actinolite & tremolite, 157
Adamite, 153
Agate, angel wing, *86*
Agate, *6, 18, 54, 77*
Aggregates, 91
Alexandrite, *124*
Allochromatism, 125–126
Aluminum (bauxite), 175
Amazonite, *14*
Amber (succinite), *9, 45*
Amblygonite, 153
Amethyst, *9, 126*
Ametrine, *23*
Ammonite fossil, *9*
Amphibolite, 55
Analytical balance, *120*
Andalusite, 53, 158
Andesite, 39
Anhedral crystals, 98
Anhydrite, 45, 48, 151
Antimony, 139, 143, 175
Apatite, *31, 105,* 153–154
Apophyllite, 158
Aquamarine, *15, 76*
Aragonite, *43,* 148
Arborescent minerals, 101
Arsenic, 139
Arsenopyrite, 141
Asterism, 123
Augite (pyroxene), 158
Aurichalcite, 147
Austinite, 154
Autunite, 154
Axinite crystal, *97*
Azurite, *6,* 147

B

Barite, *11, 102,* 152
Basalt, 39–40
Bauxite, 145–146
Benitoite, *53,* 158

Beryl, *10, 15, 31, 42,* 75, 76, *86,* 158–159
Biotite, 159
Birthstones table, 77
Bismuth, 139
Bixbyite, 144
Borax, 150
Bornite, 141
Botryoidal minerals, 101
Boulangerite, 143
Boulder classification, 52
Bournonite, 143–144
Breccia, 45, 47
Brucite, 146
Buergerite, 171

C

Calcite, *62, 96, 106, 135,* 148
Carnelian cameo, *10*
Carnotite, 155
Cassiterite (tinstone), 144
Celestite, *54,* 152
Cerussite, *134,* 148–149
Chalcedony, *71, 99,* 166
Chalcocite, 141
Chalcopyrite, 141–142
Chalk, 48–49
Chatoyancy, 123
Chemically created, table, 17
Chlorargyrite, 147
Chlorite, 53
Chorite, 159
Chromite, 146
Chromium, 175
Chrysacolla, *35,* 159
Chrysolite, *164*
Chrysoberyl, *101, 123,* 146
Chrysoprase, *166*
Cinnabar, 142
Classifying, identifying, 28–57, 91–92, 104–105, 137–172
Clay classification, 52
Cleavage, 108–110
Clinohumite, faceted, *73*
Coal, 46, 55
Cobble classification, 52
Cohesive categories, 114–115
Colemanite, 150

Collecting, 61–63, 67
Collecting tools, 63–67
Collections purposes, 68–103
Collections, housing, 78–103
Color, 123–128
  Minerals, basic colors, 124–125
Concentric minerals, 101
Conductivity, 117
Conglomerate (puddingstone), 46–47
Conichalcite, 154
Constancy of angle, law, 93
Copper, 139, 175
Coquina, 49
Coral, *49,* 50
Cordierite, *39,* 159
Corundum, *34, 60,* 144–145
  In muscovite mica, *108*
  Ruby, sapphire, 75
Covellite (covelline), 142
Crocoite, 136, 153
Cryolite, 147
Cryptocrystalline quartz, subtypes, 166–167
Crystals, 87–97, 101–121
  Development in cavities, 91
  Perfection states, 98
  Symmetry
    Axial, 93
    Central-point, 3, 93
    Plane, 93
  Systems
    Hexagonal, *95*
    Isometric (cubic), *94, 95*
    Monoclinic, *96–97*
    Orthorhombic, *96*
    Tetragonal, *94, 95*
    Triclinic, *97*
    Trigonal, *96*
  Terminology, 86–87
  Twins
    Contact, 100
    Penetration, 101
    Repeated, 102
  Crystallization
    in nature, 87
    temperatures, 90
  Crystallography, 85, 92–97